SPEAKING
THE LANGUAGE OF SIGN

Also by Jerome D. Schein

A ROSE FOR TOMORROW

A COMPLETE GUIDE TO COMMUNICATION
  WITH DEAF-BLIND PERSONS (with Linda Kates)

IMPACT 1980 (with Ronald Hamilton)

FOR PARENTS OF DEAF CHILDREN (with Doris Naiman)

THE DEAF POPULATION OF THE UNITED STATES
  (with Marcus T. Delk)

THE DEAF COMMUNITY

Speaking the Language of Sign

THE ART AND SCIENCE OF SIGNING

Jerome D. Schein, Ph.D.

ILLUSTRATIONS BY MONA MARK

DOUBLEDAY & COMPANY, INC.

GARDEN CITY, NEW YORK

1984

Library of Congress Cataloging in Publication Data
Schein, Jerome Daniel.
Speaking the language of sign.
Bibliography: p. 165
Includes index.
1. Sign language.   2. Deaf—United States.   I. Mark,
Mona.   II. Title.
HV2475.S32   1984   419   81-43554
ISBN 0-385-17344-X

To the deaf people who
introduced me to the beauties of sign
and to the high art of communication
without words.

ACKNOWLEDGMENTS

To William C. Stokoe, Jr., who cast American Sign Language in a new light—
the light shed by scientific investigation.

To Mona Mark, a superb artist and a charming philosopher, whose wit and
erudition have penetrated her drawings.

And to three present and former editors at Doubleday: Joseph Gonzales, who
initiated this project; Nan Grubbs, who kept it on track with inspired editing;
and Laura Van Wormer, who enthusiastically brought it to market.

By this acknowledgment, I do not mean to implicate these good friends and
colleagues in any errors and omissions in the text. The blame for any
inadequacies is mine alone. For the individuals acknowledged above, I have
only the deepest gratitude.

CONTENTS

LIST OF ILLUSTRATIONS

Because signs involve movement as well as different handshapes, they are difficult to represent on the printed page. Throughout the book, the artist indicates the *initial* position of a sign with dotted lines and the *final* position with solid lines; arrows are used to show the direction of the movement. When attempting to make the sign, try looking at yourself in the mirror in order to gain the same perspective that the artist used in drawing the figures, or ask a companion to make the sign according to the illustration. The drawings show what you see when someone else is signing.

1

Introduction to Language, Deafness, and Sign

Suppose nobody could hear. In such an earless world, how would people communicate? Without their voices, could they make themselves understood? By what means? What kind of language would they use?

You may immediately recognize that such a world—a world without meaningful hearing—already exists. It is not a special place; it is simply the world of deaf people. About two million Americans live in silence. Some were born deaf; others became deaf after birth. For all of them, ordinary vocal communication—in person, by telephone, over radio and television—is precluded. And for an additional fourteen million Americans the reception of speech is impaired to some extent, ranging from slight to nearly total deafness. Altogether, sixteen million of our citizens have some degree of hearing impairment.[1]* This book is for them.

This book is also for all those who meet hearing-impaired people, who share homes with them, work alongside them, or have them as students in class and as clients, friends, and customers. Increasingly, our chances of encountering deaf people grow. So do our chances of becoming deaf ourselves.

What follows should interest students of language and culture. In one way or another, almost all human beings use their hands to communicate. Gestures occur in every culture. The hands may punctuate, or indicate, or convey complex ideas and the range of emotions. We will concentrate on the latter—using the hands, along with the rest of the body, for formal communication.

*Superscripts in the text refer to notes that would detract from the flow of presentation. These are grouped by chapter and gathered at the end of the text.

Our focus will be on communication by deaf people, especially those who live in the United States. Until two decades ago, American Sign Language did not have the status of a language. It was actually suppressed by educators, because its use was thought to impede speech development. It was considered, even by most deaf people, to be a substitute for spoken English—and a poor substitute at that. Once linguists accepted American Sign Language as a true language, interest in it exploded. Today, sign language appears frequently on television. It is used in public meetings attended by deaf people. Sign-language classes have sprung up all over the country and they attract substantial numbers of students; recent estimates place "sign" third or fourth among the most frequently used languages in the United States. The 1980 Tony awards were dominated by the Broadway production of a play about sign language—*Children of a Lesser God*. Further evidence of the widespread interest in sign came in 1981, when a British production repeated the play's Broadway success in London. (For more about deafness, drama, and sign, see Chapter 8.)

How did sign become so popular? Why the sudden interest in it? Where did it originate? How did it develop? Is it easy or difficult to learn? Who teaches it? Where? How can it be used? Is there an international sign language? Are there other forms of manual communication, other ways to convey messages with one's hands alone?

Answering these questions will take us through art into science and back again. Some questions about sign have no answers at present. Research in many aspects has only begun. But what has already been observed, studied, validated, and catalogued provides a thorough restructuring of some well-established beliefs and forces a weakening, if not a complete rejection, of some cherished ways of thinking: not only about our language, but about our culture. This survey of sign language will take us to the theatre, to industry, into courtrooms, among educators and rehabilitators, and, most fascinating of all, into the lives of deaf people.

So much for what this book is all about. What it is *not* is a glossary of signs. This book has a great deal to say about how to make oneself understood manually; it offers information about where to get sign-language instruction and how to identify good teachers; it will help the reader sort through the recent plethora of sign dictionaries.[2] But this is not a dictionary, not a lesson book. It introduces you to a fascinating language and to the people who use it; and it may open your mind to possibilities as yet unrealized for an ancient form of communication which has only recently been given its place in the linguistic spectrum.

What Is Language?

Since this book is about language, we should establish a definition of it at the outset. You may already know that experts do not agree on what language is. But we are not linguists, so like Humpty Dumpty we can proclaim, "When *I* use a word it means just what I choose it to mean—neither more nor less."

Actually, we will be concurring with the majority of language experts if we adhere to the following:

> *Language is a systematic means of communicating ideas and feelings by the use of conventional symbols.*

The term *systematic* refers to the rules for combining the elements of the language, the grammar. The word *symbols* in the definition conveys another critical aspect of language: it is referential. In other words, the symbols refer to something that need not be present to be discussed. Symbols allow us to communicate about events in the past or future and at a distance or hidden from the sender/receiver. The symbols may be of any kind: auditory, visual, tactual, or whatever, so long as they can be transmitted by one person and received by another. *Conventional* implies prior agreement about the meaning of the symbols among two or more people.

Our definition avoids some of the controversial issues, though not all. It tells what language *can* do—communicate thoughts and emotions—not what it *must* do. It makes clear that a set of symbols, a collection of signs, does not make a language if there are no rules for putting the symbols together. Also, the concept of language expressed here is a social one; it requires that others (at least one other) share an understanding of the language elements (syntax and signals) before the system achieves linguistic status. Sender and receiver may not be able to explicate the rules, but they demonstrate their appreciation of them by their consistent behavior in relation to them.

Some linguists require that the symbols be arbitrary, rather than iconic (representations of the form of that which is being described, like a picture of an object, an icon). An arbitrary symbol could not be understood by someone unfamiliar with the language. An iconic symbol could. Our definition does not address this point, but our discussion of sign language will.

By some definitions, a language must be useful in specific ways. We do not impose that restriction either, preferring to note that a language can be useful, though it may not be. Nor do we include the changing nature of "living" languages in the definition; the fact that as languages are transmitted they tend to alter somewhat, usually in predictable ways, is not essential to our definition. For instance, the original word for a flying machine that carries passengers was *aeroplane*; now *plane* means the same thing. The tendency to shorten or to prune words is one predictable feature of most languages. We can accept that point without incorporating it in the definition.

Speech and Language[3]

That the word *language* derives from *lingua* (tongue) betrays the common confusion about the relation between speech and language. For many earlier linguists, the words were synonymous. The notion of a language not arising from spoken communication received little attention from leaders in language-devel-opment studies, and they, in turn, heavily influenced educators of deaf children. By not accepting manual languages as languages, educators had a reason for barring sign from the classroom and, to the extent possible, from the schoolyard. Thus, the failure to separate speech from language had a profound influence on the education of deaf students.

Can there be language without speech? Yes, there are cases on record of congenital anarthria—of persons born without effective vocal apparatus. Do such persons develop language? They do. Christy Brown had language good enough to write a popular book, *Down All the Days*. Other speech pathologists have noted cases of speechless children who nonetheless understood language, spoken or written. Of course, born-deaf persons who never develop intelligible speech and who remain mute demonstrate varied abilities to read their native language.

Linguists do not beg the question about languages existing without speech by pointing out that sign languages used by deaf people have a nonvocal base yet qualify as languages. True, most linguists now agree that deaf sign languages are languages in their own right. American Sign Language, for instance, has its own vocabulary and a grammar different from English. But that conclusion was not determined by fiat; it was only reached after extensive linguistic research. We will look at the evidence in the chapters to follow.

At this point, we want to deal with the more general question: Are speech and language independent? If they are independent, then we should find speech without language as well as language without speech. To illustrate speech without language, we could point to talking birds. A parrot's utterance, for example, lacks meaning and does not intentionally express thoughts and emotions. The bird does not necessarily want to eat when it remarks, "Polly wants a cracker." Glossolalia (speaking in tongues), which is sometimes heard in some Pentecostal churches, is also speech without discernible meaning. So are phrases in many popular songs: "Vo do dee oh do!" "Hey nonny nonny and a hot cha cha!" "Tra la la!" Then, of course, there are patients with certain forms of aphasia who speak but whose words make no sense.

All right, then: If we accept the independence of speech and language, what effect does this have on our topic? Quite a lot! As we hope to make clear, unless you accept the independence of speech and language you cannot appreciate American Sign Language (Ameslan) as it truly is—a fully developed language independent of English. The fact that Ameslan is a language independent of English (if you agree it is a fact) has been the basis for the enormous mushrooming of interest in manual communication. What is more, it is having a considerable influence on the education of deaf children and the rehabilitation of deaf adults. Through a better understanding of manual communication, we begin to see more efficient ways of working with deaf people. As is usually the case in science, increasing our understanding of one thing—sign languages—will help us understand another—English. Developing better methods of education for deaf children may also help us do a better job of teaching children who can see and hear normally. Scientific advance in one area has a way of spilling over into other areas.

HEARING VS. SEEING

Our two distance receptors, sight and hearing, are so intimately a part of us that we may not have given much thought to them. When both are intact, they work in tandem like a pair of well-bred coach horses pulling a carriage; they do it so smoothly it is difficult to separate the effort of one from the other. But when either sense is seriously impaired or absent, we detect gross differences in the way the other one functions. For perceiving language, one point is clear: we hear sequentially, but we see simultaneously. That difference in temporal relations is one key to unlocking a distinction between spoken and signed languages.

If two words are simultaneously spoken, one contributes noise relative to the other. We interpret sounds in order. But when viewing a scene, we can grasp at once several of its features and their relations. When we describe it, we are forced to enumerate, to recite the features sequentially, but that is characteristic of our language and of the speech process upon which it is based. In sign language, however, more than one idea can be expressed at the same moment. We will find this characteristic useful in classifying different approaches to manual communication and understanding their impact on the development of the "silent" languages as opposed to those which are sound-based.

Classification of Manual Communication

The generic term describing the use of hands to systematically convey thoughts and feelings is *manual communication*. Sign language is one form of manual communication; fingerspelling is another. And sign languages come in several varieties.

If we place English and Ameslan on opposite ends of a line representing the linguistic distance between the two, then at points in between we would place variations on each language, along with synthetic sign languages that have been developed in the last twenty years. Psycholinguists and anthropologists would refer to some of these in-between languages as *pidgins*. "Pidgin" derives from the Chinese corruption of the English word *business*, and originally signified a combination of often mispronounced English words delivered in Chinese syntax. The simplified language was used by Chinese and English traders to transact business in Chinese ports. Pidgin carries with it the connotation of inferiority, of something makeshift (which Chinese-English pidgin certainly is), and it designates what often results when two distinct languages collide[4].

Originally, linguists considered Ameslan as an English pidgin—if they gave it any thought at all. Distinguishing a pidgin from a natural language has critical social implications. Chapter 3 discusses this point at some length. It is raised here because we need to outline our approach to the principal languages we will be discussing, English and Ameslan. We need to recognize that they are both natural languages, that they interact, and that the results of their interaction can be observed, in part, in the various pidgins which have grown out of their contiguity.

Since English is the language of the dominant majority, we order the sign variations which have grown up in the United States by how much they resemble English. At the extreme opposite end from English is Ameslan, followed by many variations of Manual English, then by spoken and written English. In our presentation, we will take up Ameslan first and in greatest detail, followed by Manual English, and then by fingerspelling—literally printing in the air. The latter form of manual communication, one that is relatively easy to learn, permits us to reproduce English as it would appear on the printed page. The difference, however, is that writing in air is evanescent and cannot be studied and reevaluated as writing on paper can.

DISCIPLINES

The study of sign language is not the sole province of linguists. Anthropologists of all kinds, educators, neurologists, psychologists, sociologists, and others have begun to look at manual communication to provide enlightenment on language and on human interactions. Ever since the revolution in physics, scientists have recognized the centrality of language to their activities. Their newly aroused interest in sign language comes naturally.

Our treatment of the subject will try to avoid the jargon of the disciplines which have now embraced manual communication—linguistics, education, rehabilitation, psychology, anthropology—and will try to find common paths through the academic maze. As we examine some of the technical terms used, we shall assume that the reader is unacquainted with them, so each will be explained as it is introduced. What is more, we will attempt a comprehensive view of sign, eschewing detail in favor of breadth. To compensate, we include a guide to the growing literature, a guide that should enable readers to pursue their enthusiasms.

SEMIOLOGY

If we had to select one name for a discipline solely devoted to the study of sign it would be *semiology*. The Oxford English Dictionary and Webster's New World Dictionary, both distinguished lexicons, do not agree as to the meaning of this useful, seldom used word; nor do they agree as to its spelling (*semeiology* in the former and *semiology* in the latter). The Oxford's first meaning for the word is "sign language." The Webster's sole definition is "the science of signs in general." They do agree on the Greek root, *semeion* (sign). It would appear that semiology could accommodate our interest in sign *language* as well as in sign *codes*, a distinction that, if not clear now, will become so in the chapters to follow. Semiology also seems to fit our concern with both the scientific and the cultural aspects of sign. For some reason, authorities in this area have not adopted semiology as the name for the study of the art and science of sign. It seems a worthy candidate. I offer it here without foreboding, but with some anticipation of minor controversy. If it arises, that will be to the good, for such debates typically stir increased attention to a subject, and the subject of semiology has been ignored too long by large segments of the scientific and artistic communities that should find its study fascinating and rewarding.

WARNING: This Book May Be Dangerous to Preconceptions

It may seem a bit farfetched to issue a warning of possible emotional upset. But is it? Language is a very personal thing. An insult to a person's language usually arouses powerful reactions. How we use language is taken as an index of our intelligence and clearly marks our social position. George Bernard Shaw makes that point in his popular drama about language, *Pygmalion*. The musical version of that classic keeps the original lines of the eponymous hero as, in Act I, he refers to Eliza Doolittle in her flower-girl rags:

> You see this creature with her Kerbstone English: the English that will keep her in the gutter to the end of her days. Well, sir, in three months I could pass that girl off as a duchess at an ambassador's garden party. I could even get her a place as a lady's maid or a shop assistant, which requires better English.

In his preface to the play, Shaw comments, "Finally, and for the encouragement of people troubled with accents that cut them off from all high employment, I may add that the change wrought by Professor Higgins in the flower-girl is neither impossible nor uncommon." Shaw cannot resist this added bolstering of his argument, nor would many knowledgeable persons disagree with his fundamental claim, if not his hyperbole, about the critical determination of social status by language.

In 1866, the Linguistic Society of Paris would not permit the presentation of papers which raised questions about the origin of language. To raise the issue at all was blasphemous. Language was the exclusive property of humans, the basis for our uniqueness. To question its origins was to imply that it might not have been handed down from above.[5] Even now there are theorists who react emotionally to any questions about language existing in forms other than human.[6] To them, the very attribution of such a complex function to "lower" forms of life seems to demean our own. To readers who hold that view of language, what follows may be upsetting.

Are we sometimes chauvinistic about our language? The present acceptance of English as essential to the study of most sciences reinforces such attitudes. We should remind ourselves that in Shakespeare's time English was regarded as a "barbarous, vulgar, and rude tongue without logic." It was not considered fit for scientific, let alone for polite, discourse. Four hundred years ago Sir Thomas More commented on the subject of the English language:

> That our language is called barbarous is but a fantasy, for so is, as every learned man knoweth, every strange language to any other. And though they would call it barren of words, there is no doubt that it is plenteous enough to express our minds in anything whereof one man hath used to speak with another.[7]

Flora Lewis, in a sardonic vein, tells a joke to make a similar observation about linguistic insularity:

> Refusal to accept anyone else's language as worth knowing reflects the same narrow-gauge kind of head, the same stubborn ignorance, as that of the fundamentalist I heard about who denounced people speaking in other tongues, saying, "If English was good enough for Jesus Christ, it's good enough for them." The story is apocryphal in both senses.[8]

Governments have seen control of language as a means of dominating the citizenry. The idea is not in the least absurd. If all government is conducted in a language other than your own, then you do not have ready access to that government. If you cannot understand what is said about you in court, you cannot adequately answer your accusers. If you cannot read the placards, fill out the forms, and in other respects communicate with the government, then you are the government's vassal. You will not be able to advance your status in a government whose language you cannot use. Your livelihood, and possibly your life, will be in jeopardy should a language not known to you become the basis of commerce. In addition, think of what it means when the sovereign language, whatever it might be, is touted as a superior vehicle for thought. We shall see that this idea has continually been broached by adherents of particular cultures.[9]

Remember furthermore that wars have been fought over language. For example, in Belgium, the Flemings and the Walloons have fought for nearly three centuries about whose language should prevail, and now have only an uneasy truce. In 1980, the citizens of Quebec barely defeated a proposal to secede from Canada, a move some Quebecois believed necessary to protect their French language. As it is, Canada is now a firmly bilingual country, with every official document printed in both French and English.

So at national levels and at personal levels, language is critical. No wonder, then, that discussions of it can provoke strong emotions. You need to approach what follows with an open mind. The conclusions to be drawn from revised views of our world may prove to be much more fruitful than the perspectives they replace. And even if you make no conceptual reorganizations, you will likely enjoy meeting some of your silent neighbors—in their language.

2

A First Look at
American Sign Language

In this chapter we will discuss the structure of signs, what they look like, and how they are put together. The next chapters will cover related questions—for example: What rules govern the combination of signs into meaningful units (grammar)? Where did sign originate? How did it grow? How many signs? Who uses sign language? In this chapter, however, we will concentrate on a basic linguistic description of sign.

For convenience we will use the acronym *Ameslan* to designate American Sign Language.[1] When we want to speak about sign languages in general, we will only say *sign* or *sign language*. Other abbreviations will identify sign languages from different nations—for instance, *Franslan* for French Sign Language. These abbreviations and acronyms help readability; if you forget what a particular one means, consult the index to locate its definition.

What Is a Sign?

A sign is a hand-motion configuration that conveys meaning. It is made up of different handshapes, in various positions relative to the signer's body, cast into a wide assortment of motions. As each of these—the handshape, the relative position, and the motion—changes, the meaning of the sign is altered. Signs may also be made by movements of other body parts, especially the eyes and shoulders.

Since the basic semantic unit in English is the word, we naturally seek a parallel in Ameslan. That parallel is the individual sign. Saying that the sign is the manual equivalent of the word, however, is a little misleading. Signs may represent more general concepts, with the refined nature of the concept derived from context and from extramanual cues. The fact that investigators of sign often treat signs as words is *their* interpretation; it is not inherent in sign language. Put another way, researchers approach sign with preconceptions and intellectual limitations that they tend to impose on the subject of their studies. Perhaps there is no immediately satisfactory alternative, but we should remind ourselves of this ethnocentricity whenever we encounter another culture. Ameslan takes us into another culture, even though its practitioners live with us in the same country.

When we say that the closest analog to the word in spoken languages is the sign in manual languages, we realize that the statement is correct but inexact. Nonetheless, that view will be useful as a premise to our analysis. We need to consider the physical aspects of sign before taking up the semantic.

Components of Sign

A sign can be analyzed into three basic parts: the shape of the hands, the motion of the hands, and the position of the hands relative to the signer's body. William Stokoe, whose name we shall encounter frequently in connection with sign, has given brief labels to each of the three characteristics of a sign: *dez* (the handshape), *sig* (the motion made with the hands), and *tab* (the position of the hands relative to the rest of the body).[2]

Because signs involve movement as well as different handshapes, they are difficult to represent on the printed page. Throughout the book, the artist indicates the *initial* position of a sign with dotted lines and the *final* position with solid lines; arrows are used to show the direction of the movement. When attempting to make the sign, try looking at yourself in the mirror in order to gain the same perspective that the artist used in drawing the figures, or ask a companion to make the sign according to the illustration. The drawings show what you see when someone else is signing.

Figures 1 to 10 illustrate different dez-sig-tab configurations. Each set of figures uses one handshape (dez) in different locations (tabs) and with different motions (sigs). Figure 1 shows the sign for *work* or *working*. The dez is the closed

1. *Working*

fist. The tab is the front of the body, a little above the waist. The sig is a hammering motion of the right hand (if a person is left-handed, the hands are reversed, a point discussed later). When the dez and tabs are the same but the sig (motion) changes, the result is the sign in Figure 2—*necking* (you can think of the fists as heads of two lovers). Such similarities between signs permit punning, just as in spoken languages. In this case, imagine inviting an attractive person of the opposite sex to join you in working/necking!

2. Necking

Another change of motion gives a completely different concept, as shown in Figure 3, in which the hands are clenched into fists and the initial position is like that for "work" or "neck" but the motion changes to vigorously parting the two hands in an outward-upward direction. Doing so signifies *freedom*.

3. Freedom

The open hand with the thumb touching the center of the palm begins a completely new series of signs. Figure 4 shows the sign for *blue*, made by waving the open palm in front and to the side of the body. When the same handshape is drawn down alongside the mouth, the result is the sign for *brown*. The same handshape moving back and forth behind the left hand held about waist-high (the position for *working* shown in Figure 1) signifies *busy*, as shown in Figure 5.

4. *Blue*

5. *Busy*

The next set of figures shows the closed hand with a pointing finger. The same handshape (dez) and the same motion (sig) can have a completely unrelated meaning when the tab changes. Figures 6 through 9 illustrate four different signs, all having the same dez (pointing finger) and sig, but different tabs. First is *think*, a circling motion at the temple. Then the sign for *Chinese* is made by a circular twist at the side of the eye. Dropping to the nose changes the sign to *boring*. Placed at the chin, the sign becomes *sour*. One motion, but four very different concepts.

6. *Think*

7. *Chinese*

8. *Boring*

9. *Sour*

Continuing to use the pointed hand, one can sign *you* (Figure 10) or indicate *me* by directing the finger against the chest. To sign *they*, the same pointing hand sweeps an arc of 60 to 90 degrees in front of the signer. The differences in these three signs, as with the others using a particular handshape, are in the motions and where they are made relative to the signer's body. Some of the differences are small, others gross. As with distinctions in speech, the experienced signer becomes attuned to the nuances and quickly detects relatively minute changes in dez, sig, and tab.

10. You

CHARACTERISTICS OF DEZ

If you already know the American Manual Alphabet, you will recognize that the three handshapes on pages 10 and 11 are similar to letters in the manual alphabet. (If you are not, you will find the manual alphabet discussed in Chapter 6. However, you can follow this discussion without referring to that chapter at this time.) The closed fist shown in Figures 1, 2, and 3 is the letter S. The open palm in Figures 4 and 5 is either the letter B or, as will be explained later, the number 4. The pointing finger is the number 1.

Note that particular handshapes are associated with some general notions. For example, the X hand (one or two hooked fingers) tends to fit harsh, negative ideas, like *stealing* (Figure 11) and *strict* (Figure 12). (Many students of Ameslan would consider the sign for *strict* to be a sign version of American English slang, depicting "hard-nosed." The same hand position and sharp striking motion, when

11. *Stealing*

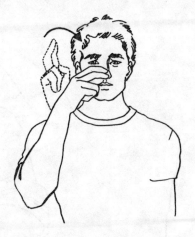

12. *Strict*

used with the opposite hand, means "hard." Substituting the nose for the passive hand makes the visual pun one motion. Otherwise *hard-nosed* could be signed by pointing to the nose, followed by signing *hard*.) The correspondences are not entirely regular, but they are worth being attentive to when learning the language.

Another general notion is expressed by the use of the index finger—for indexing, or indicating, who is being talked about, or for establishing particular reference points ("you" and "me," for instance). Linguists have borrowed a word from logic, *deictic* (proving or showing), to designate the pointing signs. Figures 6 through 10 illustrate signs using the deictic dez.

The conceptual connections between certain handshapes and some cognitive-emotional categories also occur between speech sounds and cognitive-emotional concepts in English and in other spoken languages. Think about *gr*. By itself, it is an expression of anger favored by cartoonists: "Gr-r-r!" It initiates various dour words, such as *gray, grief, grime, grubby*, and *grueling*. This association may be onomatopoeic, as in *buzz* and *hum*, or it may have other roots. To say that such imitative speech sounds occur in English does not downgrade the language. All that the coincidence of affect and sound does is to provide a clue about origins to students of the language. The same holds true for sign.

Certain other relations of handshape and meaning emerge in Ameslan. However, these relations are not invariant. There are ample exceptions. From the dez alone, one cannot necessarily determine the meaning of a sign. It takes the three elements combined, and sometimes more, to convey a sign's meaning.

CHARACTERISTICS OF TAB

The *tabula* or tab does seem to have some regularly observed relation to meaning. Its use also has its taboos in Ameslan.

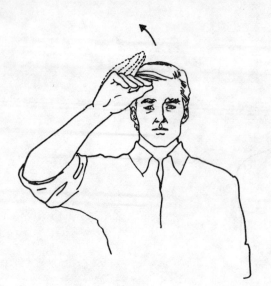

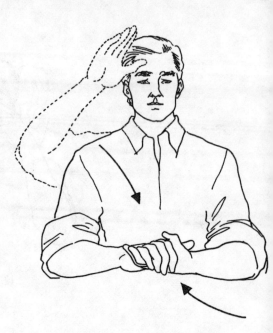

13. Man

14. Husband

Signs about the forehead usually have one of two connotations: maleness or cognition. The two concepts may be interrelated in some way, but that is highly speculative. In any case, the sign for *man* in Ameslan is given by moving a 5 hand away from the forehead and simultaneously bringing the thumb and fingers together (Figure 13). The male sign can be combined with other signs to develop further variations. *Husband* (Figure 14), for example, combines the male sign with the sign for *marry*, the two hands clasped together in front of the signer. *Gentleman* combines the male sign with the sign for *fine* or *finery* (Figure 15), which consists of the thumb touching the chest and the remaining fingers spread out. When the male sign is joined with the sign shown in Figure 16, the result is *father*, which is sometimes glossed as "the man who holds the baby." If that idea helps you remember the sign, the mnemonic can be useful, but it should not be uncritically accepted as the sign's origin.

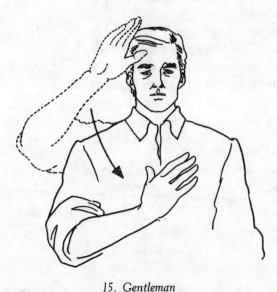

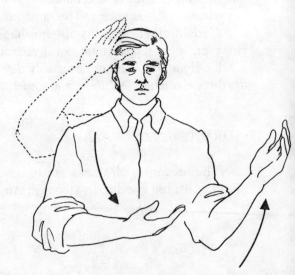

15. Gentleman

16. Father

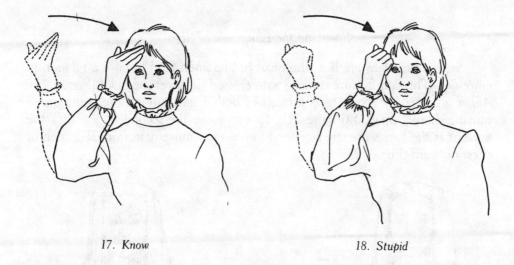

17. *Know*   18. *Stupid*

Cognitive signs in one way or another touch the forehead. Figure 17 shows the sign for *know*, which is made with a *B*-like hand directed toward the forehead. (If the orientation and motion are slightly changed, the meaning alters radically: the upright *B* hand struck against the forehead signifies "bastard"; striking it against the chin [in the female area of the head] produces "bitch." Some linguists have added a fourth component to Stokoe's triad. In addition to dez, sig, and tab, they describe the orientation of the hand [prone, supine, etc.] Other aspects of signs are also needed to complete their descriptions. Stokoe et al. [1965] anticipated the need for more details. The elegance of the first taxonomy's three rubrics, however, remains a model of scientific intuition that spurs research.) Striking the forehead with the fist (*S* hand) symbolizes *stupid*, illustrated in Figure 18. These two signs have the same tab (the forehead) and similar sigs (motion toward the forehead) but differ in dez, again pointing up how a small change—in this case, in handshape—grossly alters meaning.

Wriggling the *G* hand as it moves upward and away from the forehead makes the sign for dream (Figure 19), another kind of cognition. An illustration of a compound sign in the cognitive realm is the one for *believe*, shown in Figure 20. It is made up of the cognitive sign (index finger touching forehead) plus the sign for *marry* or *join together*.

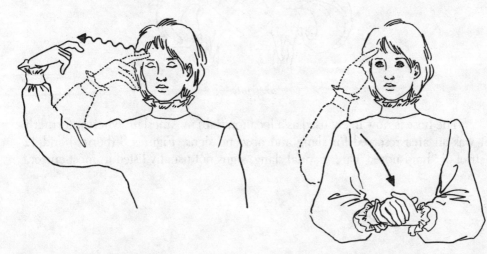

19. *Dream*   20. *Believe*

Signs whose tabs are near the heart or abdomen tend to have a relation to emotions. The sign for *love* is made with crossed fists over the heart (Figure 21). *Anger* is signed by a clutching motion of both hands around the beltline and moving sharply upward (Figure 22). To sign *hate*, the second fingers flick the thumbs as the hands execute a general throw-away movement from abdomen or chest outward (Figure 23).

21. *Love*

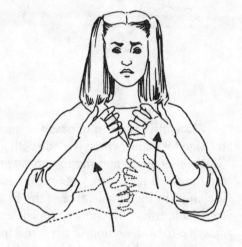

22. *Anger*

23. *Hate*

The nose is now freely used as a location (tab) in Ameslan, whereas formerly it was an area reserved for slang and obscene signs. Figures 8 (boring) and 12 (strict or "hard-nosed") are manual slang, signs not usually listed in most current

Ameslan glossaries. By contrast, other sign languages do not have the same taboos that occur in Ameslan.[3] While many signs involving the nose in Ameslan are pejorative, the Chinese, for instance, do not observe this tabular distinction. On the other hand, they regard signs about the midsection as having sexual-eliminative connotations. We will see in Chapter 6 that this grafting of cultural implications onto signs occurs even in the manual alphabets. Certain handshapes are forbidden in polite use by deaf people in some cultures but not in others.

   Again, the identification of tabs with particular meanings has distinct limitations. Exceptions abound. But the underlying idea can be helpful in learning to sign and in appreciating the structure of Ameslan.

CHARACTERISTICS OF SIG

   Motions make up the third structural component of signs. The sig varies in at least four aspects: type of motion, direction, vigor, and extent. Portraying some of these aspects in drawings is exceedingly difficult, if it is possible at all. That is one reason why, as will be shown in a later chapter, sign cannot be learned from books alone. However, the underlying principles of sig can be elucidated by means of drawings supplemented by verbal explanation, though the nuances of a particular sign are less easily conveyed. One finds, too, that much of the poetry of sign language comes from the sig. The transition from sign to sign in a smoothly flowing pattern of motions can delight the eye in the way that well-executed ballet steps do. When done well, signing seduces the eyes as singing does the ears. Unfortunately, the limits of print frustrate any attempt to portray the sequential beauty of sign.

   The directions of motions, in a simple sense, replace the functions served by word order and verb tense in English. For example, the sign for *going* is the same as for *coming*, except for the directions: when signing *going* one makes the motion away from the body, whereas in signing *coming* the motion is toward oneself (Figures 24 and 25).

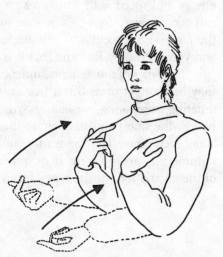

24. *Going*   25. *Coming*

Repeating the motion pluralizes; thus, doing *year* twice signifies "years." This repetition serves the same function as adding the suffix *s* or *es* in English. The repeated signs are sometimes incorrectly glossed as "year, year" instead of "years." The former interpretation makes the signer appear grossly inelegant, rather than highlighting the ingenious nature of Ameslan.

The vigor with which one makes a sign, the emphasis one places on it, and the tension of the body that accompanies it—all contribute to its meaning. Figure 26 shows the signs *small, big,* and *enormous,* the difference between them being the distance one moves the hands apart. The vigor of the movement, which is not shown, would add the intentions of "very" or "a little," as in "a little smaller piece." The possibilities for even finer shadings are obvious.

26. *Small, Big, Enormous*   27. *Dislike*

A vigorous movement can change a sign from *dislike* to *hate,* as can different facial expressions (compare Figures 23 and 27). As with vocal inflections, the energy and speed with which a sign is made alters its meaning. Similarly, one can add sarcasm, irony, "a reverse twist," and so on, to what is being signed by the manner of execution. You are familiar with this feature in spoken language and you need only imagine that it is applicable manually.

The types of movements, independent of their direction, extent, and energy, may be thought of as linear (for example, Figure 11), as jagged, smoothly undulating, supinating, pronating, wriggling (Figure 19), and so on. In using both hands, the one hand may circle the other or they may simultaneously revolve about each other. The hands may converge or diverge in a variety of basic motions: hammering, as in Figure 1, or quickly separating, as in Figure 3. The number of these variations in the type of movement, combined with the other aspects of sig and the variations in dez and tab, creates virtually endless possibilities for discrete signs. Their potential number certainly approaches, if it does not surpass, the number of English words.

Variations: Accents and Eccentricities

Those who share a common language vary widely in their expression of it. Mimics take advantage of individual eccentricities of speech to quickly identify a well-known personage. One could instantly conjure the late Ed Sullivan by saying *really big show* as "reee-lee big she-ohh!" Speakers from the South are supposed to be recognizable by their pronunciation of the phrase *you all* as "y'all," and Bostonians by their pronouncing *Cuba* "k'you-ber." These eccentricities in expression apply as well to sign.

Every individual will sign in a way that is slightly different from anyone else. Some of the variation is due to the individual's physique: longer or shorter hands and arms, and greater or lesser finger dexterity. Where the person learned sign, and at what age, are factors determining how signs will be executed. These idiosyncracies should be expected. But the extremes of dialect differences need to be mentioned, because they tend to be so much greater in Ameslan than in English. The principal reason is the limited distribution of Ameslan.

Before radio and television exposed huge chunks of the population to Standard English, dialect differences were much greater than they are at present in the United States. We have substantially reduced the variations in spoken English. The majority in the United States tends to make the same word choices and to pronounce words in essentially the same way, idiosyncracies aside.

Ameslan has not had this wide exposure. In fact, as will be noted in Chapter 4, the teaching of Ameslan is a relatively new phenomenon. For most of the last one hundred years, Ameslan was passed on informally from individual to individual, a means of transmission not apt to retain linguistic integrity. Furthermore, no simple system for writing sign has found much acceptance, so the available dictionaries have contained descriptions in English by observers who were often linguistically naïve. These scattered texts tended toward an authoritarian view of language, seeking *the correct* sign for whatever concept was noted. They emphasized the one, the sole, the only way to express each idea.

We recognize now that there is no one way to execute a particular sign, any more than there is necessarily only one correct sign for a particular concept. The *Dictionary of American Sign Language* comments: "Almost all that has been put into print about American sign language gives, intentionally or not, the impression that a sign must be made precisely so, will always be seen made that way, and admits of no variation. Nothing could be further from the truth. Individual, local, regional, and other differences operate at all levels in all languages."[4] Hence, the student of sign must learn to see the regularities underlying the discrepancies in production of signs, a skill that comes with practice.

Students who attempt to learn sign from sign lexicons will certainly be frustrated when they observe signs in continuous discourse. As with a spoken word, the articulation of a sign varies with what precedes and what succeeds it. The boundaries of the signs shown in these pages will shift somewhat when put into context. Consider signing *dream good* and *work good* (Figures 1, 19, and 30). In the former phrase, the right hand must be brought down to the mouth from a point in front and above the head; in the second phrase, the right hand moves from chest height up to the mouth. The sign for *good* will appear the same to the experienced sign reader, but may not to the novice. Indeed, the latter may not see *good* at all, taking it for the ending movement of either of the preceding signs. Because the signs one learns in isolation from other signs tend to be modified as they are used in groups, one seldom, if ever, can gain competence in signing solely from studying books. (For more about learning to sign, see Chapter 7.)

Extramanual Cues

In Ameslan, the hands do not say it all. The face is a critical component of sign. Posture also contributes to the interpretation of a signed message. These extramanual features of Ameslan may act as signs themselves (without accompanying hand movements) or as syntactic elements—i.e., as the formal components that alter the meaning of a set of signs. In English, the same set of words can be statement or question, depending on the word order: Are you the one? You are the one! Ameslan, too, has rules for changing a given group of signs to produce a different interpretation. (We will save our discussion of syntax for the next chapter. Here we want to expand our discussion of the units of Ameslan, the signs. You will note, however, that the material in this and in the next chapter necessarily overlap.)

The way one uses eyes—the direction of gaze, for instance, or squinting—has considerable meaning in the sign phrase. Signers regularly establish the individuals about whom they are speaking by assigning a specific position to them in the space to the left or right or in front of themselves. Then, by looking at that position, the signer indicates that the person in that position is being referred to as either the subject or the object of the sentence. Alternatively, pointing a finger at a particular location can accomplish the same purpose.

There are many other ways in which the eyes indicate something significant about the message being signed. It may be as integral as an adverbial portion of the message. For example, the sign for *future* (Figure 28) may be modified by squinting and pursing the lips as one signs it, thus indicating that it is far, far distant (Figure 29). Raising the brows indicates a question; drawing them down in a frowning expression indicates negation.

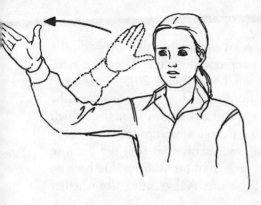

28. *Future*

29. *Far into the future*

Eye contact is another important element in manual communication. The persons to whom the signed message is addressed must maintain their gaze fixed on the signer. When they look away, they are interrupting the message, especially if they accompany their averted gaze with the initiation of signs of their own. Because they cannot communicate unless they are looking at the message source, deaf people regard diverting one's gaze as interrupting or ending the contact.

Signers use their eyes in a variety of ways. As noted, one function is to indicate the subject or object of what is being signed. Another is to emphasize what is being signed—for example, by looking away from the person addressed until one is ready to make a particular sign, and then fixing one's gaze while simultaneously making that sign. Closing the eyes has the same effect: signing *good* (Figure 30) and at the same time narrowing one's eyes signifies *very good* (Figure 31). A variation on the sign—turning the palm toward the viewer while frowning—reverses its meaning to *bad* (Figure 32).

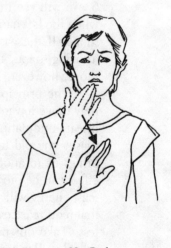

30. *Good*

31. *Very good*

32. *Bad*

In addition to eye gaze, the eyebrows play an important role. They add the question mark in questions, going up at the appropriate point. They rise sympathetically or contract with anger or to add emphasis (Figure 29).

The importance of eyes in animal communication has been considered by anthropologists.[5] They note the relatively large white sclera in humans, which makes it easy to determine the direction of gaze. People's eyes are easier to "read" than are those of many animals. Whether our eyes evolved as they did because of their communicative value or whether they have communicative value because they happened to evolve as they did is one of those irresolvable issues, like whether the chicken or the egg came first. What is no longer at issue is the importance of the signer's eyes. In Ameslan, the eyes are as critical as the hands in communicating meaning.

Bimanualism

We have only one tongue with which to speak, but we have two hands with which to sign. And Ameslan makes use of both. It has principles that govern relations between the hands and determine which does what in a broad range of signs.

When a sign requires that one hand be passive (Figure 1, for example), the active hand is always the signer's dominant hand: right for right-handed people and vice versa. Likewise, the dominant hand almost always is the one to act when only one hand moves.

Along with the dominance principle, Ameslan has a symmetry principle that is a bit more difficult to articulate. Simply put, the two hands will have the same shape whenever they are both active. This is illustrated in Figures 22, 23, 24, and 25. (When we discuss some of the recently contrived sign systems, in Chapter 6, we will see that they violate this principle in several instances.) Notice that when the left hand remains passive, as in Figure 5, the right hand has a different shape. If the passive hand provides a base or a reference point for the active (moving) hand, the handshapes will not necessarily be the same. If both hands move, however, they will have the same shape.

The principle of symmetry also holds for type of motion. The two hands may move toward or away from each other, but the type of motion they make— linear, undulating, etc.—will be the same: Ameslan does not require that you master the old trick of patting your head while rubbing your stomach. Which brings us to another principle: the principle of reduced effort. When a similar effect can be produced by two or more groups of motions, the one requiring the least energy will prevail. That notion seems to govern speech as well. Activities that require excessive energy expenditure tend to be replaced by those that expend less. Take our pronunciation of the name Barbara; its spelling indicates three syllables, Bar-bar-a. But the repetitive "bar-bar" is difficult to pronounce, so the name is usually rendered "Bar-bra." It sounds similar, but the second articulation takes less energy. Signs follow the same principle: the actions tend toward minimal effort. That largely eliminates signs in which the two hands perform conflicting motions simultaneously. One test of this principle has been made by Nancy Frishberg.[6] She studied movies of signers made early in this century and compared the signs they made to those now in use for the same concepts. She found the anticipated tendencies toward muscularly simplified signs. She also compared entries from earlier dictionaries to present-day ones, and again noted the reduced effort.

Specialized Signs

Can you swear in sign? Does Ameslan have naughty words? Is Ameslan up-to-date, with signs for the new drugs? Space flight? Medical terminology? The answer to all these questions is yes. Ameslan provides for a full range of blasphemies. There may not be a precise one-to-one relation between the swear words of English and the signed versions, but there are ample signs to cover all pejoratives and cast every curse.

No aspect of sexual behavior is without a sign, whether male or female, homosexual or heterosexual. These signs have recently been collected and published especially to aid interpreters.[7] The author, James Woodward, points out how important it can be to distinguish between various sexual signs. For example, in a court case, a deaf man was asked if he wanted to rape the woman he was alleged to have attacked. The interpreter, ignorant of the sign for *rape*, phrased the question "Did you want to *have intercourse with* the woman?" Obviously, a yes response could have resulted in the deaf man's conviction through misunderstanding.[8]

The sexual signs include names for body parts, very important to physicians examining deaf persons. The various signs need to be understood by therapists working with emotionally disturbed deaf clients. Similarly, a dictionary of terms for drug use is invaluable in counseling deaf teenagers about the effects of abuse. Woodward has provided a compendium for that area, too.[9] Special collections of signs have been developed for teaching highly technical subjects, for use in medical emergency rooms, and for other specialized purposes.[10]

Ameslan adds signs as spoken languages add words. New concepts arise, calling for distinctive ways to indicate them. Sometimes more than one sign emerges; for example, Woodward lists two ways to indicate that one is *stoned*. Ameslan sometimes borrows from English, as in the slang term *reds* for barbiturates. On other occasions, Ameslan uses abbreviated fingerspelling to signal a new idea, as for *Quaaludes*, in which the letter *Q* alone stands for that drug. Puns may also gain standing. Some deaf teenagers use the sign for *necktie* to mean "Thai-stick." Over time that awkward pun may be modified to the point that its origin is lost but its meaning retained.[11]

How Many Signs?

Any discussion of Ameslan's capacity to add signs usually prompts the question "How many signs are there?" The answer can be no more precise than the answer to the same question about English words. First, you would have to decide what would be counted as a sign (or word). Do you count all versions of *to do* or only the infinitive form? You can see that this decision alone would alter the count greatly. What about compounds? Do combined signs count as one or two signs? For example, *husband* contains two signs, *man* and *marry*. Again, how that decision is made will grossly affect the answer. One could count entries in the leading sign dictionaries. From the most extensive, the resulting figure is about five thousand.[12] But does that represent the extent of Ameslan's sign field? Hardly.

The question about the number of Ameslan's signs can be approached in another way. We might ask if there are concepts that Ameslan cannot convey, or cannot convey as accurately, as in, say, English. The answer to that question shows that Ameslan has a potential equal to any linguistic task. Where it may presently lack a particular sign—because the concept is new or newly introduced to the deaf community—Ameslan has the capability of growth. It can add signs as English does. If our question is whether Ameslan can handle communication at all levels and in all circumstances, the answer is resoundingly yes.

In 1962, Dean George Detmold, who directed student dramas as well as heading the faculty of Gallaudet College (the only liberal arts college for deaf students in the world), commissioned a tour de force to demonstrate that Ameslan had unlimited linguistic scope. He asked William Stokoe to translate into sign Act III of Shaw's *Man and Superman* (the play within a play called "Don Juan in Hell"). The act is almost wholly made up of speeches by the four characters: Don Juan, Donna Elvira, her father, and the Devil. Their discussions are largely of abstract subjects—love, hate, peace, and war. Here is a brief representative sample:

> *Don Juan:* Pooh! why should I be civil to them or to you? In this Palace of Lies a truth or two will not hurt you. Your friends are all the dullest dogs I know. They are not beautiful: they are only decorated. They are not clean: they are only shaved and starched. They are not dignified: they are only fashionably dressed. They are not educated: they are only college passmen. They are not religious: they are only pewrenters. They are not moral: they are only conventional. They are not virtuous: they are only cowardly. They are not even vicious: they are only "frail." They are not artistic: they are only lascivious. They are not prosperous: they are only rich. They are not loyal, they are only servile; not dutiful, only sheepish; not public spirited,

only patriotic; not courageous, only quarrelsome; not determined, only obstinate; not masterful, only domineering; not self-controlled, only obtuse; not self-respecting, only vain; not kind, only sentimental; not social, only gregarious; not considerate, only polite; not intelligent, only opinionated; not progressive, only factious; not imaginative, only superstitious; not just, only vindictive; not generous, only propitiatory; not disciplined, only cowed; and not truthful at all—liars every one of them, to the very backbone of their souls.

That speech, like the rest of the dialogue, was successfully signed by a talented group of deaf college students. So well did they do that they were invited to repeat their performances on the local television station, which they did to considerable critical acclaim.[13] Incidentally, you will not find a sign for every word in Don Juan's eloquent peroration; *passmen*, for example, is not only not a term in Ameslan, it is also not used in American English. Of course, Stokoe found suitable signs that were true to the playwright's intent. That problem often arises in translating a play from one language to another. The point here, however, is that Ameslan is not limited in its ability to express concepts, whether technical or artistic or whatever.

Name Signs

Proper names can be fingerspelled when they are first introduced into conversation (see Chapter 6). But continual fingerspelling of a name can become tedious. (Imagine a heated discussion about Engelbert Humperdinck!) Ameslan provides an economical solution to this problem. It is the *name sign*. Name signs signify individuals by brief gestures that usually, but not always, incorporate some prominent feature of their physiognomy or use an initial from their name. For example, a prettily dimpled lady named Enid might be given a sign consisting of the fingerspelled letter *E* touching the signer's face at places where dimples appear on Enid's cheeks. However, name signs are not always flattering. Among some deaf liberals, President Reagan's name sign is an *R* drawn across the throat.

Name signs are not formally conferred; there is no baptismal ceremony. Name signs spring up and if they appeal to signers, they stick to that person. For whatever time they are used, name signs serve as a shorthand way of designating a particular person.

Kathryn Meadow, a sociologist interested in sign and the deaf community, has studied name signs. She found the majority of deaf persons eager to investigate the topic. Her research leads her to speculate that "leaders in the deaf world might want to consider capitalizing on the positive possibilities for building identity and group identification through the encouragement and support of the notion of formal, ritualized assignment of name signs, which could reflect personal, family, and community identification and pride."[14] If as a newcomer to the deaf community you are fortunate enough to be assigned a name sign, you may learn something of how you are viewed by your deaf colleagues.

Iconicity

How do you determine the extent to which signs are *iconic* (attempts to picture the subject or action)? Pantomime is an attempt to demonstrate in action objects and activities not actually present. The mime may convey the presence of a wall by the way he reacts to a part of the space around him; or he may go through the motions of eating a meal, though no food or implements are there. When the signer expresses the thought, "I am going to the movies," does he pantomime the action or does he use arbitrarily selected signs? The question has relevance to Ameslan's status as a language, since pantomime lacks the linguistic status afforded abstract symbols. Because the subject is of considerable importance to students of sign, it has had much attention.

First of all, if signs are essentially iconic, then uninformed observers should be able to translate them. A number of studies have presented signs to persons who have never studied sign and asked them to guess what each sign means. The results have shown consistently that most signs are not transparent (their meanings are not correctly identified by naïve persons).[15]

Secondly, researchers find that signs for the same concepts are different in various sign languages.[16] Deaf persons cannot read signs from other languages on first contact; in other words, the iconic properties claimed for many signs are not immediately apparent to regular users of sign from different countries.

A third strategy for studying iconicity is to ask native signers for explanations of the signs they do use. These attempts to get at the logic, the iconic basis, of signs reveal that either (a) there are competing explanations or (b) the post hoc explanations do not accord with the established knowledge of the origins, where such knowledge exists. A case of the latter is the recently emerged sign for *bread*. As discussed in Chapter 6, young deaf students will provide an iconic explanation, even though the evidence strongly points to the origin as a condensed fingerspelling of the word.[17]

An equally compelling argument against imposing an iconic explanation of most signs is that it cannot be invoked as a factor in young deaf children's acquisition of them. Take the sign for *father*: young deaf children may never see their father wearing a hat (the first part of the sign supposedly indicates the man's hat brim or a knight's visor) or holding a baby (the presumed second half of the compound sign). Similarly, for those who regard the sign for *milk* as repeating the motions of milking a cow, the application of that iconic element is difficult to support in face of the obvious lack of experience with cows on the part of most young deaf children, who nevertheless do learn the sign quickly and easily. Most of these same children only know that milk comes from cartons stored in supermarkets, something not derivable from the sign alone.

Even if signs do contain some iconic elements, that feature does not detract from the arbitrariness of the signs. Of all aspects of man, why focus on the hat brim? (Earlier, you will recall, it was noted that some linguists posit the notion that the male sign occurs about the forehead because man thinks. The female sign is made at the jawline because woman talks. That explanation is not currently popular.) That question—Why has the particular aspect of a thing or action been chosen to represent the whole?—could be asked about every sign. What is there about the fragment of motion or minute physical feature that compels one to identify the intended referent? Those who support iconicity would need to show that there is a consistent basis for the choice of elements in the signs on which they base their argument. So far, no such consistency has been demonstrated. Furthermore, as has already been pointed out, signs tend to become more and more arbitrary over time; they change in a direction away from the imputed iconicity as they pass from generation to generation.[18]

Some researchers have found that iconicity is sometimes used by deaf people for poetic or humorous purposes. For example, Edward Klima and Ursula Bellugi describe a poetic rendering of the sign *slowly* (the right hand brushing along the left hand from fingertips to wrist).[19] The signer took nearly twice as long to make that sign as any other sign in the poem. It is the equivalent of a speaker drawing out the syllables of the word: "slo-o-owly." The way the sign was made emphasized its meaning. Native signers appear to make use of the possibilities for being "picturesque," for spicing up their signs with what may be paralinguistic features. As noted in the next chapter, some iconic-seeming elements may actually have linguistic purposes as modifiers. They differ from pantomime in that they are conventionalized, regularly conveying meaning beyond the supposedly representational aspect. What at first appears to be iconic, then, may be a grammatical construction. That this confusion occurs is demonstrated by signs that are judged to be iconic in isolation but are not correctly identified when presented in complete expressions. The result is either mistaken attribution or total absence of transparency.[20]

The Origins of Signs

Where did a given sign originate? How was the particular hand-motion configuration chosen for that concept? These are intriguing questions. As often happens in the absence of accurate information, myths arise. Nature abhors a vacuum, and some people cannot tolerate an unsolved mystery. The truth of course is that, for many if not most signs, there are no written records to search for sign origins. Yet when you take sign classes, you are apt to be given a derivation for the signs you are taught. One dictionary of signs provides an "origin" for almost every sign. The compiler of the dictionary does not reveal how these data were obtained; the explanations are presented straight-faced. And they are usually iconic.[21]

As noted above, even native signers are often incorrect when they make statements about a sign's origin. However, the practice may be harmless if it is not taken seriously. These explanations can serve as memory aids to the beginning signer, and as such they may be helpful. They might also be counterproductive, since the beginner may develop a tendency to search out iconic elements in every sign and thus become confused and fail to generalize the interpretation of the sign, when it is appropriate to do so. Take the sign for *kind*, made by holding the left hand, palm facing in, in front of the chest and circling it with the open right hand. The suggested origin is "As if winding a bandage around the arm."[22] To a present-day observer, that may seem a fair description of what the movements resemble, but it can hardly be accepted as the origin. There is no record that that is what it means. Furthermore, why bandage the arm, not the head? Why is the motion not that of kneading bread? What is potentially limiting in these speculations is the student's appreciation of the sign's fuller meanings, which include "gracious," "gentle," and "goodhearted." How do these relate to bandaging? Not too well. On the other hand, it seems innocuous to regard the sign for *year* as depicting the earth rotating around the sun: it might help someone remember that sign.

Finding the origins of words also presents many difficulties. Eric Partridge sagely noted: "That etymology is a science, no one will deny; that it is also an art, far too many deny."[23] To say that one has found the origin of a word when its Latin root has been established only postpones the question of linguistic beginnings: From whence came the Latin? In the same lecture from which the above quotation was taken, Partridge concluded most aptly: "Etymology is a perilous subject: for, reach one horizon, you find another equally distant, if not still more remote. One clue leads to another, which yields another, which yields to another, which *ad-infinitums* from days to months to years; and often one has to retrace one's steps."[24] If spoken language, which has been recorded for millennia, presents such difficulties, it is easy to understand why sign, which has been only crudely recorded for a fraction of the time that speech has, should present so many problems to the etymologist—the seeker of truth (from *etymos*) about words.

3

The Structure of Ameslan

To maintain its language claim, Ameslan first had to show that it had more than an interesting vocabulary: it needed to demonstrate consistent means of conveying ideas and emotions. Furthermore, the rules had to deviate to some extent from those of English in order to avoid the contention that Ameslan was nothing more than a code, a manual system for conveying English in much the same way that handwriting is. The discovery of unique conventions for expressing thoughts and feelings among the deaf persons who signed opened Ameslan to a different linguistic analysis than it had previously had. The earlier cataloguers of sign assumed that sign combinations that were not in correct (grammatical) word order evidenced the signer's lack of English competence. They concentrated on handshapes and movements, believing that a description of them would provide a complete account of the meaning in a signed message. Some observers complained that deaf signers were overly expressive, that they exaggerated their delivery. They did not realize that the "exaggerations" were actually manual equivalents of punctuation, of inflection, of juncture markers, and so on. What they regarded as superfluous is now recognized as essential to a full appreciation of sign. These early researchers clucked their tongues at the inability of the born-deaf person to learn proper English, never entertaining the notion that they, the linguists, lacked competence in Ameslan!

Garrick Mallery, *in 1881*, expressed this same basic idea repeatedly. In his classic monograph on American Indian Sign Language, he wrote at one point:

> It is necessary to take with caution any statement from a person who, having memorized or hashed up any number of signs, large or small, has decided in his conceit

that those he uses are the only genuine Simon Pure, to be exclusively employed according to his direction, all others being counterfeits or blunders. His vocabulary has ceased to give the signs of any Indian or body of Indians whatever, but becomes his own, the proprietorship of which he fights for as if secured by letters-patent. When a sign is contributed by one of the present collaborators, which such a sign talker has not before seen or heard of, he will at once condemn it as bad, just as a United States Minister to Vienna, who had been nursed in the mongrel Dutch of Berks County, Pennsylvania, declared that the people of Germany spoke very bad German.[1]

Methods of Investigation

What the linguists uncovered about Ameslan is fascinating. Science, however, is distinguished by its methods, and the methods themselves are of great interest. So we will inspect some of the tools that investigators use to unpack the intricacies of sign. In doing so, we might recall the character of George Primrose in *The Vicar of Wakefield.* Having gone to Amsterdam to teach English to the Netherlanders, he discovered on arriving that he could speak to no one. With chagrin, he realized that "in order to teach Dutchmen English, it was necessary that they should first teach me Dutch. How I came to overlook so obvious an objection is to me amazing."

Bilingual native users of any language can greatly contribute to an understanding of their native language. Being able to converse with the investigators in their language, the native can translate from and into the target language. The investigators may ask for an explanation of particular expressions (forward translation) or ask how to express a concept (back translation). Together, these two techniques serve as a check, one on the other, and as a means of rapidly expanding knowledge of the grammar.[2]

Note that when describing the signs I will use various English words as if the signs were meant to reproduce those words. That is the basis for ethnocentrism, explaining things in one's own language and then concluding that one's own language is the basis for all languages. We have no choice but to translate the signs into English for this book, since that is the language in which this book is written. But the signs of Ameslan have meanings independent of English and consistent within Ameslan. To translate the sign in Figure 20 *(believe)* as "mind-marry" would be ridiculous. In Ameslan that sign indicates the concept of belief. How it arrives at that is not a straightforward matter. Neither is a strictly phonological analysis of English compounds. The word *mindless* in English can be shown to be made up of two separate words: *mind* and *less*, but rendering that word as meaning "having less mind" would miss the definition ("unintelligent, inattentive, heedless"). It is a difficult problem irrespective of the languages involved.

The use of televised and filmed dialogues greatly aids linguistic research.

The recordings can be viewed repeatedly by groups of native informants. In that way, the same material can be open to many interpretations. Researchers worry about the representativeness of their native informants' language preferences. This concern grows larger when Ameslan is being studied, because there are so many different dialects in active use. A user of Ameslan in one part of the country may fail to understand a sign that is widely used in another part. Furthermore, using informants who communicate well in English, while it often eases the researcher's task, may bias the findings, since such informants' judgments about Ameslan grammar may be contaminated by their knowledge of English. For reasons such as these, the modern linguist prefers to record material and present it to many informants rather than rely on one or two, as did the earlier researchers. If signers of different ages, from different parts of the country, and with different school backgrounds all agree about a particular point, the researcher has strong evidence for the generality of that point. If they disagree, the researcher may have clues to a deeper understanding of the language by uncovering differences that relate to age, social class, and other factors.

Because it is relatively inexpensive and flexible, requiring little technical background and minimal paraphernalia, television has been widely used in recent studies. But whether on film or videotape, these permanent records also provide visual documentation of sign changes over time. Such records have been invaluable for students of Ameslan, because the written accounts of signs have not been widely accepted and because drawings are neither easily made nor satisfactorily interpreted. Even though two-dimensional, these continuous recordings of sign movements have been a major contributing factor in the development of a deeper appreciation of Ameslan.[3]

Another approach has been to observe the acquisition of sign by young deaf children who have been exposed to it. Seeing how children acquire their first language provides insights into the syntactical structure of the language, insights not easily made from observations of adults only. From 1958 to 1964, Bernard Tervoort[4] studied deaf schoolchildren in Holland and the United States, with the aid of motion pictures made while the children were signing to each other. From this study Tervoort concluded that the Dutch and American children developed separate esoteric languages, which not only had specialized vocabularies but also had syntactical rules differing from their native speech *and* sign languages. Since sign is rarely taught to deaf schoolchildren, even in schools that use sign in the classroom, the development of idiosyncratic language (Tervoort prefers to call it "esoteric") seems to stem from an inherent need for systematic conversation. The children's communication with each other hurdled the linguistic barrier of deafness by creating conventions and signs where the established ones were not yet known to them.

What about even younger children? Susan Goldin-Meadow and Heidi Feldman[5] examined six deaf children, ranging in age from seventeen to forty-nine months, whose parents did not know or use any sign language. The investigators found that these children developed a structured manual communication system without ever having seen one. The evidence strongly supports the notion that humans have a natural inclination for systematic communication in contrast to the idea that children learn their caretakers' language by imitation only.

Harry Hoemann and Rosemarie Lucafo[6] have published a transcription of a seven-year-old deaf boy's signed conversation, illustrating the remarkable fluency that can be acquired at that age. In the one-hour interview, which was videotaped and later analyzed, the boy used nearly seven hundred signs and his spontaneous remarks ranged unhesitatingly over topics usual for children his age, but with unusual facility.

If a child had one parent who was deaf and one who heard, would the child learn to speak or to sign first? Two researchers studied a child in precisely that situation.[7] At seven months the little girl, whose hearing was normal, demonstrated her first word—in sign. Over the following year, she alternated in her acquisition of speech and sign, showing that learning the one did not interfere with learning the other. Learning to communicate with their hands seems to be easier for children than learning to speak; that is, children who are exposed to both signing and speaking in infancy develop signed communication first. Another study reported that Davey, a normally hearing child of normally hearing parents who signed and spoke to him from infancy (the parents were teachers of deaf children who used sign in their work), had acquired his first fifty words by sign at 15 months of age, and by speech at 16 months of age.[8] A normal control group exposed only to speech attained the fifty-word level (for average male children) at 22.1 months of age. In fact, Davey had acquired a combined total of fifty spoken and signed words by 14 months of age—an amazing 8 months ahead of the normal pace of vocabulary development. Another team of linguists videotaped deaf parents during the first year of their six infants' lives and noted that signed communication developed among all six of the children studied, regardless of whether they were hearing or deaf.[9] These naturalistic observations of early language acquisition are only beginning to reveal some of the linguistic treasures that may be buried under earlier prejudices against manual communication. Clearly, sign holds primacy in early language development.

Once data are in analyzable format, the researcher's ingenuity comes to the fore. Consider an hour or two of storytelling in Ameslan: What do you focus on? The possibilities are as numerous as the researchers. Robin Battison, among others, looked for physical constraints on signs.[10] In spoken English, for example, a consonant sound is seldom, if ever, repeated consecutively. When such repetition does occur, it is usually for purposes of humor ("K-K-K-Katie!"). A similar group of prohibitions has been drawn up for Ameslan.

Another approach to analyzing signs has been "to look them in the face." Charlotte Baker has noted that identical signs are given different meanings by slight facial changes.[11] Figure 33 shows the sign *late*, and Figure 34 *not yet*. In the latter, the difference between the two concepts is signaled by a slight protrusion

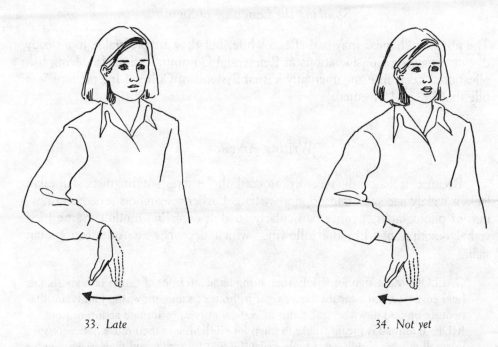

33. *Late*   34. *Not yet*

of the tongue. Linguists now feel that, at least for some signs, the descriptions are not complete without specification of the accompanying facial expression.[12]

All of these syntactical considerations and many more to be discussed below arise from intensive attention to detail and from a questioning attitude. The linguistic mapping of Ameslan still leaves some areas uncharted, but what is known is intriguing. We will consider a few basic grammatical principles of Ameslan that parallel English, and introduce some that fall outside the realm of a spoken language. These will help illustrate Ameslan's claim to status as an independent language. We will also show how Ameslan confronts the problems that all languages must solve—how to indicate past, present, and future actions, for instance, and how to distinguish among objects by sex, number, and so on—and how it does so systematically.

Incidentally, the scientific approach to sign has its light side. The young researchers who are attracted to this field often tend to be iconoclasts and to express themselves humorously—or at least without the pedantry that dulls readers' senses in many other scientific disciplines. Consider only the titles of some recent publications to catch the flavor of their style:[13]

"The case of the missing length."
"Time on our hands."
"On the other hand."
"How many seats in a chair?"
"A good rule of thumb."
"What's not on the other hand in American Sign Language."
"Some handy new ideas on pidgins and creoles."

The puns on "hands" may pall after a while, but they are preferable to a steady diet of "Diglossic Considerations in Referential Communications Involving Implicational Lects in Fundamentally Visual Systems of Cultural Interactions"—a title that I hope I invented.

Writing Ameslan

Because it has only recently aroused the interest of linguists, Ameslan lacks a widely accepted transcription system. Earlier researchers relied on drawings or photographs, neither particularly good at depicting motion. Some tried verbal descriptions—like the following, which describes an American Indian sign:

> GALLOP. Make sign for RIDE; then bring hands in front of center of body, hands held edgewise, left near the body, right in front of same; move the hands simultaneously up and down several times in vertical curves, to imitate action of horse.
> RIDE. If animal is meant, make the sign for HORSE and then move hands forward in small curves. If riding a vehicle make the sign for same, and then make sign for SIT on left palm.[14]

As you can see, such descriptions must be either very long or imprecise. The sign for *gallop* is described in terms of the sign for *ride*, which in turn requires that one know the sign for *horse* and signs for various vehicles, as appropriate. The greatest difficulty arises when this system is used to recount a signed sentence. Consider the number of words needed!

Several conventions have been created that use English words to indicate the equivalent signs. The idea seems reasonable only if you accept a word-sign equivalence. That way of looking at Ameslan, however, leads to some of the errors made by students of sign in the past: directed by their search for word equivalents, they missed some of the critical features of sign.

Photographs are seldom satisfactory, because they do not depict movement well. Oddly enough, photographs also suffer because they include too much detail. Drawings are much better. Supplemented by arrows to indicate direction of movement, they can give a fairly clear idea of the distinguishing features of a sign. They still lack a third dimension, and if the sequence of movements is complicated they can become so cluttered that they are very difficult to read. Making a sequence of drawings helps, but it is also cumbersome.

Why not write sign? Researchers in the field need a shorthand to record their observations of signers. Making accurate sketches requires skills many do not have. Besides, it would take much time and cause the observer to lose many further observations. The solution would be some written form, much more incisive than our alphabetical system but similarly compact. Professor William Stokoe created such a system. It is displayed in Appendix B.

The British Sign Language Workshop has adapted Stokoe's notational system to British Sign Language, adding a fourth category—orientation *(ori)*, which expands the description of the hands' positions relative to each other.[15] Linguists in other countries, too, have made similar adaptations of Stokoe's system, retaining its basic concepts and most of its symbols. That it cuts to the bone of the anatomy of sign is attested by its widespread use among sign researchers of many nations. We have not used Stokoe's notations in this book because it takes time to learn the system (and a great deal of practice to write it rapidly). Furthermore, it has not been widely adopted. It is presented here to illustrate what can be done. Someone, somewhere, is probably working on a more appealing system that will eventually satisfy the field and be adopted by signers.[16] Until that system arises, we will content ourselves with a combination of drawings and verbal descriptions, realizing at the same time that they cannot replace direct exposure to signing. The same is true of efforts to write speech sounds. We seldom realize how complicated our orthography is because we are so familiar with it. We also have become accustomed to its shortcomings, and especially its ambiguities. If the last statement puzzles you, recall that *ough* has no single pronunciation: *bough, cough, dough, rough.* You probably have your own list of English inconsistencies. We tend to ignore the inadequacies of English orthography, because, while not perfect, it does the job.

When an English word is substituted for each sign, the resulting expression often looks stupid. What is at fault is the recording, not the grammar of Ameslan or its ability to convey nuance. Take an example from another language—say, German: *Was geht mich das an?* Word for word, it translates as "What goes me that on?" But what is grammatically correct German is incorrect English. The proper translation is "What does that have to do with me?" or "What business is that of mine?" One good idiom deserves another.

Translations of signs into words can make Ameslan seem primitive, ungrammatical. For example, to indicate the plural form in Ameslan the sign is repeated (as discussed previously). Seeing this repetition, a translator may incorrectly write "man, man," when the correct English equivalent is "men."

Or take a simple statement: I like my coffee black. Figures 35A–D show that sentence in Ameslan. If each sign is (inappropriately) rendered directly into English, the sentence reads, "Like coffee black me!" That is an example of word-for-sign substitution. It is incorrect. It ignores the fact that Ameslan and English have different grammars. Such a translation also makes the deaf person sound dull-witted. The fact is that the translator, not the deaf signer, is ignorant—of proper Ameslan. Translations of any language always risk some loss of meaning or even misunderstanding. We will discuss the problem further in Chapter 7. Suffice it to say here that translators seldom have done full justice to signs. Successfully shifting from one language to another requires great care and considerable empathy, as well as intimate knowledge of both languages.

35A *Like*

35B. *Coffee*

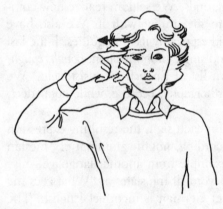

35C. *Black*

35D. *Me*

Managing Space

To some extent, the analogous parts of sign and spoken language are space and sound. The signer must manage the visual space in order to communicate effectively; the speaker manages the auditory space.

The length of the signer's arms determines the boundaries of the visual space, the *frame*. The size of the frame—the breadth of the signs—governs how "loud" or "soft" is the communication. One can readily indicate magnitude, as illustrated in Figure 26. The size of the sign will indicate something about what is meant and will also determine at what distance the signs can be read. Addressing a large audience, signers make larger signs than when conversing intimately with one person seated across from themselves. Thus, the *relative* size, spread, and vigor with which signs are made, not these absolute qualities, determine how the sign should be interpreted. The person receiving the signed communication must be alert to shifts in the signer's posture or facial expression and to relatively small changes in the beginning or end of a sign. Much meaning can be incorporated into a single sign by these physical variations, greatly extending its semantic range.

PRONOUNS

Signers also use the space around them to indicate other persons and objects that will be part of the communication. The area directly in front of the signer is reserved for first and second person, for "you and me." Third parties can then be placed to the signer's left or right. By glancing at that previously designated place or by pointing to it, the signer indicates that the utterance refers to that person or object. The sign space can also be used to indicate subject-object re-lations. The direction of signs can indicate the direction of the action. "I gave you" and "You gave me" can be distinguished by the way *give* is signed. If the signer wishes to express "You give him," the direction of the verb is from the space directly in front of the signer to the appropriate side. This highly efficient method serves the function of pronominalization. Researchers, intent upon finding sign-for-word equivalences in Ameslan, missed that feature. Careful observation of signers, however, confirms that this use of the signer's space is well understood by those conversant with Ameslan.[17]

TENSE

How does the signer indicate the time at which an action is or was occurring or will occur? The verbs in Ameslan do not generally inflect to indicate tense. "Go," "gone," "will go"—all are made with the same sign verb. What the signer does to mark time is to signal it at the outset of the communication, only indicating when the time reference changes. When initiating a conversation, then, the signer establishes the temporal context. That time remains in effect until the signer signals that a different period is in effect. This system makes attentional and me-morial demands on the receiver that are not made by English, which constantly marks time by the verb form.

Linguists have described Ameslan's "time line"—the space that is at head-level on the signer's dominant side. The signer indicates the future by a forward motion, much like that of a quarterback throwing a short pass. The present is immediately in front of the signer. The farther forward the motion, the more distant the future. The past is indicated by a short movement of the dominant hand toward the signer's rear. A very long movement is difficult to execute at shoulder height. However, by means of facial expressions, the distant past or future can be shown (see Figures 28 and 29).

The duration of an activity or condition can also be shown without adding adverbial phrases. The way in which a sign is made gives one indication. Making the sign *to fly* with a very slow, prolonged motion would tell the observer that the flight had been a very long one, just as making it very briefly and vigorously would suggest that the signer had taken the *Concorde* across the Atlantic. Moreover, making a sign close to the body tells that the event has very recently happened. The abruptness with which the sign for *now* is made and the proximity to the body (as well as facial expression) can vary its meaning from "sometime in the near future" to "at this very second!" (Figures 36, 37, and 38). As we will discuss next, these same signs may convey even more information.

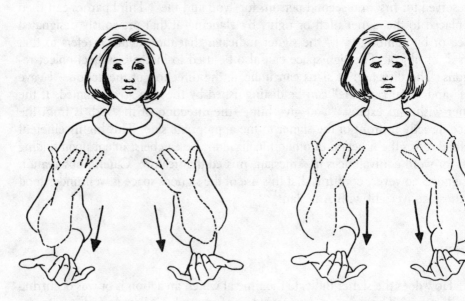

36. *Now*   37. *Now?*

38. *Now!*

AGGLUTINATION

Linguists refer to languages which combine into a single word a number of linguistic elements as *agglutinative*. The Reverend Eugene Dyer has published a brilliant comparison of Ameslan and Turkish, showing that the two have many common characteristics linguistically.[18] Their agglutinative tendency results in considerable expressive economy. Dyer illustrates the point with the Turkish verb *vermek*, which means "to give" in its citation form. The verb has 114 positive variations in the indicative mood and 59 positive variations in the subjunctive mood. These can be doubled by shifting to the negative, resulting in 346 variations! He then points to one of its forms, *vermemeliymissiniz*, which translates "It is said that it might not be necessary for you to give." The economy is apparent: the one word spoken in Turkish expresses a thought that requires thirteen English words. That Ameslan has similar agglutinative properties has already been alluded to in Chapter 2.

Take the possibilities that can be derived from the single sign *now* (Figure 36). Asked with a questioning look, it can be translated as "Do you want it done at this time?" (Figure 37). In addition to the facial expression—arched eyebrows and direct eye contact—the hands hold the sign for a longer period than would be true were *now* an answer or command. If the signer leans forward, with a slight thrust of the head toward the person being addressed, the question is changed to "You mean right now?" Or, if the question is one of incredulity ("Do you really mean *now?*"), the signer would make the sign closer to the person addressed and would do so more slowly than for a simple response. Of course, all the preceding questions require the inquisitive look, the arched eyebrows, the eye contact, and body posture. To change the *now* to a direct order, the signer assumes a more commanding expression and makes the sign with a firm, downward stroke. A "pinched face"—pursed lips, knit brow, slightly narrowed eyes—adds the necessary emphasis (Figure 38). Using these variations in making the sign, the signer can express the thought "Do it at once and no fooling around!" or "Yes, this would be a good time to get it done." The way the sign is made, the accompanying facial expression and posture, and the context must all be read along with the sign to grasp the full implications in the single gesture.

EXPRESSING NUMBER

As explained previously, the plural form can be expressed in Ameslan by the repetition of the sign. Making the sign for *man* twice results in "men"; sign *year* twice and the meaning is "years." Another way to differentiate between singular and plural is by the extent of the sign. Point for "him," but sweep the indexing hand in an arc to mean "them." A further means of forming the plural is to combine the noun with the sign for *many*. In this use, the *many* sign should be considered a quantifier that is not necessarily translated as "many" but serves to convert a singular noun to the plural form. Thus, the sign phrase *many soldiers* might best be rendered in English as "the soldiers."

NEGATION AND ASSERTION

Ameslan has a number of ways of asserting and negating statements, as does every other language. Stating something is true, of course, is easy to conceive, but Ameslan offers several opportunities for distinctions that are contained within the sign. A signer can express thoughts varying from simple acquiescence to vigorous assertion by the way in which he makes the sign. The same holds true for negation.

In some respects all that is required to deny a statement is to make it with a headshake from side to side, also a signal of negation to users of English. One can merely shake one's head while signing "I love you" to mean that one does not. Figure 39 shows the sign for *rejection*. It is usually glossed as "refused," but it has a more general sense of negation. It can be combined with other signs to indicate their obverse. Of course, Ameslan has signs for *not, cannot, none,* and the like, along with conventions that also serve to negate statements. These grammatical aspects of Ameslan have been amply mapped and are well understood by linguists.

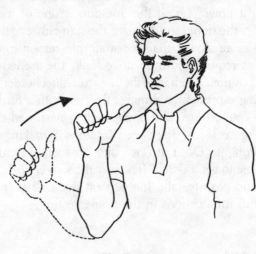

39. *Rejection*

WORD ORDER

The rules for creating sentences in Ameslan differ from those in English. Initially, researchers considered that Ameslan simply lacked restraints on how it put signs together. They did not realize the significance of different arrangements. It is likely that further studies will uncover other distinctive features of Ameslan grammar. What is unequivocally known is that Ameslan has consistent rules for word order that affect the meaning of the signed utterance.

The statement "I like my coffee black" (shown in Figures 35A–D), if read in the order signed, says "Like coffee black me." Not very English-like! But then neither is French or German. The correct translation of the four signs is as first noted. You can see, however, why the first English observers of sign thought it ungrammatical. They looked for English, and their native informants probably did what they thought was expected—that is, gave them a word-for-sign interpretation.

The appearance of a basic grammar[19] has quieted most arguments that Ameslan does not have a distinct structure. However, some linguists[20] have advanced the idea that presumed rules for word order in Ameslan are merely conveniences and that these patterns are not essential to meaning. Carol Padden[21] has cogently replied with an impressive analysis of Ameslan sentence patterns that leaves little doubt of their syntactic necessity. Implicit in her presentation is that the tendency to seek English-like rules for Ameslan is at the heart of the misconceptions. Ameslan, as pointed out earlier, tends to resemble languages like Turkish and Greek. Furthermore, an adequate investigation of Ameslan requires that attention be directed beyond the hand signs to grammatical elements conveyed by the eyes and body position, as pointed out in this chapter. A more complete understanding of Ameslan grammar lies in the future, but Ameslan's language claims are now indisputable.

QUESTIONS

In English, we usually indicate a question by the initial adverb—what, where, how, and so on. In Ameslan, on the other hand, the question word may appear at the end (but not the questioning facial expression). Take the example in Figures 40A–C. The signs read, "That girl name what?" (obviously an incorrect English

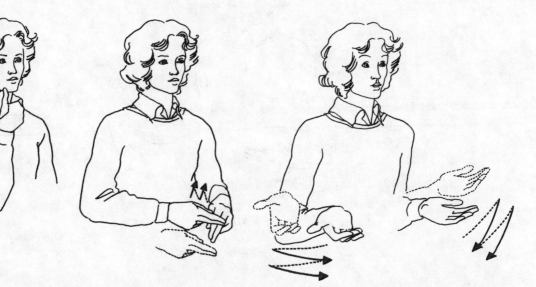

40A. *Girl* 40B. *Name* 40C. *What*

rendering). They mean, instead, "What is that girl's name?" Incidentally, the determiner *that* is not actually signed but indicated by the gaze of the signer.

Another interesting feature of Ameslan is that some question words have a more general meaning. Read independently, the signs in Figures 41A and B are *live* and *what*. In the order shown here, and with that questioning look, the translation is "Where do you live?" (In colloquial Ameslan, the same sign may mean *where* or *what*.) Again, note that the interrogatory adverb appears at the end of the utterance.

41A. *Live*

41B. *What*

CONDITIONAL STATEMENTS

Contingency statements are made, as in English, with the conditional first, followed by the consequent. This conceptual order is represented in Figures 42, 43, and 44. In 42, the condition is shown. Though there is only one sign, *rain*, the facial expression and posture of the signer convey tension, saying in effect that something more is coming. Then follows the resolution. In Figure 43 it is the sign *go*, for "Will you go?" (The signer's face provides the question mark.) In Figure 44 the sign is *stay*. In sequence, Figures 42 and 43 would be translated "If it rains, will you go?" Figures 42 and 44, in that sequence, yield "If it rains, I will stay here." In each case, two signs provide fairly lengthy English equivalents.

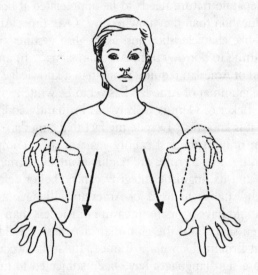

42. Rain

43. Go

44. Stay

The compactness, however, as already pointed out, comes in part from concentrating solely on the hands. The adverbial and adjectival variety emerge from the way the sign is made and from the extramanual expressions. These are, unfortunately, almost impossible to produce coherently in drawings. The reader is therefore asked to accept much that cannot be illustrated here.

Summary

The above samples of Ameslan grammar are intended only to make the case for its status as a language—a language that is independent of English. Of course, Ameslan does share characteristics with its sister language, but it deviates sufficiently to cause native users of Ameslan considerable difficulty in acquiring English competency. Its separate nature needs to be appreciated if born-deaf people are to have a better education than they now receive. Over time, Ameslan will acquire additional English-like characteristics, just as English gestures have borrowed (and will probably continue to borrow) from Ameslan signs.[22] In any event, it is clear that an appreciation of Ameslan requires more than a knowledge of its vocabulary.

The definitive grammar of Ameslan has yet to be written, though the excellent work of Charlotte Baker & Dennis Cokely has brilliantly codified the consensus with respect to what is known. [23] Despite the fact that Ameslan's grammar attracted linguistic attention only in the last twenty years or so, a complete account of it should emerge soon. Once its rules are readily available, Ameslan can be taught more consistently and its linguistic integrity can be better defended. Soon those who want to teach English to users of Ameslan will have a sounder basis for instruction and should have a greater measure of success than they now achieve.

What has been said about the grammar of Ameslan holds also for the sign languages of Great Britain, Denmark, France, Ireland, Sweden, Thailand, and other nations whose sign languages have been subjected to linguistic analysis.[24] What emerges from these studies is that all of the sign languages face the same basic communication problems—transmitting the concepts of time, number, gender, and so forth—and all use different strategies to solve them. They all have grammars, but the grammars are not the same for all.

4

A History of Manual Communication

How old is sign? As old as humankind—and possibly older. Anthropologists who have speculated about the origins of language and who accept an evolutionary concept of its development now theorize that gesture preceded vocal utterance in human communication.[1] That is why studies of animal communication (which we will discuss later) have such strong implications for linguists. They suspect that our ancestors communicated with their hands before they communicated with their voices. The opposing view is that language came full-blown from the mouths of prehistoric humans. Some linguists have even brushed questions of language origins aside with a reference to a "mutation" that accompanied the emergence of the earliest humans. But others choose to believe that our language has followed an orderly development. The link to other life forms could be manual.

Kinds of Scientific Evidence

What kinds of evidence do scientists use to support one or another position? Several disciplines contribute to the reconstruction of our beginnings.

Paleontologists study the anatomy of hominids, using bones from specifically dated eras. These examinations suggest that the vocal space of early humans—australopithecine and ramapithecine—would not accommodate the complex speech apparatus we now have. At the same time, the skeletal structure seems consistent with having facile hands.[2]

Cave paintings and other ancient graphic evidence can be interpreted as showing people gesturing. Nonalphabetic scripts, like the now famous Minoan

Linear B, seem to indicate an attempt to translate gesture rather than speech.[3]

What about animal communication? As mentioned earlier, current studies of animals can provide an important link between human precursors and ourselves. If other primates—apes and chimpanzees, particularly—can communicate gesturally, that would suggest a similar capacity in our ancestors and would strengthen the argument that they used it. The issue of animal communication, however, has not been fully resolved. To some extent, experimental results are influenced by the experimenter's approach. Some who have found what they regarded as substantial evidence of chimpanzees' ability to learn and use sign have credited their success to the way they arranged conditions: "Indeed, it seems that the more freedom we allow in our experiments for the subject to participate, rather than constraining the subject either in a confining apparatus or experimental procedure, the more interesting are the results, and the more impressive is the evidence for apparently higher-order kinds of cognitive operations in the chimpanzee."[4]

One of the most exciting demonstrations of the use of signs by a chimpanzee is also highly controversial, largely because the trainer denies the interpretation placed on his data. Nim Chimpsky's exposure to sign came shortly after his birth and proceeded through his first four years or so. Nim did use signs consistently, but Herbert Terrace, the animal project's director, concluded that Nim's signs were imitative and did not reflect a grasp of language principles.[5] Gregory Gaustad reviewed Terrace's book and countered that Terrace's initial bias against the idea of animal communication blinded him to Nim's accomplishments.[6] Terrace retorted: "In searching for evidence that Nim was using sign language, Gaustad apparently fails to grasp that both speaking and signing children, but not apes, provide rich corpora of spontaneous utterances that allow one to ascertain the degree to which a child's utterances are rule governed."[7] Gaustad responded: "It is a wonder that any spontaneity was exhibited by Nim. However, when chimpanzees are raised in a way that more nearly resembles the rearing conditions of human children, the chimpanzee's utterances are spontaneous . . ."[8] And so the debate between scientists continues.

Challenges to animal communication are not new. A nineteenth-century linguist pontificated: "The one great barrier between the brute and man is *Language*. Man speaks, and no brute has ever uttered a word. Language is our Rubicon, and no brute will dare to cross it."[9] By contrast, a modern linguist, reviewing studies of apes' attempts to sign, concedes that, though all the evidence is not in, "perspectives on the nature of man's relationship to other animal species have changed dramatically."[10] Certainly, today, a philosopher is hardly likely to assert that animals "would not dare to cross" the language barrier!

Jane Hill, an anthropologist, urges that we take an evolutionary view of language development. "It seems clear that human languages, like other behavioral systems, are the products of evolutionary processes. To make such a statement does not degrade human language any more than it degrades the beauty of the colors of butterflies if we point out that they function in defense or in sexual attraction."[11] To accept the ability of animals to use language does not *degrade* human language. That word, *degrade*, provides a clue to the reasons for the incredible anger that the very idea of animal communication arouses in some individuals, laymen and scientists alike. Nor is the controversy fueled solely by animals who closely resemble ourselves. James Gould points out that, despite impressive evidence of language in bees, some scientists cannot accept that notion. Gould might as well have been speaking about primates when he says:

> Some of the resistance to the idea that honey bees possess a symbolic language seems to have arisen from a conviction that "lower" animals, and insects in particular, are too small and phylogenetically remote to be capable of "complex" behavior. There is perhaps a feeling of incongruity in that the honey bee language is symbolic and abstract . . . Especially in ethology, it is difficult to avoid the unprofitable extremes of blinding skepticism and crippling romanticism.[12]

At least one scientist, Harvey Sarles, sagely questions the very essence of the issue: "What has, in effect, stopped us has been a firm belief in the uniqueness of man as the only creature with language. How could we know that?"[13] A doubt well worth expressing in view of all the evidence rapidly coming to hand.

The problem of language beginnings can also be addressed by applying the principle from biology that *ontogeny recapitulates phylogeny*. The notion that individual development from conception follows an evolutionary course is a powerful research tool, bringing the irretrievable past under present scrutiny. By studying the development of individuals from fetal stages through infancy and early childhood into adulthood, scientists can test ideas about the probable behavior of humans in prehistoric times. Linguists are now paying keen attention to the earliest language behavior of very young children and have noted some fascinating regularities.[14] These regularities also appear in the development of sign language by deaf children. The adult forms of languages—as we know them—emerge from considerable social buffeting. The childlike forms appear to be wired into the organism. Roger Brown believes that his studies and those of other linguists show a "universal development sequence" in language development. He comments wryly about his own painstaking efforts: "The quite surprising degree to which results to date support this vision has sustained the researcher when he gets a bit tired of writing down Luo, Samoan, or Finnish equivalents of 'That doggie' and 'No more milk.' "[15]

Occasionally, researchers stumble upon natural experiments that they would not, could not, set up. Rolf Kushel found a deaf man on a remote Polynesian island, Rennell, where the inhabitants' oral history covering twenty-four generations had no previous record of a born-deaf person. The deaf man, Kangobai, has developed systematic signs that he has been able to teach to his hearing compatriots, and thus established communication with them. Amazingly, Kangobai's signs parallel the island's spoken language. The Rennellese have no one term for fishing; it is an activity too vital to their economy to be left unspecified, except, as Kushel points out, when a Rennellese is speaking to "an ignorant anthropologist." Kangobai, similarly, has no general sign for fishing. Instead, he has at least ten distinct signs that range in meaning from "to catch a fish with a spear" to "to net flying fish by torchlight."[16] The study of this isolated man's naturally developed signs can be as provocative to the linguist as the studies of first signs in children.

What about first contacts between persons from cultures that have had no prior communication? Gordon Hewes reviewed accounts of early explorers' interactions with the natives they encountered. He was interested in how they managed to establish meaningful intercourse without knowing each other's languages. He found that through signs they communicated with a high degree of accuracy: "Thus, when some Eskimos indicate by signs that they will return to a particular place after three days, and they do in fact show up as they promised, both parties appear to have understood the message in the same way. Navigators, including Christopher Columbus, acting on signed information, have found islands in the direction and at distances indicated."[17] Hewes regards the study of these initial encounters between people who have no shared language as highly important to our understanding of language origins. He also suggests an answer to a futuristic question: How would we communicate with a visitor from outer space? No doubt about it: we would sign!

Another tool of anthropologists is comparative linguistics. By contrasting and comparing how languages have developed under various circumstances throughout the world, linguists can gather some useful hints as to what is and is not likely to have happened from earliest times until today. This is not simply etymology (the study of word origins) but the broader investigation of how language problems are dealt with in different cultures—for example, how a particular language handles the concept of time. By what means does a speaker indicate that an action has taken place, is now occurring, or will take place later? Do all cultures have such concepts? And what about gender, age, and other human attributes? Discovering *language universals* can direct us toward our beginnings and toward the essentials of communication.[18]

Linguists also study disordered persons, including aphasic, cerebral-palsied, and congenitally deaf children. How does the human organism react to injury and deprivation? Answers to such questions can illuminate earlier stages in the origins of our species. Observing how the deaf child, for example, manages to communicate without hearing language provides clues to what is essential to communication.[19]

Added together, all the evidence—from anthropologists, paleontologists, psychologists, linguists, and professionals from related disciplines—creates a telling argument for the primacy of manual communication in the human species. No single piece of the puzzle would, by itself, be convincing in reconstructing the unrecorded human past. Cryptographers have unlocked the secrets of ancient writings, but their theories depend on supporting facts from other disciplines for confirmation. The ideal of multidisciplinary scientific endeavor is best illustrated by the recent flurry of research in manual communication—a field in which the talents of many specialists have come together to mine its hidden riches.

Which brings us to the sometimes overlooked value of studying manual communication. In uncovering its mysteries, we may be contributing to our understanding of how language became the great tool of man that it is, how it took its present shape, and how we might continue to shape it more effectively in the future. The anthropologist Gordon Hewes has summed up very well the arguments for more intensive study of this topic:

> The problem of language origins is one of the most important in the study of human evolution, not only because the use of language is the sharpest behavioral difference between man and other animals, but because language underlies so much of human cultural achievement, including man's efforts to understand the world.[20]

Prehistoric Communication

One critical aspect of anatomy is posture. Until an organism is erect, it must use its four appendages for mobility; so chimpanzees are considered especially good subjects for learning sign language, but other apes are not, because they propel themselves on all fours. When hominids (including humans) became erect, their hands were freed—for tool using as well as communication. Consequently, anthropologists regard the onset of *homo erectus* as a probable date for the beginning of sign language—about a hundred thousand years ago.

The conditions surrounding early humans also had to affect their choice of a language modality. When they hunted on relatively open plains, it makes sense to assume they could and would use signs. They could see each other, and the silent communication would not alert their prey. But when they entered the woods or hunted in high grass, verbal signals became more important. To communicate in sign requires good visual conditions, adequate light, and unobstructed views.

Of course, there is no reason to believe that using gesture precluded using speech, or vice versa. Anthropologists now seek language origins, rather than looking for a singular origin. The factors favoring and shaping language development are likely to be complex—acting, reacting, and interacting. In prehistoric times, as now, people probably used both speech and gesture. Whether or not their use of gestures reached the stage of formal language, permitting full communication without vocalization, is an unanswered question. Some evidence supports the notion that sign languages have existed among humans since very early times. The crucial data, the unequivocal findings, have not yet appeared.

Sign Language B.C.

Aristotle's pronouncement on deafness cursed deaf people for the next two thousand years. Reasoning that speech and language are one and the same, Aristotle concluded that those who could not speak were unteachable. Children born deaf were often exposed to the elements and left to die by the ancient Greeks, and deaf children's minds were similarly left unexplored by other nations influenced by Aristotle.[21]

Aristotle's influence on attitudes toward deafness extended well beyond Hellenic culture. Rome, for one, denied citizenship to those who were born deaf. Similarly, the ancient Hebrews denied full religious standing to deaf persons who did not speak. The proscriptions were largely paternalistic, an attempt to keep unscrupulous persons from taking advantage of those presumed to be intellectually incapable of managing their own affairs. Thus, in the Talmud, born-deaf Jews are lumped together with mentally retarded persons in the category of those who cannot legally make a contract. Such laws must be considered in their two-thousand-year-old context: they were promulgated at a time when deaf children were not educated. The attempt to circumvent the exploitation of deaf people made them, in effect, wards of the state, with all the protections intended by that status. Today, most Jewish religious liberals ignore or reinterpret this bit of tradition. Deaf Israelis are educated in excellent facilities and enjoy the benefits of citizenship, much as deaf people do in Greece and Italy. Ironically, the headquarters of the World Federation of the Deaf, an organization devoted to advancing the status of deaf people, is in Rome, the city that once denied them basic civil rights.

While attitudes toward those who could not hear and did not speak were, from our perspective, harsh in those early days, sign language had gained (or regained) a fair measure of acceptance. Luigi Romeo points out that records exist of signs used by religious orders during the twelfth century and even earlier. Recognizing the difficulties of obtaining and translating ancient texts, Romeo nonetheless believes that "sporadic studies so far have not yet tapped what could be a cache of treatises on gesture languages used during the Graeco-Roman era of inquiry and even more productively during the Middle Ages. A systematic investigation would uncover a gold mine of texts, which in part could contribute to the understanding of the nature of signs and their 'universals' as well as of 'diachronic' generalities, at least for Western cultures."[22]

The Renaissance

Not until the sixteenth century did educators call into question the wisdom of Aristotle. The Italian physician Girolamo Cardano is not known to have treated a single deaf patient himself, but he countered the Aristotelian dogma on deafness in writing. His influence in contrast to that of the mighty Greek philosopher was inconsequential, so our mention of this Renaissance man is rather to acknowledge his courage, historically, than to mark any great accomplishments on his part. Still, he set forth what might have been a Magna Carta for deaf people when he said that "the mute can hear by reading and speak by writing."[23] Putting those revolutionary ideas into practice fell to the credit of two Spanish priests: Juan Pablo Bonet and Pedro de Ponce.

Silent religious orders have used manual communication for centuries.

Originally developed as signals for particular situations, over time these signs have begun to take the shape of natural languages. Robert Barakat has studied communication in Cistercian monasteries, in which silence is a required part of life but in which signs have been permitted since at least 328 A.D.[24] The resulting sign language is a peculiar mixture of natural and artificial characteristics, some aspects resembling sign languages in general, and others the language of the country in which a particular monastery is situated. The existence of sign language in religious retreats eventually led to modern education for deaf children. A silent environment, such as the Cistercian monasteries provided in ancient times, made a hospitable residence for deaf children. So far as we now know, however, the conjunction of those virtues produced no benefits for deafness education until the middle of the sixteenth century.

Pedro de Ponce entered the Monastery of San Salvador de Oña in 1526. Inadvertently, in 1545, the monastery became the first school for deaf children in recorded history. That year, the powerful head of a well-placed Castilian family, the marquis Juan Fernández de Velasco, brought his two sons to live at the monastery. Don Pedro was about eight years old, and his brother Don Francisco was about twelve. Their parents had eight children, five of whom were deaf. The three girls all spent their lives in convents. Placing their deaf children in these religious retreats served to prevent their procreating and to put them out of sight. When their father placed Pedro and Francisco in the monastery, he very likely had no plans, no hopes, for their education. But the kindly priest Pedro de Ponce almost immediately and instinctively took charge of them and began their education.

How did he proceed? What methods did he use? Pedro de Ponce wrote a book describing his methods, but the manuscript—which has never been published—was lost, possibly burned, possibly mislaid in some storehouse of ancient documents. All that is known (based on a great deal of supporting evidence) is that he succeeded. Both of the deaf boys learned to read and to speak—Francisco, who died at an early age, spoke a little; Pedro, who lived past thirty years of age, not only spoke—he reportedly sang in the monastery choir! He also read and wrote, not only Spanish but also Latin and to a lesser degree Greek. His good work brought the priest many new pupils—of the nobility, of course.

Secondhand reports (one from the physician to King Philip II of Spain) confirm that Pedro de Ponce began his pupils' education with instruction in reading, using fingerspelling. A manual alphabet was already available to Pedro de Ponce in his religious order. After establishing the concepts of language, he attempted to teach his students to speak. Not all did so, but all who are known to have studied with him did gain some competence in Spanish, at least. It is almost certain that Pedro de Ponce used signs, as they also were a part of the monastic environment. An eleventh-century text, Wilhelm's *Constitutiones Hirsaugienses*, gives directions for making over four hundred signs. In one of the rare surviving documents that he is known to have written, Pedro de Ponce told what, but not how, he taught his deaf charges ("the sons and daughters of great noblemen and important people"):

> I taught them how to read and write, count, pray, serve at Mass, understand the Christian doctrine, confess orally, and to some Latin and others Latin and Greek and to one even Italian . . . Besides, they were very knowledgeable in the history of Spain and other lands and they made use of the doctrine, politics and the discipline that Aristotle denied them.[25]

Those last words, "the discipline that Aristotle denied them," indicate Pedro de Ponce's awareness of his iconoclasm. He challenged established wisdom, the twisted pronouncement of Aristotle, and he won! When he died, after serving fifty-eight years as a monk, he was accorded honors usually reserved for heads of monasteries. Inscribed on his headstone is the inscription, "Here lies the venerable Fray Pedro Ponce worthy of eternal remembrance for the gift bestowed upon him by God of making the mutes speak."

The pioneering work of Pedro de Ponce might have gone to waste had it not been for another Spanish priest, Juan Pablo Bonet. Bonet did publish his methods, and that work survives to this day. Like his predecessor, Bonet drew his pupils from the noble and wealthy families of Spain. He taught them to read, to speechread, and to speak. In doing so, he used the manual alphabet and signs. In fact, the alphabet that he used is little changed to this day (see Chapter 6). Though Pedro de Ponce holds precedence in the education of deaf children, Bonet holds equal or higher status, because he published—a lesson that should not be lost on any young academician.[26]

Instructional methods have been altered over the last three centuries. What survives—the great legacy—is the faith of Cardano, Pedro de Ponce, and Bonet in the ability of born-deaf persons to acquire language. Not necessarily speech, but definitely language. The intellectual courage of these Renaissance men stands as a bulwark against the Aristotelian views of deafness. Their labors on behalf of deaf people produced excellent results, results we enjoy to this day. Young deaf people can learn; their deafness, even at birth, is not an insuperable barrier to their education. That is the message that spread from Italy and Spain into France, Germany, England, and eventually to the United States.

The Eighteenth Century to 1880

The name that lightens the darkness surrounding the education of deaf children is that of another priest, a Frenchman named Charles Michel, the Abbé de l'Epée. His interest in the problem of early deafness arose from a chance visit to a parishioner. The lady was not at home when he arrived, but her two daughters indicated that he might wait for her in the parlor. The Abbé noted that neither girl said anything to him, a fact that struck him as very odd. The mother quickly, and gladly, dispelled the mystery upon her return: both girls were deaf. Seeing his curiosity, and having no one else to turn to for help, the mother implored the Abbé to undertake her daughters' education. He did, and he changed the historical course of deafness education.[27]

The Abbé's classical education was coupled with an inventive turn of mind. He questioned the established wisdom that said deaf children could not be taught, and arrived at an amazing (for that time) conclusion. In his own words, "The natural language of the deaf is the language of sign; nature and their different wants are their only tutors in it; and they have no other language as long as they have no other instructors."[28]

But the Abbé did not know sign language. What was he to do—create one? In a way, he did. He began, however, by studying the signs already being used by deaf Parisians. That was his genius, recognizing that deaf people were communicating without speech. He gathered a group of deaf people together, including his two young charges. With their assistance, the Abbé both learned signs and developed a signed version of spoken French. His insight into communication enabled him to see that a thought can be represented by an arbitrary manual gesture as readily as by a spoken utterance, but he failed to see that the deaf Parisians had more than signs. They had a language—an independent vocabulary and grammar. Missing that point, the Abbé imposed French grammar on the selected group of signs, leading to some awkwardness that might have been avoided had he realized that a grammar already existed. On the other hand, even if he had he might not have changed his approach. We are all vigorous proponents of our own language, of its beauty, its expressiveness, its inherent correctness. Such an attitude merely reflects the human condition, and we have no reason to doubt that it afflicted the Abbé much as it had countless persons before him. (Even today, efforts are made to put signs in English word order—a topic that will be discussed later in this chapter as well as in the next.)

Whatever one may think of the Abbé's educational strategy, a review of the historical record will show that he astonished his countrymen and, indeed, many learned people throughout Europe by the performance of his deaf students. Contrary to Aristotle, deaf youngsters showed they could learn the language of their country. History records that the demonstrations stirred great excitement. The Abbé single-handedly raised the social status of deaf people and, in the process, earned himself a secure niche in the ranks of noted humanitarians. Here is what a distinguished linguist and scholar, Professor Harlan Lane, says of the Abbé de l'Epée:

> Why do we revere him? Because he did two things that are terribly important: first, because he was a priest, and because he was concerned with the poor, he saw that he would have to bring the deaf together to educate them . . . And as a by-product, he created the deaf community. He created the essential circumstances in which a language could develop. Not because he understood this necessity, but for an adventitious reason . . . If Epée's first accomplishment was the formation of a deaf community, his second was to call attention to that community . . . He held public demonstrations in which the deaf transcribed the signs that he dictated into French, Italian, Spanish, and, of course, Latin, the language of the church. These dem-

onstrations brought about a tremendous flurry of efforts in behalf of the deaf. This was a time when mental retardation was believed untreatable; when deafness and the ignorance of the deaf were considered similarly invincible; and here was a man who taught the deaf to converse in the tongues of the world, or so it would appear to the casual observer. The casual observer included kings and princes and emissaries from throughout the world.[29]

The Abbé's fame spread to other nations in Europe, and they sent scholars to learn his methods. In turn, some of the Abbé's disciples traveled to other lands where they established schools. Soon after his work became known, they opened schools in Holland, Poland, Sweden, and Ireland, to name a few. But not England or Scotland. That detour around Britain is another story, and it will give us the solution to a seeming paradox (that deaf persons from the United States find it easier to communicate with deaf French than with deaf English persons). But let us trace the French lineage a bit further before we look at some other countries and eventually at our own.

The Abbé was well along in years when he began his work with deaf pupils. Soon it was necessary to find a successor. Among his teachers at the Institut National de Sourds-Muets (National Institute for Deaf-Mutes), as the French Revolutionary Assembly called it, was Roche-Ambroise Cucurron Sicard. Sicard had come to the school from Bordeaux, and he quickly earned the reputation of a brilliant teacher. His most adept pupil was a deaf shepherd named Jean Massieu. Sicard wrote that, as he taught Massieu the formal signs developed by l'Epée, Massieu taught Sicard sign *language*. Sicard carried l'Epée's procedures a critical step further, from learning signs to learning sign *language*—from the deaf students.

All of this revolution in the education of deaf children was taking place amidst the political revolt. The French National Assembly had declared l'Epée's school a national institution in 1782. Sicard, however, soon fell from grace. About 1796, during the Reign of Terror, he was seized by the mob and dragged before a tribunal. Since he was a priest, Sicard had little defense against the charge that he was a counterrevolutionary. He was jailed to await the guillotine. Then appeared Massieu with a petition that, even today, cannot help but move the reader. Lane's translation preserves Massieu's eloquence, the more remarkable because he was born deaf and his education did not formally begin until he was twelve years old:

> Mr. President, the deaf and dumb have had their instructor, guardian angel, and their father taken from them. He has been locked in prison like a thief, a criminal, but he has killed no one, he has stolen nothing. He is not a bad citizen. His whole time is spent in instructing us, in teaching us to love virtue and our country. He is good, just, and pure. We ask for his freedom. Restore him to his children for we are his. He loves us like a father. He has taught us all we know. Without him we would be like animals. Since he has been taken away we are sad and distressed. Return him to us and you will make us happy.[30]

Upon hearing the petition read by the clerk, the National Assembly rose to its collective feet and cheered. The vote to release Sicard was *pro forma*. Unlike a stage play, however, the story does not end there. In those chaotic days, the order of the highest legislative body was ignored. Sicard was saved from beheading, but his discharge from prison occurred a week and a number of misadventures later. He did at last appear before a revolutionary committee that recognized him as a teacher of deaf students and arranged for his safe return to the school and his grateful students. The experience understandably scarred Abbé Sicard, so when Napoleon returned from Elba, Sicard took his two best pupils on a tour outside France. He was in London when a young clergyman from Connecticut came to hear his lecture. The meeting forged the French connection in the education of this country's deaf children.

Thomas Hopkins Gallaudet, the Connecticut clergyman, had sailed to Europe at the request of a successful Hartford physician who had a young deaf daughter, Alice Cogswell. Untrained as a teacher, Gallaudet had nevertheless made some progress instructing Alice. Her father determined to open a school for deaf children, and he sent Gallaudet to England because that was the natural place from which to borrow culture. Furthermore, a Scotsman named Braidwood had established a school for deaf children in Edinburgh, and it was his reputation that provided the specific attraction. The Braidwood method followed the tradition which depended upon teaching speech and lipreading. When Gallaudet arrived to learn the procedures, Braidwood proved ungenerous; he refused to permit Gallaudet to observe his methods, unless Gallaudet agreed to sign on as a teacher for three years or to enter into a partnership with Braidwood to open a similar school in the United States. Disappointed, Gallaudet was in London, contemplating his return to Hartford empty-handed, when he saw an advertisement for a lecture by Sicard.

Unlike Braidwood, Sicard was generous. He invited Gallaudet to join him in Paris, where (now that Napoleon was defeated and the monarchy restored) Sicard would return to reopen his school. Gallaudet had read about Sicard's methods, so when the Abbé indicated there would be no charge for instructing him, Gallaudet accepted the invitation. In doing so, he allied the United States with Ireland, which also adopted manual instruction—in contradistinction to England and Scotland, which chose Braidwood's oral method.

Gallaudet remained in Paris about five months. When he prepared to return to America, he invited Laurent Clerc, one of Sicard's best teachers, to emigrate to Connecticut. It may seem somewhat like stealing the host's silverware for Gallaudet to recruit one of Sicard's best teachers; but Sicard approved of the plan, insisting only that Gallaudet give Clerc a written contract for his projected services.

What Clerc brought to America was Franslan (French Sign Language), as well as the teaching methods of Sicard and, most importantly, visible evidence of their success. Clerc himself was deaf. His remarkable development as a scholar undoubtedly had a strong positive effect on the New Englanders who met or heard about him. The visit by Clerc and Gallaudet to the Connecticut legislature resulted in that body's enactment of the first public support for special education in the United States—a grant to the Hartford school of five thousand dollars. Added to private donations, that sum enabled Gallaudet in 1817 to open his school in Hartford. It survives to this day and is now called the American School for the Deaf. (The school is actually in West Hartford, but we will abide by custom and refer to its location simply as Hartford.) For his role in the education of deaf children, the United States Post Office honored Thomas Hopkins Gallaudet, in 1983, with a postage stamp bearing his portrait.

Did Clerc and Gallaudet bring sign language to America? Yes and no. The sign language they brought did not fill a vacuum. Deaf people in the United States already used manual communication. Deaf immigrants from European countries brought their native signs. These collided with each other and with American Indian Sign (Amerind), resulting in early versions of Ameslan.

The rather charming recent historical discovery of an entire island—Martha's Vineyard—where everyone signed, confirms the early use of sign language in the United States. Martha's Vineyard was settled about 1640 by a small group of English immigrants, who mingled with the native Wampanoag Indians to rapidly expand the population over the next few generations. Local custom dictated intermarriage, and the birthrates over the next hundred fifty years were unusually high, with families often having twenty children. Among the numerous offspring were many who were deaf. In fact, so many were deaf that deafness itself was not thought noteworthy. Nora Groce, a graduate student studying the island population, reports:

> Vineyarders themselves, used to a sizable deaf population, saw nothing unusual in this, and many assumed that all communities had a similar number of deaf members. Almost nothing exists in the written records to indicate who was or was not deaf, and indeed, only a passing reference made by an older islander directed my attention to the fact that there had been any deaf there at all.[31]

With as many as one in twenty-five persons deaf, how did the islanders adjust? The answer is beautifully summed up by one eighty-year-old resident interviewed by Groce: "Oh, there was no problem at all. You see, everyone here spoke sign language."

Delightful as that bit of history is in its own right, our interest is in the nature of the language that was used. A complete reconstruction of the Vineyard sign language is being attempted. While this may never be fully accomplished, the reconstruction so far makes it clear that it was unlike Manual English *and* unlike Franslan. It appears that Vineyard sign, like the Vineyarders themselves, had grown in isolation and fostered unique elements. Clearly, deaf people were using sign long before the importation of Franslan.

That deaf people in the States signed before the school at Hartford was founded does not reduce that school's impact on sign language—regularizing it, promoting its use, and popularizing the education of deaf children. Before Hartford, only sporadic attempts had been made to open schools for deaf children. After Hartford was established, schools quickly sprang up in the neighboring states:

in New York in 1820, in Massachusetts in 1821, in Pennsylvania in 1822, and in Ohio and Kentucky in 1823. Today, the education of deaf children is mandated by federal law and extends throughout the United States, in public and private schools, encompassing more than eighty-four thousand deaf students.[32]

Shortly after the Hartford school was founded, Gallaudet left in a dispute with the trustees. Clerc, however, remained for over forty years. He not only instructed deaf students; he was also responsible for teaching sign to new teachers and to those from other institutions who cared to learn it. His influence and, through him, the influence of the two Abbés on Ameslan must have been great. To some extent, the reverse must also have been true: Clerc learned Ameslan from the deaf persons he met here. Thus, the Ameslan of today has demonstrable French origins, but the prevailing structure is probably more of a local outgrowth than an import from Paris. Clerc early abandoned the methodical approach of l'Epée for the grammar of Ameslan. His decision in favor of Ameslan is once again coming into fashion, after being reversed over the last century and a half. The fortunes of Ameslan in education have altered as often as those of a soap-opera heroine, but Ameslan's place in the deaf community has remained constant.[33]

Gallaudet College

No history of sign language is complete without reference to Gallaudet College, still the only liberal arts college for deaf students in the world. The founder of the college was the son of Thomas Hopkins Gallaudet and a deaf mother, Sarah. Edward Miner Gallaudet, Thomas and Sarah's youngest child, came to Washington, D.C., at twenty years of age to head a school for deaf children established by a politician turned philanthropist, Amos Kendall. Kendall had encountered a man who was putting deaf children on display, ostensibly to raise money for a school. Kendall has written his own account of the events:

An adventurer brought to this city (in 1856) five partially educated deaf mute children whom he had picked up in the state of New York, and commenced exhibiting them to our citizens in their houses and places of business. He professed a desire to set up an institution for the education of unfortunates of that class in the District of Columbia, raised considerable sums of money and gathered a school of about sixteen pupils.

Apparently to give respectability and permanence to his school, he sought and obtained the consent of some of our leading citizens, to become its trustees. It soon appeared, however, that he had no idea of accountability to them, and only wanted their names to aid him in collecting money to be used at his discretion. On being informed by the trustees that such an irresponsible system was inadmissable [sic] he repudiated them altogether. In the meantime the impression had gone abroad that he mistreated the children, and it led to an investigation in court, ending in the children being taken from him and restored to their parents, except the five from abroad, who having no parents or none who seemed to care what became of them, were bound to me by the orphans court and formed the nucleus of our institution.[34]

Having accepted full responsibility for the five orphans, Kendall established a school to educate them. In May 1857, he brought Edward M. Gallaudet and his mother to Washington. Edward's mother was essential to the arrangement, because Kendall did not feel it proper to entrust the living arrangements of the deaf students of both sexes to a young unmarried man. Sarah Fuller Gallaudet had been a student at the American School for the Deaf; she married Thomas upon her graduation. Sarah has received little credit from historians for her probable role in starting the Kendall School and inspiring her son to struggle for an institution of higher learning for deaf persons, as well as adding her much-needed skills in sign language to her son's first educational effort. Without her, in effect, that early elementary school might not have survived nor, consequently, would its role as the seedbed for the college have been fulfilled.

In 1864, with the United States still torn by civil strife, Edward Miner Gallaudet prevailed upon the Congress to charter the National Deaf Mute College, a name later changed to Gallaudet College in honor of Thomas Hopkins Gallaudet. President Abraham Lincoln signed the act on April 8, 1864. From that date to this, Gallaudet College has been the bastion of sign language in the United States. Edward Gallaudet believed that the accomplishments of the college and of its graduates clearly proved the worth of manual communication in the education of deaf students. He remained president of the college until March 1910, a distinguished career of fifty-three years' duration.

The International Congress on the Education of the Deaf, 1880

So far, we have described the introduction of sign language into the education of deaf children as if it had been unopposed. Not true. The use of manual communication in deafness education has had foes from its inception. Even Bonet, who is regarded as manual communication's founding father, coupled its use with the teaching of speech and lipreading. The British adopted the latter and rejected the former. The *oral approach*, as it came to be known, also accepted the educability of deaf children. The quarrel became one of how to proceed. The Abbé de l'Epée fought a long battle by mail with the German educator Samuel Heinecke on the educational roles of sign and speech.[35] Wherever deaf children were educated, the issue was joined: speech vs. sign. The opposition came to a head at the International Congress, held in Milan in 1880. That gathering saw the culmination of many earlier attacks on manual communication. The meetings were attended by the leading educators of the day. They passed a resolution that affirmed "the incontestable superiority of speech over sign for integrating the deaf-mute into society and for giving him better command of language." After the vote favoring the oral approach, a delegate rose and proclaimed, "Vive la parole!"

Following Milan, teaching speech became the educational goal, not only in Europe but in the United States as well. Teaching *language* became secondary to teaching *speech*, a distinction not then acknowledged. American schools that had formerly used Ameslan bowed to the wisdom from Milan, and sign faded as a leading instructional tool. At the turn of the century, at another congress—this time in Paris—Edward Gallaudet again sought a compromise as he had in Milan. He proposed that instructional methods be tailored to suit the deaf person's needs and abilities, thus supporting both oral and manual approaches. His efforts to resolve the conflict failed by a vote of seven for and one hundred against!

Deaf people in the United States quickly responded to the challenge from Milan. It is not coincidental that, in August 1880, the National Association of the Deaf (NAD) came into being. The deaf leaders who called that first meeting had in mind the continuing use of sign language in instruction and, equally important, the maintaining of positions for deaf teachers in schools for deaf children. If speech became the principal goal, it was felt, then the deaf teachers' jobs would be in jeopardy. And the decline in the number of deaf teachers after 1900 proved that prediction sadly correct.

The NAD stands as its own affirmation of Ameslan. It is an organization *of* deaf people, not just *for* deaf people. In its hundred-year existence, the NAD has fought for the rights of deaf people, not only in education but throughout civilian life. That it has grown to its present size (over fifteen thousand members) and remained viable for so long testifies to its success in achieving its objectives. Among these are the defense of Ameslan and the encouragement of its development as the principal mode of communication of deaf citizens in the United States.[36]

The principal argument against the use of sign with born-deaf children runs something like this: if they learn to communicate in sign, they will not learn to speak, because signing is easy for them to learn and speech is difficult. Dee, Rapin, and Ruben in 1982 followed eleven born-deaf children about two years of age for twelve to eighteen months after their parents began to sign to them. Instead of impeding speech development of these young children, sign appeared to facilitate it! What is more, instead of finding the children's language development delayed (which is usual for born-deaf children of hearing parents) the investigators found the children's language at or close to the norms for their years. The latter finding is consistent with the belief that *the more language one knows, the easier it is to acquire more language*. What sign language seems to have done for these children is to aid their acquisition of English. Of course, the study has limitations inherent in research with humans. Controls cannot be absolute. Adherents of sign will point to the parents' limited signing ability, and opponents will argue about the sampling (for example, all the children came from middle-class families). In a matter so critical as the development of language in children, polemics should yield to careful investigation. A single study is unlikely to resolve all doubts about so complex a subject, but acceptance or rejection of any treatment on an emotional basis should have no place in the education of deaf children.

1960: *The Return of Ameslan*

From 1880 to 1960, manual communication generally was suppressed. To appreciate that suppression from the educator's side, consider the opening remarks of the keynote speaker at a symposium on British Sign Language, held in England in April 1980: "We are now at last—or perhaps once again—at a point of history in Britain when it is reasonably safe to discuss the use of sign language with most educators."[37] The choice of the phrase "reasonably safe to discuss" conveys the chill on positions contrary to the established one, especially disturbing in a twentieth-century democracy like Great Britain. But the advocates of oral approaches were not less devoted to the education of deaf children than those who approved of the use of sign; the oralists appealed more to the national majority. Even schools that used sign emphasized their efforts to teach deaf students to speak and speech-read. Deaf children and their parents were made to feel that using sign was a bad thing, giving up to sloth and lower forms of existence. A brilliant deaf scholar, Barbara Kannapell, recounts how she came to appreciate Ameslan as a true language and not simply a system for rendering English manually. Her bitterness at the narrow education she had does not appear as such in her writing, but one quotation reveals the depth of her emotions and, most likely, the emotions of other born-deaf persons:

> The stigma of the deaf person is intimately related to his or her language. The deaf person can sometimes "pass" until he starts to sign.[38]

The change in attitude toward Ameslan in this country can be specifically dated: the year is 1960. That is the publication date for William Stokoe's *Sign Language Structure*, a monograph presenting the then novel thesis that Ameslan was indeed a language, not a coding system for the manual representation of English. In 1964, Stokoe and his associates followed with the classic *Dictionary of American Sign Language*. That second work hammered into place the position of Ameslan, a place secure from logical lexical assault. The impact of those two works on the deaf community was substantial. They generated an entirely new approach to language, one that will doubtless benefit all of us in the long run. In the short run, the improved status of Ameslan reflected favorably upon the self-image of the deaf community: its language was acceptable as a language; what its members preferred was legitimate; hence, they themselves were legitimized. If their language was not inferior, neither were they. William Stokoe had made the single greatest contribution to deaf people's welfare since Edward Miner Gallaudet and Laurent Clerc. But initially, deaf people did not see it that way.

Reflecting on his earlier experiences, Stokoe confided to his linguistic colleagues how his research was received at Gallaudet College, where he was (as he still is) a professor of English when he published his seminal works:

> This, of course, was only the comedy's first act curtain. Publication in 1960 [of *Sign Language Structure*, Occasional Paper 8] brought a curious local reaction. With

the exception of Dean Detmold and one or two close colleagues, the entire Gallaudet College faculty rudely attacked me, linguistics, and the study of signing as a language. My function was to teach English, they told me in a meeting to which I had been invited to talk about the occasional paper. If the reception of the first linguistic study of a Sign Language of the deaf community was chilly at home, it was cryogenic in a large part of special education—at that time a closed corporation as hostile to Sign Language as [it was] ignorant of linguistics. Even the general public joined in the outcry. One instance: When the National Science Foundation first granted support for research in Sign Language, two letters attacking the foundation, the grant, and the research purpose appeared in the *Washington Post*. Both letter writers, descendants of A. G. Bell, based their objections on the claim that grandfather had proved once for all that Sign Language is useless and pernicious in the education of the deaf . . .[39]

Linguists, however, respected what Stokoe had done. Not all of them, to be sure, but in sufficient numbers to encourage him to continue, which he has with spectacular results over the last two decades. At the hundredth anniversary of the NAD's founding, the Deaf Community officially made amends for its earlier opposition. Stokoe was given a tribute most fitting for his accomplishments and most suited to his personality: his students and friends secretly prepared a *festschrift*, a collection of essays published in his honor, *Sign Language and the Deaf Community*. The essays all begin with sketches by the authors recounting their experiences with this great teacher-researcher. Probably the most touching tribute, and possibly the one most valued by Stokoe, comes from the deaf playwright Gilbert Eastman:

> . . . Dr. Stokoe taught me to be aware of Sign Language and to appreciate its beauty. I developed basic Sign Language courses, wrote plays, and went all over the country to conduct workshops on Visual-Gestural Communication and to give speeches about my work. But it was Bill Stokoe who helped me to develop pride in my language and my activities, and it was he who encouraged me to tell the truth. Dr. Stokoe is not a fluent signer, yet he has never stopped learning our Sign Language. Dr. Stokoe was the first linguistic researcher in Ameslan, and he became an internationally known advocate of deaf people and Sign Language. We should all honor him as the Father of Sign Language linguistics.[40]

Our lifetime will probably not see a repetition of the Reign of Terror that occurred in the French Revolution. But if Bill Stokoe, like the Abbé Sicard, ever needs a friend to plead for his life, the above statement leaves little doubt that Gil Eastman would welcome the opportunity.

Other deaf people, too, will in time come to recognize Stokoe's pronouncements as their Declaration of Independence. As for those of us who are not deaf, the history of sign language has much to teach us about ourselves.

5

Manual Codes for English

Ameslan is a *natural* language. No one invented it. It originated from the need for visible communication. While its originators are unknown, deaf people are its principal users. The language suits their hands and their eyes, just as spoken languages are adapted to the vocal mechanism and the ears. That critical point needs to be borne in mind as we investigate the *artificial* manual languages that have recently come into vogue. To be more precise, they should be called *codes*, since each is intended as another means of conveying a spoken language.

The idea of making spoken language visible is not new. Chapter 4 discusses in some detail the attempts of the Abbé de l'Epée, among others. It needs to be emphasized that he did not borrow the grammar of Franslan but invented a form of sign that paralleled, on the hands, spoken French. That meant adopting the same syntactical structure, the same grammar, the same underlying punctuation as were used in his country's spoken or written language. The Abbé thought like a person who had always heard, who grew up with and depended upon the French language for communication. Naturally, his ideas of language were based upon that linguistic model. His success in educating deaf children, as noted in the preceding chapter, was demonstrated by their abilities to read and write French, not by their use of Franslan, the natural language of born-deaf French people. The manual system he used, then, was an artificial one.

Returning to the United States in 1816, Gallaudet brought the Abbé's system, modified by putting signs in English word order. We will refer to the latter strategy as *Manual English;*[1] that is, substituting signs for words, following the oral language's syntax. The alternative is to sign in a different order, using a different grammar. (On this point, you may wish to refer to Chapter 3, especially the examples in Figures 41, 42, 43, and 44.) Notice that the word order is not all that changes in Ameslan. Ameslan also condenses utterances. Several words may be required to translate the meaning of one sign correctly into English. That feature of Ameslan—simultaneous or nearly simultaneous presentation of relatively more information than is given by single words—relates to the difference between the functioning of eyes and ears. Ears require temporal separation; eyes do not. Ameslan takes advantage of that fact.

Still, the most popular form of manual communication in the United States today, whether in classes for deaf children or on television, is not Ameslan but Manual English. The simple explanation for what may seem a paradox is that Manual English is far easier for English-speaking persons to learn than is Ameslan. To learn Ameslan takes the same amount of time and effort as would be required to learn, say, German or Spanish. To learn Manual English requires only learning the manual equivalents for English words. To understand Ameslan, one has to acquire not only a new vocabulary but also a different syntax—a time-consuming and complicated process. Teachers of deaf children are usually persons who can hear, so they prefer Manual English. The same preference holds for interpreters, counselors, and other professionals who communicate with deaf persons. What is most important, 90 percent of the parents of deaf children can hear. (For more on this, see Chapter 9.)

Of course, there is another rationale for preferring Manual English to Ameslan. English is the language of the dominant culture in the United States. The dominant group naturally opts for its language over that of all lesser groups. When opposing linguistic groups become nearly equal in power—as in Belgium, for example—battles may be fought. Or the country may become bilingual, with two official languages rather than one, as in Canada, where today all government communications must be printed in both French and English. The Canadian decision, in favor of two languages rather than one, recognizes the political strength of the French minority, a strength great enough to overturn a century of discrimination against their preferred language. Nothing similar to that is apt to occur with respect to Ameslan. Deaf people are a very tiny minority numerically, and very weak politically. Except in the rare situation that occurred on Martha's Vineyard, deaf persons can expect little concession to their language preferences. As a matter of fact, many accept the introduction of Manual English into the classroom for deaf students as a great concession by the speaking majority.

There are several varieties of Manual English. Since most of them represent a compromise between English and Ameslan, they can properly be referred to as pidgin English. The term *pidgin* should not arouse animosity; linguists do not use it as a pejorative. It connotes a mixing of vocabularies and grammars, usually dictated by commerce, that arises naturally, as members of one linguistic community adapt to another. A related term is *creole*. Creolized languages develop when two groups speaking mutually unintelligible languages remain in lengthy contact. Pidgin or creole contrasts with artificial languages, which are created through conscious efforts. In this sense, English is a natural language and Esperanto is clearly artificial. With that distinction in mind, let us look at some specific forms of Manual English.

Paget-Gorman Sign System (PGSS)

The historical grandfather of the current attempts to invent sign languages is the Paget-Gorman Sign System (PGSS). We mention it first out of respect for its precedence. Sir Richard Paget became interested in the education of deaf children. Recognizing the difficulties of the oral approach, in which heavy reliance is placed upon speechreading for language reception, he turned to manual communication. Put off by British Sign Language's different grammar, Sir Richard set to work inventing a systematic way to reproduce English on the hands. His efforts were first published in 1951.[2] After Sir Richard died, Lady Paget invited Dr. Pierre Gorman, a brilliant, born-deaf, Cambridge-educated psychologist, to complete the system.

In PGSS, as presently formulated, each sign represents an English word or part of a word. The inflections found in spoken English are represented in PGSS by adding signs representing various suffixes. Most important, the signs are presented in English word order. The latter feature distinguishes all the various invented forms of Manual English, much as it did the Abbé's version of Manual French.

Seeing Essential English

A few years after the publication of PGSS, David Anthony, a young deaf emigré to the United States from England, made his own adaptation of Manual English. He called it Seeing Essential English, or SEE. First published in 1966 and later in an expanded form in 1971, SEE has had a considerable vogue in the United States.[3] Unlike PGSS, SEE basically uses the signs of Ameslan, though with a number of restrictions. It also adds various function words absent from Ameslan: pronouns, forms of the verb *to be*, articles, and so forth.[4] SEE's purpose, like that of PGSS, is to represent spoken English as closely as possible on the hands.

Within a year after its introduction, SEE was followed by two other invented versions of Manual English. One took the name Signing Exact English. Because the resulting acronyms are identical, the second system has come to be known as SEE II, and the first as SEE I. In addition to the similarity in the abbreviations, SEE I and II also have similar rules of organization and invented constructions.[5] A third version of Manual English created in the United States is distinguished from SEE I and II more by its name than by differences in its structure. Called Linguistics of Visual English, the system is known by its acronym, LOVE.[6] Nor do these three exhaust the number of versions of Manual English. We could add Siglish, Ameslish, and Signed English.[7] Some are the work of individuals and others of committees. A particularly careful version of Manual English has come out of the Texas Education Agency's Statewide Curriculum Project, an attempt to develop a unified curriculum for all deaf students in Texas. The comprehensive dictionary, rationale, and recent supplement produced by the project evidence the thoroughness with which English can be adapted to manual forms. The linguistic savvy of the project's communication team is reflected in the signs, all of which are labeled in both English and Spanish—an indication of the large proportion of deaf students in Texas with Hispanic backgrounds.[8]

Basic Manual English Conventions

With so many versions, one would expect the systems of Manual English to vary among themselves to some extent. They do, but not so much that we cannot consider them in terms of their basic similarities, ignoring the minor differences. In what follows, then, we will attempt a synthesis of the varieties of Manual English, while aware that each has acquired modifications not shared by the others. They are, however, very much alike in their philosophy: they all attempt to provide a precise analog of spoken English on the hands.

VERB FORMS IN MANUAL ENGLISH

Since Ameslan, unlike English, does not use auxiliary verbs in forming the perfect tenses, Manual English must invent them. One of the first problems of Manual English, then, is to modify verb signs so they illustrate tense. Various strategies are used. Figures 45, 46, and 47 show three forms of the copula *to be* in Manual English. In Ameslan, one sign—the index finger moving straight out from the lips—signifies the various forms of *to be*. Ameslan uses that sign only to indicate existence, not as a combining form with another verb. Another modification of verbs is needed to put them in their participial mode, which in English is accomplished by adding *-ing* (in the present tense) or *-ed* (in the past). To

45. *Is*   46. *Are*   47. *Were*

indicate the present participle of any verb, Manual English follows the verb sign with a sign indicating *-ing* (shown in Figure 48). The past participle can be managed in several ways, one of which is to use a sign meaning *-ed*, as demonstrated in Figure 49.

48. *-ing*   49. *-ed*

AFFIXES

English has a large number of affixes, which Ameslan lacks. Manual English solves the problem by inventing signs for suffixes and prefixes. These are handled in the same way they are in English—that is, the affix is signed either before or after the word. Figure 50 displays the affix *-ee*, as in standee. To sign the latter, one would first sign *stand* and then *-ee*. The possessive in English is indicated by the addition of *'s*, a solution followed in Manual English, as shown in Figure 51. Again, note that the noun is signed first, then the sign for *'s* is made with a twist of the hand as it forms the letter. Prefixes are formed by making the sign for the affix, then the root sign. *Return* would be expressed by signing *re* and then *turn*.

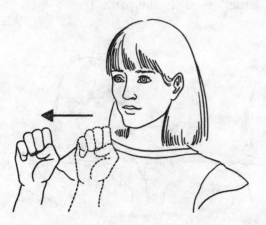
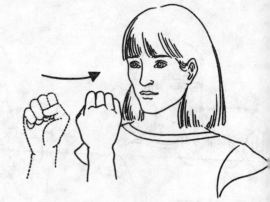

50. *-ee*   51. *'s*

PRONOUNS

Ameslan uses the same sign for *me* and *I*. Manual English distinguishes between them, as shown in Figures 52 and 53. *My* (not shown) is signed with

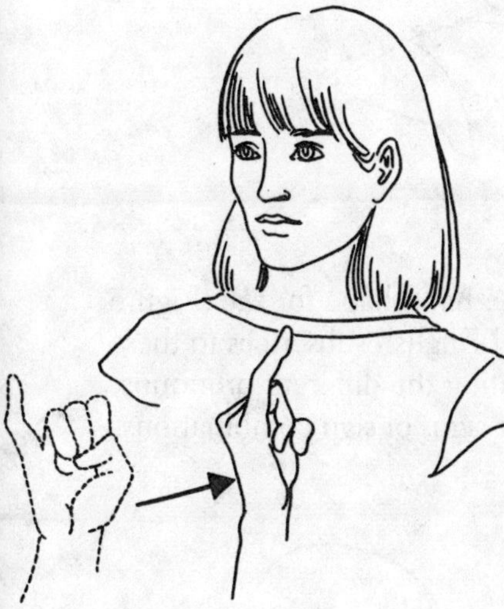

52. *I*

53. *Me*

the palm flat against the chest. The third-person forms in Ameslan are differentiated by the means discussed in Chapter 3, principally by indexing. This strategy does not satisfy most versions of Manual English. Using positions around the head and handshapes from the manual alphabet (for which see Chapter 6), Manual English differentiates the seventeen pronouns of English with seventeen different signs. Following Ameslan's distinction for the sexes, Manual English makes the signs for the masculine third person near the temple, each with the same movement away from the head on the dominant side. Figures 54, 55, and 56 illustrate, respectively, *he*, *him*, and *his*. The female signs approximate Ameslan's stroke

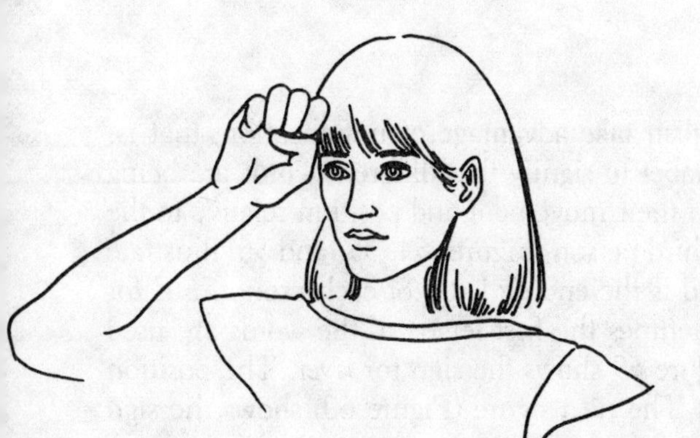

54. *He*

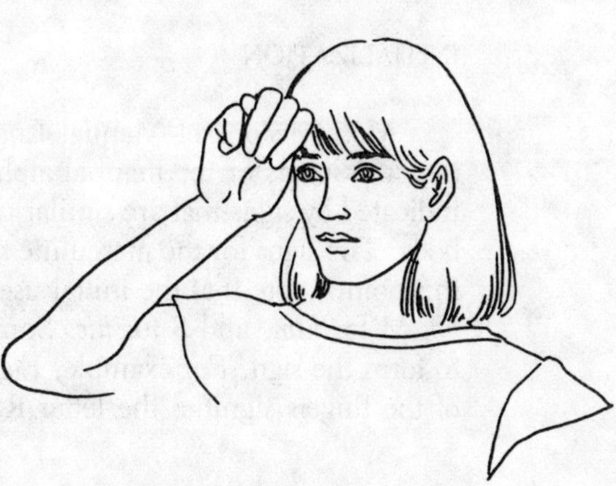

55. *Him*

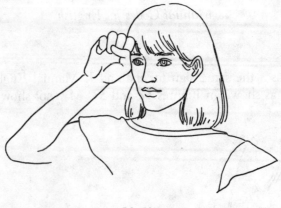

56. *His*

along the lower edge of the jaw, with changes in the handshape for *she* (Figure 57) and *her* (Figure 58). Not every version of Manual English subscribes to these same forms, but each does have some way of indicating the different pronouns, just as the verb forms can be distinguished by separate signs or sign combinations.

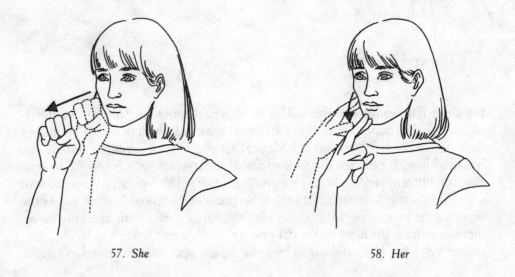

57. *She*   58. *Her*

INITIALIZATION

Most versions of Manual English take advantage of initialization; that is, they use letters of the manual alphabet to signify that different words are being indicated by signs that are similar in their movement and position relative to the body. The signs for the masculine third person (Figures 54, 55, and 56) illustrate this point. Note that the initial used is the ending letter of each pronoun: E for *he*, M for *him*, and S for *his*. Sometimes the first letters of the words are used to form the sign. For example, Figure 59 shows the sign for *river*. The position of the fingers signifies the letter R. The next figure (Figure 60) shows the sign

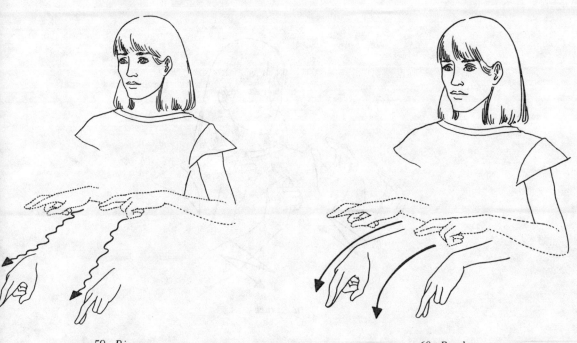

59. *River*

60. *Road*

for *road*. Again, the hands are in the same shape as for the letter R. The different movements signal different words. The handshape also can change as the sign moves from its initial to its final position; the result is a wide variety of possible words. Figure 61 shows the sign for *fun*. As made in this version of Manual English, the sign ends with an *n*. To differentiate *fun* from *funny*, the final handshape for the latter would be changed from N to Y.

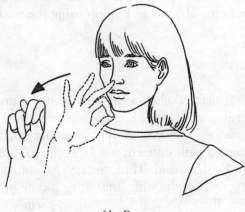

61. *Fun*

What happens when a single letter is too often used to make differentiation clear? Figure 62 displays one solution: use two letters, one in each hand. The drawing is for the SEE II sign for *truck*, with the left hand shaped for *t* and the right hand for *c*. This particular arrangement seems to violate two principles of

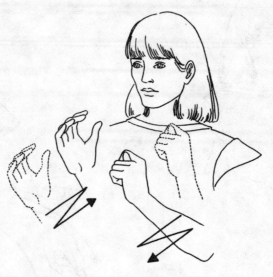

62. *Truck*

Ameslan (see Chapter 3). The first is that both hands usually have the same shape, except for a few basic handshapes of the passive hand, of which *t* is not one. The other is that the dominant hand, usually the right, contains the definitive information. In this sign, the dominant hand has a secondary letter. Ameslan's rules likely developed because they suit the eyes and the hands in the way that spoken English adapts to the ears and the vocal apparatus. Thus, the rules probably reflect limitations in the receptors and effectors, rather than esoteric semantic principles. Repeated deviations from what have been observed as regular rules or features of Ameslan lead to the prediction that either these features will be dropped (or ignored) or the versions of Manual English using them will fall into disuse.

ONE WORD, ONE SIGN

PGSS and SEE II make explicit a rule that seems to underlie some of the decisions in other versions of Manual English: one word, one sign. Ignoring the fact that English words often have more than one meaning and that the same meaning can be expressed with different words, both PGSS and SEE II permit only one sign for each English word. Thus, the sign for sailing vessel (*ship*) serves both for that meaning and for the suffix indicating a state or quality (town*ship*, friend*ship*). In practice, then, Manual English signs town*ship* by adding the sign for *ship* to that for *town*. If that does not seem an odd rule, think of the interesting possibilities with the word *left*, which in SEE is always indicated by the Ameslan sign for direction, even when it connotes the verb ("She left," or "He left the book on the table").

This rule has provoked considerable humor, and a little bitterness, among users of Ameslan. They find it odd to use the same sign for concepts that have different signs in Ameslan. In Manual English, "It turned out all right" uses the same sign for *right* as in "They all turned right" (Figure 63). In Ameslan, two distinct signs are used. The rule also raises objections from linguists, who point out that it increases the time required to transmit a particular thought, thus attenuating one of the advantages of Ameslan—its economy. SEE has also been criticized by linguists who feel that this convention makes it more difficult for deaf adults to learn it, without a compensating demonstration that deaf children find it easier to learn than Ameslan.[9]

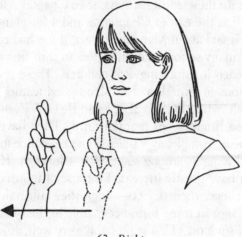

63. *Right*

CRITIQUE OF MANUAL ENGLISH

What these systems amount to are manual codes for English. A *code* designates a group of symbols, signs, signals, or devices that are used to transmit language. Naval signal flags send messages interpretable in many languages. The Morse code's dots and dashes represent alphabetic characters that in turn spell the words of any language reproducible with those letters. Manual English uses hand signs to transmit English. The code is manual; the language remains English.

The decisions that have led to the various forms of Manual English are arbitrary ones, unlike the decisions of a natural language like Ameslan. For any given linguistic problem, many solutions are possible: the developers of the several Manual English systems have simply chosen one, without regard to why such a rule does not exist in Ameslan. Adding signs may prove, in the long run, to be more confusing than edifying. The aim of reproducing English may be a chimera and, like that mythical beast, one not worth pursuing.

One alternative to Manual English that has not been sufficiently tested is *bilingualism*.[10] Deaf children might be better off if they are allowed first to develop a thorough understanding and appreciation of Ameslan, and only then to build English upon that firm base. As for those hearing persons who later learn manual communication, they would be better advised to choose whichever language they prefer, Ameslan or Manual English, rather than to believe that one or the other alone represents the extent of proper linguistic choice. Between Ameslan and English lie the varieties of pidgin English that probably are used by most of the normally hearing persons who learn sign late in life. The pidgins preserve to some extent the virtues of Ameslan: they are relatively uncluttered to the eye, while being easily learned because their grammar is close to that of English, the predominant language for these adult learners. (See Chapter 7 for a fuller discussion of this point, as well as the earlier Chapters 3 and 4 for grammatical highlights.)

Whatever else is said about Manual English, it has had considerable influence on the decisions of many school administrators to shift from an oral approach to a manual-oral approach in educating deaf children. These systems have overcome most of the objections to Ameslan. Ameslan, as educators who resisted it have noted, is not English, while PGSS, SEE I and II, LOVE, and the other versions are English—precise English—in manual form. They have the advantage over spoken English of being completely visible. Some resistance to any form of manual communication still remains among some U.S. educators. However, these signed versions of English have greatly increased the use of manual communication in the classroom. Whatever their defects—linguistic, cultural, or whatever—these systems have made sign in some form acceptable to the broad share of educators responsible for deaf students. That is probably very well, since research indicates that manual communication has important advantages over other methods in the instruction of deaf children.[11]

Gestuno—International Sign Language

Is sign language universal? Can deaf persons from different countries communicate easily with each other? Or are sign languages unique to particular countries?

Margaret Mead—the late, deeply revered anthropologist—has written that sign language should be considered for filling the need we have for an international language.[12] Dr. Mead was hardly naïve about sign language; she knew that each country has its own signs and that signs vary even among deaf persons in the same country. Nonetheless, she urged that sign be considered as a way around the attachment people have for their native tongues. She reasoned that a competing manual language would be less threatening than a spoken one.

The potential correctness of Mead's suggestion is attested to by a recent creation—*Gestuno*. Gestuno is the product of a committee of deaf leaders brought together under the auspices of the World Federation of the Deaf (WFD).[13] The WFD committee that assembled Gestuno consisted of members from England, the United States, the Soviet Union, and Denmark and was chaired by a delegate from Italy. Within a very short period, the committee selected about sixteen hundred signs—all of them natural signs taken from several sign languages, including Swedish and Finnish sign languages as well as the members' native signs. These form the basic vocabulary of Gestuno.

What does Gestuno look like? Figures 64 to 71 show eight international signs that differ from their Ameslan counterparts. Each may be compared to the Ameslan version shown elsewhere in the text. Our using these eight signs as illustrations, however, should not obscure the fact that many of the signs from Gestuno are identical to those from Ameslan. A representative from the United States, Willard Madsen, was a member of the committee that selected the signs, and he prevailed as often as any of the other members who championed their own language.

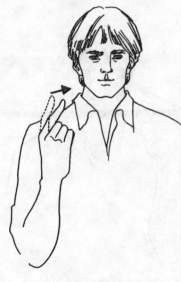

64. Come

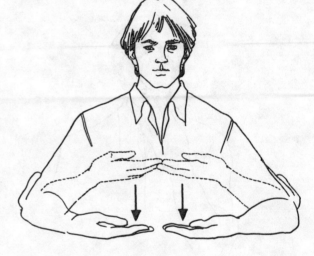

65. Now

66. Good

67. Bad

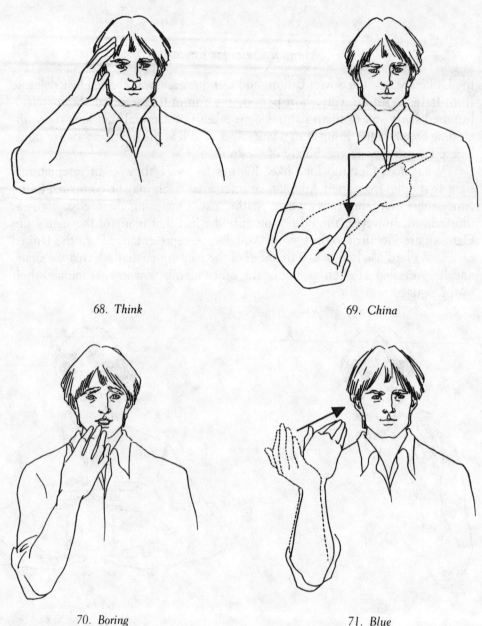

68. *Think*

69. *China*

70. *Boring*

71. *Blue*

What about syntax? The commission finessed this issue. As the chair noted, "This use of signs in isolation presents both a problem and a challenge to newcomers to the situation."[14] True, but it seems to have been a challenge eagerly met and a problem rapidly overcome, to judge from the use of Gestuno at international meetings of the WFD, where it is the third language, French and English being the other officially adopted languages. When using Gestuno, signers put the individual signs in the order most congenial to themselves, allowing the viewers to make of them what they will. In practice, Gestuno is not as difficult to understand as it may seem, particularly for deaf persons, for ambiguity in communication is part of their daily experiences.

Outside of WFD meetings Gestuno has not grown to any popularity. But it is too early to say whether it will eventually join Esperanto as a noble but failed experiment or whether it will reach the hoped-for status of a truly international language. Even before the advent of Gestuno, deaf people were successfully communicating with their foreign peers. A combination of signs and pantomime generally yielded very good results in face-to-face meetings. Cesare Magarotto, Executive Director of the WFD, has written: "Through the language of gestures, which they practice and keep alive, deaf people are able to establish friendly relations across any frontier."[15] He goes on to point out that the fifty-four countries making up the WFD arrived at a constitution expeditiously, despite the lack of a common language. About the founding meeting, convoked in 1951 to adopt the WFD's constitution, Magarotto comments: "No political issues, no partisan views, no legal quibbles hampered their clear, precise argument."[16] Such a delightful meeting stands in contrast to the discordance of the United Nations, and it must arouse the envy of all who have observed delegates wrangling endlessly and fruitlessly over even petty details. Perhaps the approach to hastening an effective world order is to use Gestuno.

6

Let Your Fingers Do the Talking

For every letter of the English alphabet there is a corresponding hand configuration. The twenty-six letters of the American Manual Alphabet are shown in Figure 72. Because there are several other manual alphabets, we shall call this one *Amanubet* as a short expression of the longer name American Manual Alphabet, giving us an acronym parallel to Ameslan.

Using Amanubet, a person can reproduce manually any English word, no matter how long or complicated. It is like writing in the air. (Notice, in fact, that two of the letters are drawn: *j*, with the little finger, and *z*, with the index finger.) Amanubet, then, is another English code. It uses signs for letters, rather than signs for words, as Manual English does.

Fingerspelling

Seeing the letters in their static position on the page gives a misimpression—that one reads the letters one at a time. In practice that is not the case. You do not hear the separate phonemes of a word when you listen intelligently. You put them together to spell something meaningful. For example, what you hear is not "k / ae / t" but "cat." So it is with fingerspelling. The memory load would be extreme if you actually observed fingerspelling as a series of discrete letters. Imagine trying to follow a conversation that went along these lines: "p-l-e-a-s-e-p-a-s-s-t-h-e-s-u-g-a-r-a-n-d-c-r-e-a-m"! Of course, fingerspellers break up the spelled words by inserting pauses between each. The pauses are minute, just as they are in speech, but the experienced fingerspeller groups the letters into meaningful units.

 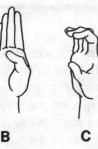 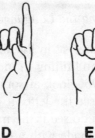  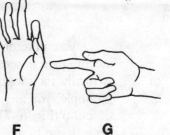

A B C D E F G

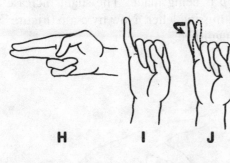 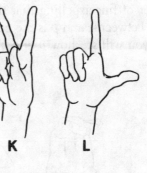   

H I J K L

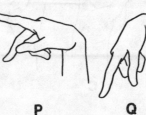 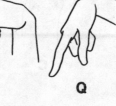

M N O P Q

R S T U V W

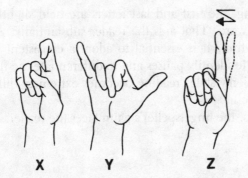

X Y Z

72. *American Manual Alphabet/Amanubet*

Also, in reading fingerspelling—as in listening to speech—the viewer becomes accustomed to seeing patterns and filling in movements that are so fast they are virtually indistinguishable. If you look at someone spelling the word *cup*, for example, you are not likely to see the letter *u* when it is quickly produced. Try it: c-u-p (Figure 73). What you do see is the movement of the hand as it passes from the *c* to the *p*, the latter made with a downward thrust of the wrist. It is this last movement as much as the actual handshape that cues the experienced reader of fingerspelling that the letter *p* is being made. The slight increase in time between *c* and *p* is the cue for the missing letter. Now try c-a-p (Figure 74) and you will see how *u* and *a* are distinguished.

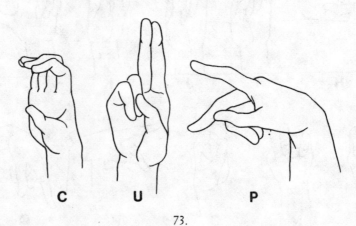

C   U   P

73.

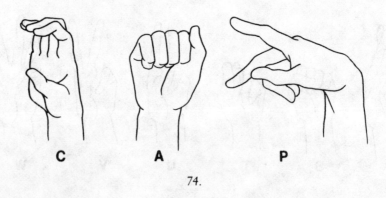

C   A   P

74.

In fingerspelling, the first and last letters are held slightly longer than the interior letters in a word. That aids the reader substantially. Another important consideration is rhythm. It is essential to adopt a consistent rate of spelling in order for the reader to identify pauses and to differentiate the first and last letters. If the speller has a jerky style, reading becomes extremely difficult. It is similar to unrhythmic speech.

For most letters, the fingerspeller's palm faces the reader. The arm must not move about wildly, forcing the reader to search for the next letter. Confine movement to the hand and wrist, not the arm. Some fingerspellers hold their right wrist with their left hand in order to keep it steady while spelling (as in Figure 75). Others rest their right elbow in the palm of their left hand for the same reason. Whatever the means used, the fingerspeller should concentrate on keeping the hand confined to a relatively narrow space: unlike print, fingerspelling does not move from space to space but remains in one place. Two exceptions to that rule: (1) to indicate a capital letter, move the hand horizontally a very short distance, and (2) to indicate an abbreviation, make a small circle with the hand while maintaining the shape of the letter.

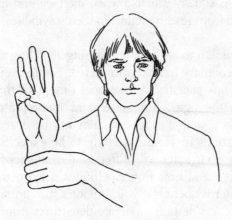

75. *Stabilizing hand*

Spelling can, of course, be done with either hand. Most people spell with the dominant hand, occasionally shifting to the other hand for variety or to relieve fatigue. To emphasize a point, one can also spell with both hands—the same letters, naturally. It is a bit like shouting in speech, so it should be reserved for special effects.

Learning Amanubet

Like any physical activity, fingerspelling requires extensive practice to develop proficiency. An excellent way to practice is to spell in front of a mirror. That way you can observe how your spelling looks to others. You will still need an instructor to provide corrective feedback, because practicing errors or idiosyncracies is worse than no practice at all.

Using the mirror for practice has another great advantage: it helps you learn to read fingerspelling. Memorizing the twenty-six letters is fairly easy, taking perhaps half an hour of concentrated study. But developing skill in reading fingerspelling is another matter altogether. Some people claim they cannot learn to read fingerspelling, regardless of the time invested. They may be correct. Nonetheless, the situation resembles that of learning to read Morse code. Sending (spelling) comes rapidly; receiving (reading), slowly. In learning to read fingerspelling or Morse code, one experiences plateaus—periods in which no learning, no change in acquisition rate seems to occur regardless of the effort expended. Then comes a burst of speed in reading as one jumps to the next level of proficiency. To hasten these jumps and to reduce overall learning time, the assistance of a knowledgeable instructor is valuable. Specific exercises have been found to be helpful. La Vera Guillory[1] has prepared such lessons in a guide that can be used for self-study; it is equally valuable when used with an instructor. The lessons strive to advance one from reading letters to seeing syllables, then grasping whole words.

Teachers of Ameslan today believe that fingerspelling should only be taught after a basic sign vocabulary has been mastered. Some even suggest that fingerspelling not receive any specific instructional time, but that students learn the letters as they learn the signs. Since the signs incorporate many of the hand positions of Amanubet, such a procedure may not be unreasonable.[2]

Individual variations in handshapes are to be expected. As in speech, the way a person makes each letter will differ somewhat, depending upon the size of the hand, dexterity, and how fingerspelling was learned. Slight variations of style in the beginning may befuddle you, but after substantial experience you will be able to identify letters despite moderate departures from the forms you have learned. You will recognize that this situation parallels that of speech, where a difference in accent can make comprehension a problem.

ABBREVIATIONS

To show an isolated letter, as in an abbreviation, one makes the hand position and draws a small circle with it. Figure 76 shows six letters that illustrate an amusing game. Say the six letters aloud: they form a sentence that might be of interest to a member of the opposite sex. Many deaf students enjoy these word games, which depend on the way the letters sound and on what the sounds indicate as words. Thus, being adept at this game flouts one's auditory disability. That is why you will see some deaf students spell, as they depart, "C-U!"

U   R   A   B   U   T

An abbreviation that has become very popular among hearing people, especially politicians, is shown in Figure 77. Jimmy Carter used it during his 1976 presidential campaign. (The fact that he did not use it during his unsuccessful bid for renomination in 1980 may be a mere coincidence.) The sign is based on three fingerspelled letters—*I, L, Y* (see Figure 78). When you make the three letters quickly in succession, they blend into the configuration shown in Figure 77. By drawing a circle with the hand in that shape, you are expressing a lovely thought—"I love you." You can appreciate why politicians like to wave that to a crowd.

77. I love you

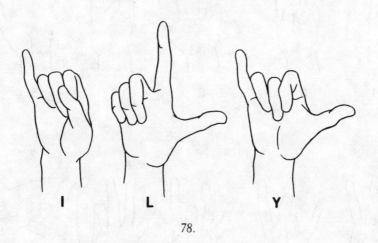

I   L   Y

78.

COUNTING ON THE FINGERS

Using the fingers to indicate numbers seems simple enough—if one does not go over five, with one hand, or ten, with both. On the contrary, Amanubet is not at all limited as to how high a number you want to express; you can signify trillions and beyond. For the sake of clarity and to allow for an infinitely large number, Amanubet adopts a slightly different set of conventions than you might guess.

Zero to Ten. Amanubet uses the shapes shown in Figure 79 for the first ten digits. Notice that 3 is not made in the popular manner; if it were, it would be confused with 6. A brief inspection of the chart will illuminate the logic of the system. For the first five digits you hold up the requisite number of fingers. After that, you indicate the 6, 7, 8, and 9 by touching in turn the little finger, ring finger, middle finger, and index finger with the thumb. Holding up the thumb and twisting it announces the number 10.

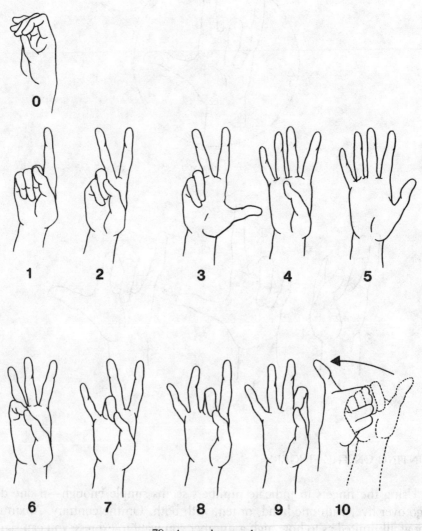

79. *Amanubet numbers*

Eleven and Beyond. By spelling 10 and 1, you make 11; 10 and 2, 12. In practice, these are made with a flicking motion of the index finger against the thumb *(11)* or first and second fingers against the thumb *(12)*. For numbers in the teens, the *10* sign is followed quickly by the sign for the correct digit. The motion is rapid and uninterrupted, to indicate a single number. For twenty, you produce 2 and 0, or you make a pinching motion of thumb and finger. Numbers 21 to 29 are signed by making the sign for *L* followed by the appropriate digit. For thirty, 3 and 0; forty, 4 and 0, and so on. The system is easy and logical. One hundred is shown by the letter *C;* one thousand, by *M;* one million, by *MM;* and so on. Any number can be shown with one hand.

ORDINAL POSITION, TIME, AND MONEY

Amanubet allows for any other linguistic convention with which you are familiar. By drawing a shallow "u" with the index finger, you indicate "first." Doing the same with the number 2 signifies "second."

Touching the wrist of the left hand with the right index finger and then holding up the sign *8* indicates *eight o'clock* (Figure 80). To say *eight cents*, you tap the forehead with the index finger and make the shape for eight as the hand moves away (Figure 81). Additional conventions account for any mathematical notion one can express in spoken or written language.

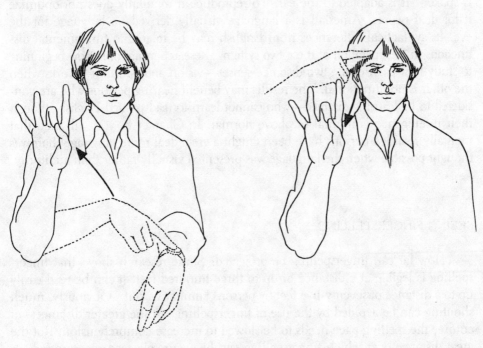

80. 8 o'clock   *81. 8 cents*

Use of Fingerspelling

The ease with which fingerspelling can be learned and its close mirroring of any spoken language may make it seem like the logical contender for first choice in manual communication. It is not. Why? First, fingerspelling is difficult to read for very long. It is fatiguing to the viewer. The sender, too, may experience fatigue after a while, as it is laborious to spell, spell, spell. There are, of course, shortcuts: abbreviations, conventions, elisions. A good rule in spelling a message is to watch the receiver closely. When that person appears to have comprehended a word, skip to the next. Take this message: "The King of Constantinople has died." After spelling K-I-N-G O-F C-O-N-, if it is apparent that the receiver knows to whom you are referring, you can pause briefly (very briefly) and then spell the next word, assured that the message will be understood. Despite such conventions and many abbreviations, fingerspelling remains a tedious way to carry on a conversation. We typically speak at a rate of a hundred and fifty words per minute. Intelligibility is not a problem at that rate. But fingerspelling at a rate greater than two hundred *letters* (or about fifty words) per minute rapidly induces fatigue and cuts intelligibility sharply. As will be pointed out in the discussion below, the Rochester Method, which relies partially on fingerspelling for communication in the classroom, has not enjoyed a great vogue in the education of deaf children. The major reasons seem to be its slow pace and the fatigue it induces.

A more subtle point sometimes goes unnoticed. English is a language that is spoken. It is adapted to the ear. To reproduce it manually does not optimize it for deaf people. Ameslan is a language visually derived—a language for the eye. Its syntactical differences from English may be related to fundamental distinctions in the operation of these two systems. Researchers are only now beginning to study how each of the two distance senses—vision and audition—works when the other is nonfunctional. The results may benefit hearing persons who are considered to be learning-disabled—who cannot learn to read printed English, though their intelligence is normal or above normal. In Chapter 8, you will read that mentally retarded persons have been taught a great deal more language than was thought possible when the language was presented visually rather than auditorily.

SEEING FINGERSPELLING

How far can fingerspelling be projected? Some research shows that fingerspelling is legible at a distance of up to three hundred feet! It can be read easily up to a distance of seventy-five feet by persons familiar with it.[3] Obviously, much shouting can be avoided by the use of fingerspelling. At the greater distances, of course, the spelling pace needs to be slowed to increase comprehension. But the great distance over which fingerspelling can be accurately read recommends its use in noisy situations or where sender and receiver are separated by distances which would fatigue the vocal chords to overcome. By comparison, however, the legibility of sign over distances is much greater than that of fingerspelling.

KEEPING SECRETS

Manual alphabets have been used for centuries by religious orders whose members have taken vows of silence.[4] Youngsters who have learned fingerspelling from Boy Scout manuals or from deaf persons delight in using it in situations where speaking is forbidden. They can fingerspell to each other across a playground or during a class. Discreetly passing messages in full view of others has great appeal, but the fingerspeller who desires confidentiality must be sure that possible viewers do not know the alphabet being used. As noted, fingerspelling is legible at a considerable distance.

Obviously, one way to keep fingerspelling confidential is to keep it out of sight of all but the intended receiver. This can be accomplished by spelling behind an extended coat flap or beneath a table edge. Whatever obstructs the view of possible "eyes droppers" will suffice. Some deaf people also become adept at "whispering" with their fingers. They make tiny finger movements, much as one lowers one's speaking voice. Such fingerspelling is very difficult to understand, if the context is not known. The clandestine pair can also switch to the British two-handed alphabet (which is described later in this chapter), with the sender using the receiver's hand as the passive hand. Since the experienced receiver can then read the letters by touch, the hands can be completely out of sight of everyone. A deaf couple I know have such conversations in crowds; to the casual observer, they merely appear to be holding hands.

LEXICAL BORROWING: FROM AMANUBET TO AMESLAN

Deaf people who sign use fingerspelling sparingly. One major exception is the spelling of proper names. Once established in conversation, the names are usually not spelled again but indicated in various other ways (see Chapter 3). Research by Robin Battison has shown, however, that Amanubet has had a considerable influence on Ameslan's vocabulary.[5] His research on *lexical borrowings* (the linguist's term for influences of one language on another) shows numbers of instances in which it is reasonable to suspect that the present-day form of a sign has been modified by aspects of Amanubet. Some common two-letter words— *if, oh, O.K., or*—have become highly stylized when signed, but remain identifiable as fingerspelling in origin. Other signs have been traced to their fingerspelling origins. Take the sign for *job* (Figure 82). It has become so reduced that it is hardly recognizable as a modification of *j-o-b*. It now looks like *i-b*, with a twist

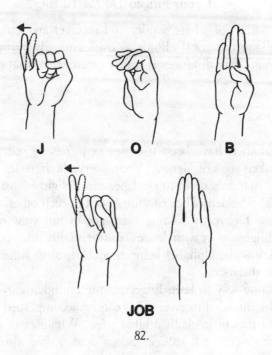

J O B

JOB

82.

of the forearm as it moves from the *i* to the *b* position facing the speller. As shown in Figure 82, the sign has only a faint resemblance to its fingerspelling origin. These transformations of fingerspelled English words into Ameslan are probably commoner than has been supposed.

The changes from spelled words to signs sometimes involve more than a reduction in the fingerspelling to a simplified version. Some lexical borrowings have taken on altered meanings. One sign idiom is made by repeating the letters *d-o*. In Ameslan, this takes on the meaning "What do we do now?" Or it may be used to express "What should we do?" In a group of teenagers sitting around with time heavy on their hands, someone may suddenly use the sign to mean "What do you want to do?"

Amanubet used with Ameslan extends the range of the latter. The combination results in some fascinating variations that are not all they appear to be on the surface. Uncovering their full meaning requires careful study. Battison points out that his informants were occasionally unaware of the genesis of some signs recently derived from fingerspelling, offering plausible but inaccurate explanations of how the signs evolved. He illustrates the point with the borrowed sign for *bread* (see Figure 83). Its appearance is like that of the numerals 5 and 8, repeated two or more times. Careful analysis indicates that the sign comes from the fingerspelled *bread*, with the *rea* dropped out and the *d* modified somewhat. When asked how the sign came about, some of Battison's younger informants said they thought it came from the pinching motion one would make to test a bread's freshness. Their

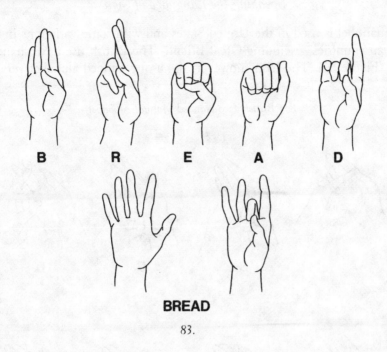

BREAD

83.

resort to an iconic explanation does not fit the etymology, so far as Battison could determine it.[6] The anecdote offers a caution, again, to those who attempt to guess at the origins of signs, typically seeking concrete explanations which, aside from being incorrect, maintain the fiction of Ameslan as an essentially iconic language.

Other Alphabets

One possible disappointment you can avoid comes from believing that by fingerspelling you will make yourself completely understood by any deaf person. Not necessarily. Remember that you will be spelling English words in English word order; therefore, how well the deaf person understands the fingerspelled message depends upon how well he or she knows English. It may be clearer than if you only spoke to the deaf person, forcing that individual to rely on lipreading. Knowledge of the spoken language, however, is the limiting factor for comprehension of fingerspelling. When you go to France, you will find you can sign intelligibly to deaf French natives, but not fingerspell intelligibly—unless you know French. You can learn the British two-handed alphabet and you will be intelligible to many British deaf people. Using Ameslan with British deaf persons will not be as effective as with the French—a paradox that can be explained by looking at the history of manual communication. You may find that what you expect, based on what you know of spoken language, will not apply to manual communication.

Amanubet is used in the United States and with some variations in several European countries, excluding Great Britain. The British use a two-handed alphabet (Figure 84). The Irish, however, use a one-handed alphabet very much

84. British Two-Handed Manual Alphabet

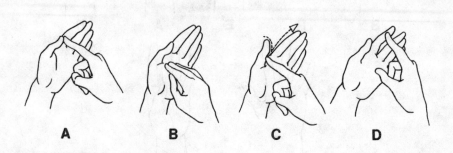

A   B   C   D

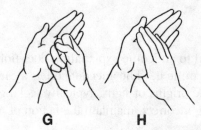

E   F   G   H

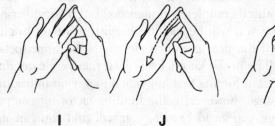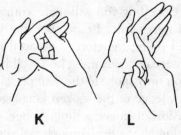

I   J   K   L

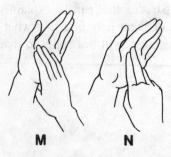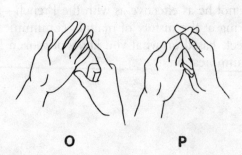

M   N   O   P

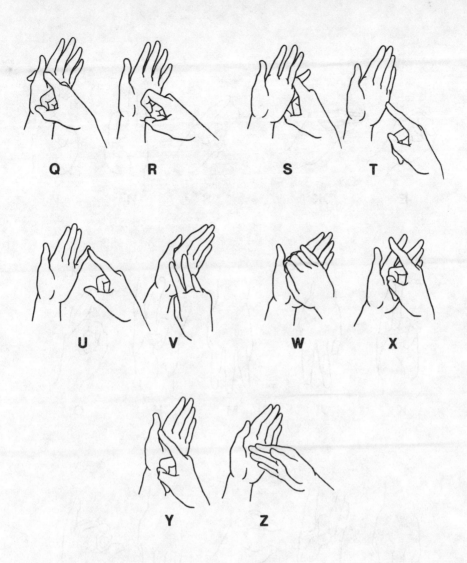

Q R S T

U V W X

Y Z

like our own. In fact, Ireland's and our manual alphabets have the same country of origin, France. The French alphabet, in turn, came from Spain. The Russian alphabet probably came to that country from France, along with sign language, but it had to be expanded to allow for representation of the additional letters in the Cyrillic alphabet. The result is shown in Figure 85. In recent years, countries without a written alphabet, like Thailand and China, have developed fingerspelling which reproduces their spoken languages. As is true of sign, the possibilities inherent in fingerspelling are virtually limitless.

85. Russian Manual Alphabet

А Б В Г Д

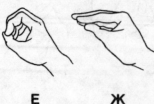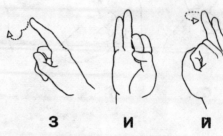

Е Ж З И Й

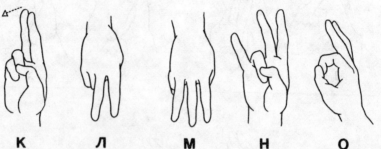

К Л М Н О

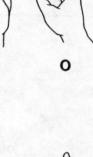

П Р С Т У

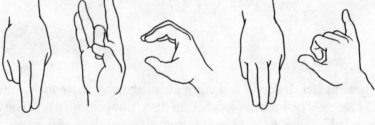

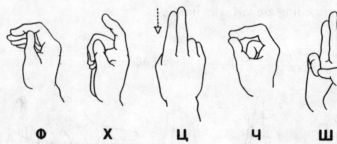

Ф Х Ц Ч Ш

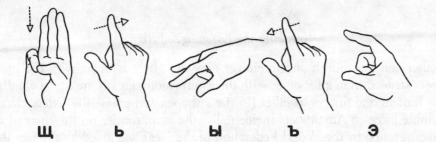

Щ   Ь   Ы   Ъ   Э

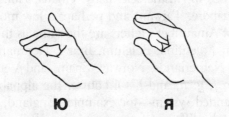

Ю   Я

THE INTERNATIONAL MANUAL ALPHABET

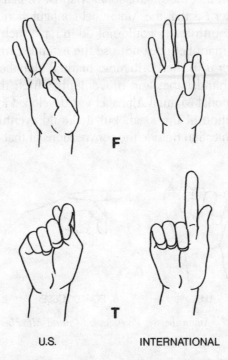

F

T

U.S.   INTERNATIONAL

86. *Amanubet vs. International Manual Alphabet*

The World Federation of the Deaf has established an International Manual Alphabet. It is almost identical to Amanubet, except for two letters: *f* and *t* (see Figure 86). In the International, *f* is made with the three extended fingers close together and the thumb and forefinger crossed. The *t* is made with the index finger extended from a fist made with the thumb alongside (in the *a* shape) rather than holding the fingers together (in the *s* shape). Otherwise the letters closely resemble those in Amanubet. Incidentally, the compromise on the manual alphabet reached by the World Federation of the Deaf was aided by the fact that Amanubet is already used in Austria, Germany, Ghana, Hong Kong, Ivory Coast, Liberia, Nigeria, Singapore, Taiwan, and perhaps a few more countries. In addition, the majority of Amanubet's letters are the same as those in the alphabets used by deaf people in Argentina, Belgium, Brazil, Denmark, Finland, France, Ireland, Mexico, the Netherlands, Norway, Spain, and Venezuela. The differences occur mostly in *f*, *g*, *h*, and *t*. Of course, the alphabets of the countries that rely on a two-handed system—for example, England, Scotland, and Yugoslavia—are completely different from Amanubet. But countries that have a one-handed alphabet tend to have one that resembles Amanubet. The major exceptions are countries that have larger or smaller alphabets, such as Poland, Russia, the Philippines, Japan, and Thailand.

The major reason that the International Manual Alphabet adopted a different handshape for the letter *t* is that the Amanubet configuration is an obscene gesture in many European countries. It would not do to have such a symbol in general display. Similarly, Amanubet does not use the extended middle finger, a shape that signifies the letter *a* in the Portuguese manual alphabet (Figure 87). There are other taboos in handshapes and movements which the International has avoided. The International Manual Alphabet was developed for use at the meetings of the World Federation of the Deaf, but it should eventually prove an aid to international communication outside the convocations of that distinguished body.

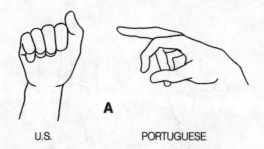

A

U.S.   PORTUGUESE

87. Amanubet vs. Portuguese Manual Alphabet

The Rochester Method

In 1878, Zenas Westervelt introduced a compromise between the two extremes warring over the education of deaf children.[7] He was an advocate of oralism (the position that speech should be the basis of instructing deaf children), but he recognized ambiguities inherent in lipreading and sought to supplement it with fingerspelling. He was doubtless influenced in that decision by Alexander Graham Bell. Bell, who preferred to be listed in *Who's Who* as a "teacher of the deaf" rather than as the inventor of the telephone, supported the use of fingerspelling:

> Spoken language I would have used by the pupil from the commencement of his education to the end of it; but spoken language I would not have used as a means of communication with pupils in the earliest stages of education of the congenitally deaf, because it is not clear to the eye, and requires a knowledge of the language to unravel the ambiguities. In that case I would have the teacher use written language, and I do not think that the manual language differs from written language excepting in this, that it is better and more expeditious.[8]

As superintendent of the Rochester (New York) School for the Deaf, Westervelt was able to put his approach to a full test. The simultaneous use of fingerspelling and speech remained the method of instruction at the school until Westervelt's death in 1912. Despite reports of its great success, the method faded after its innovator's demise. It is revived from time to time, and a few schools for deaf children in the United States employ it today. Its tediousness probably accounts for its lack of popularity with educators. It has other disadvantages, aside from being slow. Its performance requires great dexterity; hence, it is difficult to initiate very young deaf children in its use. They lack the requisite fine motor control. In that regard, it should be noted that spelling is a skill that usually develops after children have acquired language proficiency. Trying to advance spelling and language proficiency simultaneously does not seem to work especially well. Very young deaf children do learn to spell—sort of. That is, they can usually—if they are taught—make finger movements closely resembling their names at two years of age, or even earlier.[9] Spelling one's name, of course, is a distant remove from spelling word after word in grammatical English. Nonetheless, proponents of Westervelt's method, though few, persist. It is not, however, the method used today at the school after which it is named.

The Russians have recently "invented" the same method and named it *neo-oralism*.[10] Early research reports from the Soviet Union gave glowing accounts of its results. Little has been said about it in the Russian literature of the 1970s. Why it has fallen from favor is unexplained.

Cued Speech

Lipreading (or speechreading) has frequently been proposed as an alternative to manual communication for born-deaf persons. The deaf observer interprets clues on the speaker's face—mostly the changes in the shape of the lips. The idea intrigues most people, until they realize that only sixteen different lip shapes are discriminable. These sixteen must serve to represent the thirty-six phonemes of English—a difficult task.[11] To clarify the point, look in the mirror as you successively say "bop," "mop," "pop": visually they are nearly identical. Or try to distinguish between "dime" and "time" by lipreading. If that configuration appears along with a questioning look on a speaker's face, do you reach for your wallet or your watch? (You might also want to see if you can choose, by lipshape alone, between "wallet" and "watch.")

In 1966, Orin Cornett conceived of an ingenious technique for improving lipreading accuracy. He reasoned that deaf children, like all humans, need a formal communication system at an early age. Sign language could fulfill that need, but parents might be slow to acquire it. Even Manual English requires time and effort to achieve a reasonable competence. What about a simple technique to aid lipreading? Such a technique would focus on English, a language congenial to most parents of deaf children, and would be quickly mastered by them. The result—Cued Speech.[12] It uses four hand positions to distinguish eleven English vowels, and eight handshapes to differentiate twenty-five consonants, plus movements for some diphthongs (Figures 88, 89, and 90). The user of Cued Speech need only distinguish between three lip shapes—open, flattened-relaxed, and rounded. The hand position then identifies the intended phoneme among the look-alikes. Nonetheless, there is much for the user to learn, and much to keep in mind besides communicating when using the system. Cornett recognizes that point and urges that his approach "be learned initially by students who already have a language foundation, as a system for clarifying words and statements which are misunderstood." He refers to Cued Speech as a "back-up system."[13] And so it appears to be, having achieved a modest success but having made no greater impact on the education of deaf children than was planned by its innovator.

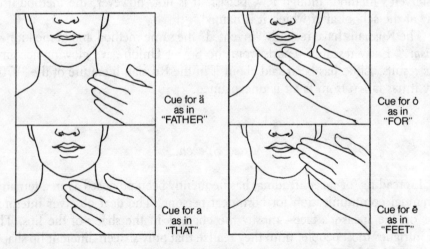

88. Cued Speech vowel cues

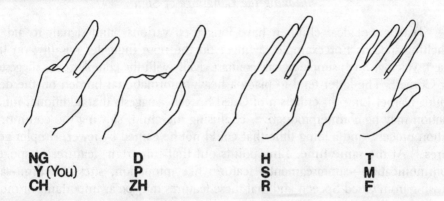

NG
Y (You)
CH

D
P
ZH

H
S
R

T
M
F

G
J
TH (Thin)

N
B
HW

K
V
TH (The)
Z

L
SDT
W

89. Cued Speech consonant cues

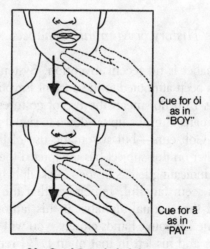

Cue for ŏi
as in
"BOY"

Cue for ā
as in
"PAY"

90. Cued Speech diphthong cues

Teachers of deaf children have long used various hand signals to aid in teaching speech. For example, a finger on the nose indicates nasality; on the chest, voicing. Such simple signals contrast vividly with the complex cues suggested by Cornett. The latter tend to place a heavy informational burden on the deaf child. Daniel Ling, in criticism of Cued Speech, suggests that additional information may be counterproductive, confusing the child, slowing the communication process, and adding little that could not be gained by fewer, simpler gestures.[14] At the same time, Ling points out that important features of spoken communication—suprasegmental features like intonation, stress, rhythm—are missing from Cued Speech and that these features may be as important, or more important, than the cued information.

Historically, Cued Speech is the end of a line of compromises between strict oralism and supplemented oralism. Two French educators in the nineteenth century thought it likely that a system of hand signals to indicate which consonant was being spoken would improve the education of deaf children.[15] The intention was to use speech in teaching deaf children, with the hand signals resolving the difficult-to-distinguish lip configurations. Because fewer handshapes would be involved, they reasoned, the system would be easier to learn and faster to apply. In Denmark, Georg Forchhammer created a similar system that he named the Hand-Mouth System.[16] It has been used in Danish schools for deaf children for most of this century. Interestingly, the system has not been adopted by other Scandinavian countries. Under Cornett's dedicated leadership, however, Cued Speech may have a greater and longer-lasting impact. One major difference between Cued Speech and its predecessors is its developer's willingness to submit it to rigorous scientific tests to establish its merits. If it passes these successfully, Cued Speech will become a strong contender for preeminence among manual-oral communication methods.

History of Manual Alphabets

The manual alphabet is no recent invention. Systematic use of the hands for communication has been attributed to the ancient Egyptians, Hebrews, Greeks, and Romans.[17] By this I do not mean the use of gestures or one- or two-hand positions—like the Romans' thumbs-up or -down to signal pleasure or displeasure with gladiators in the Coliseum—but systematic use of the hands for communication. One early writer on this subject has interpreted the handshapes of various pre-Hellenic statues as indicating letters of the Greek alphabet or of its precursor.[18] If such interpretations seem fanciful, remember that the great sculptor Daniel French used letters of the manual alphabet in his famous statue of Abraham Lincoln. If you examine Lincoln's hands closely, you will see that his right hand is in the shape of an A and his left in that of an L.[19] French had received great esteem for his sculpture of Thomas Hopkins Gallaudet teaching the manual alphabet (specifically, the letter A) to Alice Cogswell. Centuries from now, the historian who guesses that these hand positions illustrate letters of Amanubet will be correct. Might not the guesses about ancient Greek sculpture also be on target?

At any rate, unequivocal evidence of the use of manual communication can be found in the writings of the seventh-century historian the Venerable Bede.[20] He describes three different systems known to himself. From that day to this, evidence abounds of the use of manual alphabets. Monks in the Middle Ages learned finger alphabets for communication after taking a vow of silence, and may also have used them to keep their exchanges confidential.

Incidentally, some of the ancient alphabets would appear remote from Amanubet. The letters were indicated by pointing to parts of the body: for example, the vowels were signaled by touching the tips of the fingers (A—thumb, E—ring finger, and so on). The English two-handed alphabet still uses the fingertips for the vowels, with the consonants now made by the right hand in the palm of the left hand. Other variations use parts of the left hand for every letter of the alphabet.

Who first used the manual alphabet to teach deaf students is not known. Credit usually goes to the Spanish priest Juan Pablo Bonet. The reason: he wrote the first book on educating deaf children, *Reducción de las Letras y arte para Enseñar a Hablar los Mudos*. The book contains a diagram of a one-handed alphabet. That alphabet is the progenitor of Amanubet. The Abbé de l'Epée adapted it to the French language, and thence it came to the United States with Laurent Clerc and Gallaudet. Did Bonet invent the alphabet he used? He makes no such claim; instead, he discusses options other than the one-handed alphabet— for example, one that uses the Latin names of body parts: A—auris (ears), B— barba (beard or chin), C—caput (head). The profusion of alphabets already known suggests that Bonet adapted an existing one-handed alphabet to his purposes rather than inventing one (see Chapter 4, especially the section on Pedro de Ponce).

Why the English chose the two-handed, as opposed to the one-handed, alphabet as the vehicle for instructing deaf children is not clear. In 1644, the English physician John Bulwer published a monograph describing a communication method used by a deaf man and his wife; it was a two-handed alphabet. Bulwer's later book, printed in 1648, describes six other alphabets, so the British had ample choices. Later publications emphasize the two-handed variety. A booklet that appeared in 1698 offered "the most compendious, copious, facile and secret way of silent Converse ever yet discovered Shewing how any two persons may be capable in half an hour's time, to discourse together by their Fingers only, as well in the dark as the light." Since the anonymous author identified himself (or herself, as the case might be) as "a person who has conversed no other wise in above nine Years," it seems likely that the book, *Digiti Lingua*, was written by a deaf person. The alphabet recommended therein closely resembles the one in use in England today.

The two-handed alphabet has some distinct advantages over the one-handed. First of all, it is potentially more private. Conversations can go completely unnoticed by others. It can be used in the dark. This second advantage, independence from both sight and sound, makes it an excellent vehicle for use with deaf-blind persons. Some are able to read the one-handed alphabet by placing their hands over the speller's, but for some deaf-blind persons the two-handed alphabet is preferable.[21] The advantage of unobtrusiveness becomes a disadvantage when the two-handed alphabet is used in communication with a group. The one-handed alphabet is probably more visible over greater distances. Another disadvantage is that the two-handed speller cannot eat and talk comfortably at the same time. When using Amanubet, you can work or carry things with one hand and spell with the other.

Whether one-handed or two-handed, fingerspelling has great utility in silent conversations. Where a precise, easily learned code for English is required, Amanubet or its British cousin clearly meets the need. It enables the communicator to fill any gaps between Ameslan and English. In 1648, when John Bulwer wrote *Philocophus*, he subtitled the book "The Deafe and Dumbe Man's Friend." The words remain apt three centuries later.

7

Learning to Sign

If you have become enthused by this introduction to sign language, you may now be thinking about learning to sign. Where will you find classes? With whom? How will you be taught? Which variety of sign will you learn? All these questions will be examined here. In the next chapter we will consider commercial uses of sign: how to convert your knowledge of sign into a career.

First, be assured that learning to sign is no more difficult, and perhaps no less, than learning any other language.[1] Some people find that hand-eye coordination is more difficult than ear-tongue coordination, while others find it easier. Obviously, those who are hearing-impaired usually will be better able to handle the former than the latter. But the difficulties of one means of conveying language as compared to the other should not be overemphasized. The basic factors in learning sign language—patience and persistence among them—will prevail. Learning sign, like learning any new material, will require time and a good deal of effort.

Sign Classes

Until 1964, when the Metropolitan Washington Association of the Deaf set up its first classes for the public, there were few places where one could go to learn sign.[2] Today, it is safe to say that you can get instruction in sign in almost every major metropolitan area in the United States at some time during the year. In cities like New York, Los Angeles, Dallas, and Washington, D.C., you will find classes almost every working day, often offered by more than one organization—a community college, a high school, or an organization of deaf persons. If you are looking for a sign class, you will often have several choices.

As with any other course of study, sign classes are apt to be taught well by accredited institutions of education. Adult continuing education courses are a very good bet; they are designed to manage a limited scope (assuming all you want is the sign language and not a degree in rehabilitation counseling or the like), and most do not insist upon prior academic credentials or specific course prerequisites. Such programs are offered by community colleges and universities. Occasionally high schools and technical institutes offer adult continuing education courses. Your local public library will have a list of the possibilities in your vicinity.

Service organizations and clubs for deaf people also have classes in sign language. Some are excellent—equal to or better than in many of the colleges and universities—but the majority, frankly, are not as good. It stands to reason that the institutions where education is a full-time concern are more likely to do a better job of it than the service organizations and clubs where education is only an incidental undertaking. The latter often initiate their sign programs because no other institution has offered classes in their region. However, circumstances are changing. Today, sign has become a popular offering. Classes are filled, and often oversubscribed, as soon as they are announced. The very popularity of sign should make you wary of the instructional possibilities. Student demand may, for a time, outstrip instructor supply.

Opportunities to learn sign have also grown in other countries. The Royal National Institute for the Deaf and the British Deaf Association sponsor sign classes throughout the British Isles. Along with a number of important research projects, sign classes may be found in such cities as Edinburgh, Bristol, and Newcastle, as well as in London.[3] Many other countries throughout Europe have begun to expand the teaching of sign beyond the realm of professionals interested in its use in the education of special populations. An exception appears to be Italy, where the government-sponsored educational programs respond antagonistically toward sign. However, in Africa, in the Antipodes, and in several countries in Asia, Japan foremost among them, sign instruction is becoming increasingly available.

Selecting an Instructor

Aside from choosing a reliable institution, whenever possible you should also consider the instructor. The probabilities of getting a poor one are rapidly declining, but you can still run into sign instructors who know little more than you do. Not very many years ago, I encountered a teacher from a nearby school district who had taken a summer class in sign at New York University. She excitedly told me that on the strength of that six-week course her superintendent had put her in charge of teaching sign to the remainder of the staff in her school! She expected me to be as pleased and proud as she was. I am afraid my dismay showed through. Imagine having as an instructor of Spanish or French, for example, someone who had no more knowledge of the language than could be obtained in thirty instructional days!

Deaf persons are a fertile source for supplementing the ranks of teachers. Those who have been signing since early childhood have a competence analogous to that of native users of any language; they usually "think in sign." And they usually have competence in Ameslan. They may not, however, be good teachers. Knowing a language and being able to convey that knowledge do not necessarily go together. Planning an instructional course and managing students' idiosyncracies do not automatically accompany language competence. As tutors or simply as persons with whom to practice sign, most deaf people can serve very well. Once in a while, a small group of parents of deaf children or other persons motivated to learn sign have banded together and hired a deaf adult to teach them, and the result has been excellent. If good formal classes are not available or if you want extra instruction, contacting deaf adults is a feasible option.

How can you be assured that your instructor is qualified? A few judicious questions will be in order, beginning of course with "Where did you learn to sign?" You will also want to know whether your potential instructor has had formal preparation to be an educator. Knowing how to sign is one thing, but being able to teach sign is something else.

Scientific evidence supports the commonsense importance of motivation in learning languages. *You learn what you want to learn* is a sound basic notion. One of the language teacher's critical functions is maintaining students' morale during instruction. The teacher must balance the maintenance of motivation against the student's tendency to feel complacent over insignificant progress. Keeping the lessons interesting and giving adequate but not undue praise for achievement are among the demonstrably successful means of sustaining the students' desires to learn. In selecting a sign teacher, you should assess the candidate's personality as well as his or her knowledge of Ameslan and instructional experience.[4]

Another indication of teaching competence is certification by the National Association of the Deaf. The association recognizes that it is in the best interests of deaf people to have sign taught well, and it has accepted some responsibility to meet the need for qualified sign instructors. In addition to sponsoring programs that develop sign teachers, the NAD conducts certification examinations and maintains a register of those who have attained any of the various levels of competence. If you can get a certified teacher of sign, you have assurance that you will be receiving instruction from a thoroughly prepared professional.[5]

Methods of Instruction

Language teachers have long known that the student's initial exposure to a language should be substantial. Berlitz has developed a technique called "Total Immersion," in which the student conducts all communication, for several hours at a time, solely in the language to be learned. The same principle is followed by the State Department in preparing diplomats for a Foreign Service assignment, and by the Mormon Church in teaching new languages to its missionaries.

At New York University, we have found concentrated instruction to be the method of choice for beginners.[6] Since 1972, we have held Intensive Sign Language Institutes (ISLI) in which students spend eight hours a day for one week, Monday through Friday, in classes that use sign as the sole means of communication. The regimen can be stressful at first, but the important thing is that almost every student who undergoes the experience has a fair (or better) grasp of sign at the end of the five days. A popular variation is the ISLI retreat. Students assemble at a resort where not only their days but also their nights are occupied with sign. Signs prevail at mealtimes, at coffee breaks, and in after-dinner games, as well as in classroom settings. During the retreat, students agree not to talk, except at specified "speech breaks"—a diversion found necessary to overcome occasionally drastic frustration. Through the years, some students have returned to three or more ISLI retreats. The ISLI program no longer accommodates only beginners; the technique has been found useful for students who want to transcend a plateau they feel they have occupied too long. The result has been that ISLI programs now cover various levels, from beginning to advanced.

Where will you find a similar instructional strategy? At present, only in few locations. You may want to lobby for such programs in your area if none currently exists. Of course, there is also much to be said for spaced classes. But meeting once or twice a week (sometimes referred to as the "slow-drip method") is of greatest value to those who already have some competence in the language. For them, it is an excellent way to sharpen their skills and expand their vocabulary. Without a good start, however, spaced instruction can often be so slow to produce results that the individual becomes discouraged and drops out of the program. The intensive approach tends to maintain motivation much better. By quickly learning a fair number of signs, the individual can begin to practice outside class, to use the language, and, most important, to have fun with it. Once the student has a bit of fluency, the addition of signs becomes increasingly easy and the incentive to learn more is self-renewing.

Which Sign System?

At present it is much easier to obtain instruction in Manual English than in Ameslan. But that situation is changing. More and more, people are demanding the opportunity to at least be exposed to the "true" sign language, as opposed to learning a system for manually encoding English. The difference between the two—manually encoded English and Ameslan—is substantial. As shown in earlier chapters, Ameslan differs greatly from English, has its own syntax, and thus creates what the psychologists call *proactive inhibition* to learning (the material learned earlier conflicts with the material to be learned). Simply put, learning Ameslan means learning a foreign language.

The systems of Manual English, to varying degrees, require only that the student learn a sign-for-word substitution. That is clearly not as difficult as also learning a new grammar. But there are other reasons for choosing Manual English over Ameslan. Many school systems that formerly resisted the use of sign in the classroom now have adopted it for use with deaf children, because Manual English is "English written in the air." When Manual English is thought of in that way, school administrators can no more oppose it than they can oppose the introduction of print. The precise representations of English, like SEE, have broken the monopoly of speech over the deaf students' educational scene. So those who plan to become schoolteachers or otherwise to work in school systems would be well advised to learn one or more of the artificial systems of Manual English.[7]

Does that settle the issue? Hardly. Several good reasons remain for learning Ameslan. First, it is the preferred language of deaf persons. If you wish to become better acquainted with deaf culture and to be more readily accepted in the deaf community, Ameslan is the better entrée. Ameslan, as we have seen, grew empirically, just as English did. But Ameslan has developed as a visual system: it is accommodated to the eye. English arises from speech: it is accommodated to the ear. The difference in the languages must, in part at least, reflect the modalities for delivering each. One learns Ameslan, then, for the same reasons one learns any foreign language: to become familiar with the culture, to be able to interact meaningfully with its users, to develop a valuable proficiency.

The best option would be to learn both Manual English and Ameslan. In effect, having learned Ameslan it is easy for a native English speaker to acquire Manual English. The reverse, learning Manual English and switching to Ameslan, does not hold: the person proficient in Manual English will still have to make a considerable effort to acquire Ameslan. Whether or not it is worth the effort is, of course, a highly individual matter.

Second-Language Learning

For most students of Ameslan, its study falls under the heading of Second-Language Learning. The *codes* for English can be visual (like signal flags or print), auditory (like Morse code), or tactual (like Braille); these codes provide alternative means of transmitting the spoken language. But for the native English speaker, learning Ameslan is like learning Greek. It is not code shifting, as in learning to write one's native language; it is learning a new language *and* a new code form.

Scientific interest in second-language learning is of fairly recent origin. The major second-language teachers in the United States have not produced any research. The State Department's Foreign Language Institute, the Peace Corps' Action program, and the Mormon Church's Language Training Mission have taught foreign languages to thousands of native English speakers, but they have not published their methods or studied the factors that influence their results. Linguistic researchers, on the other hand, have undertaken a great deal of research, partly fueled by the acknowledged backwardness of the United States in the study of foreign languages.[8]

Some of the research has looked at the charge that bilingualism might be intellectually debilitating. To the contrary, studies from Canada, Israel, New York, Singapore, South Africa, and Switzerland lead to the conclusion that bilingual individuals have cognitive and linguistic advantages over those who are monolingual. In one Canadian study, the children who were bilingual in English and French outperformed those with only French on verbal and nonverbal tests of intelligence, on academic achievement tests, and on tests of French language competence, in spite of the two groups' having been carefully equated on social class, intelligence, and language achievement. What is more, the bilingual students seemed more flexible and diversified in their thinking than the monolingual students. The findings in this and in the other investigations apply only when both languages that are acquired are valued socially by the individuals who command them. When one of the languages is denigrated, the result can be a *subtractive* rather than an *additive* bilingualism; that is, if one of the languages is not respected, then it interferes with, or subtracts from, intellectual activity.[9] The latter qualification may account for the finding that among some groups, like Mexican-Americans in the Southwest, bilingual children often do less well in school than do their monolingual peers. In the Southwest, Spanish has not been a highly regarded second language. Efforts are being made to alter that attitude; if they succeed, the region may be rewarded by gains not only in the Mexican-American children's self-esteem but also in their academic achievements. The application of this reasoning to born-deaf children is equally pertinent if Ameslan is considered their first language and English their second.

But what about the adult who decides to learn Ameslan? First of all, the studies at hand indicate that adults approach second-language learning differently than children do. Adults tend to be more deductive, preferring to be given the grammatical rules and then applying them. Children seem to proceed inductively, discovering the grammar through experience. Does this mean that adults will learn less well than children? Not exactly. Adults, of course, set higher standards than children. Adults also have distractions (work, family) that children do not have. So far, the ideal age for acquiring a second language appears to be adolescence,[10] a conclusion that is apt to startle teenagers and their parents. The evidence should encourage any adult who desires to learn a second language. The old adage that, in learning a language, younger is better does not hold up to close, systematic examination. The adolescent and the adult both have an edge when mastery of a language is the objective. So if you have been concerned that you may be too old to acquire Ameslan, set that worry aside. Science says your age is no barrier to learning to sign.

As already noted, motivation plays an expectedly large role in language learning. The sign teacher can aid you by making the classes interesting and by reinforcing your early approximations of correct Ameslan. But you can help yourself by some introspection to determine your own reasons, your real reasons, for wanting to learn sign. Are you expecting too much or too little? Learning Ameslan may cure your shyness in public; it may lead you to an exciting career; it may gain you new friends or a spouse. Then again, it may do none of these things. After all, Ameslan is a language. Do you have any interest in it for its own sake? If you do, you are far more apt to master it.[11]

Another psychological variable that may affect your ability to learn Ameslan is *empathy*—understanding another person's feelings without feeling what that person feels. You may, for example, know why someone is angry without feeling angry yourself. Empathy requires sensitivity to aspects of another person's behavior. This sensitivity, in turn, seems to be a factor in acquiring a second language, or at least another spoken language.[12]

Most persons born or brought up in the United States will have some added difficulty learning sign, because we have cultural proscriptions against broad hand gestures in communication. In that respect we are the opposite of, say, the Italian or French people, who do gesticulate extensively in conversation. We tend to be more like the English, who frown upon conspicuous displays. You will certainly be conspicuous, or feel conspicuous, when you sign in public for the first time. Once this cultural bias is faced, it should be readily overcome. You need to prepare yourself for some stares from strangers and some unkind remarks from family and acquaintances. If you understand the basis for *their* embarrassment, you will have little or none of your own.

Researchers may one day have some practical advice for second-language learners based upon seemingly impractical experiments on cerebral localization. Ever since Pierre Paul Broca, in the nineteenth century, established that the left side of the brain had primary control of speech in right-handed people, neuropsychologists have speculated about the locus for language. Bilingual persons who suffer damage to the brain provide a source of information. One theory has it that language representation is spread thinly across both hemispheres in bilingual persons. Some case histories of brain-injured bilingual individuals seem to support that view: these persons become aphasic far more often than would be expected, regardless of the laterality of the injury. But other cases contradict these findings, leaving the question open.

More direct and satisfactory research has been done with intact individuals. For example, persons were asked to read aloud some material while tapping with their right or left hand. The monolinguals' tapping with the left hand did not disturb their reading aloud, but their tapping with the right hand did. For persons who had become bilingual later in life, however, the tapping was disturbed on the right when the reading sample was in their native language, and on the left when in their second language. If this result proves reliable, it would demonstrate that language, not just speech, is localized on the side contralateral to the dominant hand for the native language, and on the opposite side for the language acquired later. In other words, for the right-handed majority the primary language function is located on the left side of the brain, and the secondary one on the right side.[13] This possibility is supported tangentially by the observation that persons bilingual from early childhood processed information more quickly on the right than on the left side of their brain (based on electroencephalographic recordings), and the reverse held for those who became bilingual later in life.[14]

The evidence on cerebral localization of language is not yet conclusive. When it is more so, it may have some implications for the ways in which we teach second languages. The left side of the brain is thought to be more accessible to meaningful auditory stimuli; the right to pictorial materials. A teacher may therefore conclude that more gestalt-like approaches should be used for second-language instruction. The thought is intriguing, but not yet practical.

Signing vs. Reading Sign

Persons who have tried to learn a foreign language or who have studied Morse code know that it is usually much easier to learn to send than to receive. The same holds true for signing: you can quickly acquire some skill in making signs and still be very poor at reading them. The difficulty lies partly in the different amounts of practice acquired. You will have much more meaningful practice signing than observing sign. When you sign, you know what you intend to say and you thus have practice in coupling the sign with its meaning. But when you are observing someone else sign, you lack the meaning: it is what you must supply yourself. So learning to read sign may be a very big problem.

In developing your receiving abilities, films and videotapes can be particularly helpful. This will be especially true if you can use them alone, with the option of replaying them as you wish. The solitary nature of the practice reduces the embarrassment that arises when you must expose your ignorance by asking another individual to repeat and repeat and repeat. After the second or third time someone signs something you do not understand, you are apt to smile and pretend you do understand. Sad, because the opportunity has been lost to learn something, but most understandable in the context of human relations. With the videotape or filmstrip, you can replay the sign as often as you please—without any social discomfort.

Self-Help

So far nothing has been said about learning to sign by oneself. The reason is that learning a language from a book rarely succeeds. First of all, sign is a matter of motions, and these are very difficult to accurately portray on a two-dimensional surface. Besides, merely copying an isolated sign from the page does not convey the flow of motions that signing must become in practice. Putting the signs together is a critical step in learning to sign.

What about television and motion pictures? These can be much more helpful, but again it is doubtful that one can learn from them alone, since they provide no feedback. You may watch a signer on the screen and believe that you are faithfully copying the motions. But you may not be, and so you spend much time practicing errors. Another subtle point is that you must mentally reverse the image on the screen, shifting from the viewer's orientation to the signer's. Some people do this easily, others do not. For those interested in videotapes and films, a list is provided in Appendix C. They are undoubtedly useful as supplements to classroom instruction and as refreshers once you have learned to sign.

Finally, signing involves not only motion, but emotion. One critical factor in learning Ameslan, or any language, is feedback. The instructor and classmates can provide the support most of us need to sustain our progress during the early, difficult days of language learning. You especially need others for practice; a mirror offers insufficient feedback. You must avoid practicing errors as you learn signs; you need to be told if you are signing properly. You aid your classmates, and they you, in providing the hours of correct repetitions needed to shift a language from the conscious to unconscious level of execution. In some respects, learning Ameslan is easier than learning other languages. One reason is that, in the case of Ameslan, less conflict occurs between old and new learnings—the kind of conflict you experience when you encounter words that sound (or appear) similar but have different meanings in the native and foreign languages. In French, for example, *tin* means "block of wood," not a metallic element. The German *Boot* means "boat," not a foot covering. Among the languages that share the twenty-six letters of our alphabet, such confusions are inevitable. But similar conflicting meanings are unlikely between the handshapes and movements of sign. The other facilitating aspect of sign learning is its novelty. Speaking with hands is different. A good teacher can capture that excitement and maintain interest ahead of the frustrations that beset the journey to competence.

8

Putting Sign to Work

Sign proficiency is now a marketable skill. Less than two decades ago, sign had little commercial value, but today a knowledge of sign can be the basis for an occupation or can enhance an already existing one.

Signing has come more and more to public awareness, and as the number of persons who use it is now perceived to be substantial, professionals and business people have begun to regard knowledge of sign as an asset to their practices. The lawyer who can sign has obviously great appeal to members of the deaf community. The same holds true for physicians, accountants, dentists. Tradespeople such as barbers, hairdressers, and restaurateurs can increase their commerce with deaf persons by learning sign. Several travel agencies and a few tour operators have found it worthwhile to advertise the availability of personnel who can sign. Macy's department store, in New York City, recently advertised that they had a store shopper who could sign to deaf customers. The list could be extended, but the point is clear: sign now has financial appeal.

The potential for opening new markets and increasing sales to deaf persons by learning sign has brought many persons to sign classes. We need to note here, however, that what would pass for sufficient sign competence in many social situations would not begin to satisfy the demands of a professional practice. Gaining proficiency in sign adequate for a psychiatric interview, for example, is vastly different from learning a few signs for typical in-flight situations. Most airline personnel can learn enough signs for their purposes in a week of concentrated study, while the psychiatrist would need years of study to attain a level of sign proficiency that would satisfy the intricate demands of interpersonal therapy. Yet communication is often vital to the delivery of many services. What is to be done?

The Congress has mandated that rehabilitation clients be served in "their native language or preferred mode of communication." That phrase in the Rehabilitation Act Amendments of 1978 has been interpreted to mean that rehabilitation agencies must provide personnel who can sign to deaf clients. But what does the agency do if it has no one on staff who can sign? Does it place the deaf client "on hold" until a counselor completes a quick course in Ameslan? Does it deny services to the deaf client? The federal regulations exclude both options in favor of a third that does not penalize the deaf client.

The agency must employ a sign-language interpreter to bridge the communication gap between deaf clients and the professionals who are available to them.[1] The same solution—use of an interpreter—could cover most of the instances demanding high levels of linguistic competence. A logical idea, but a relatively new one. Indeed, the whole notion of interpreting as a profession, as a means of making one's living, has only emerged in the past twenty years.

Sign-Language Interpreting

The interpreter is the bridge over the communication gap between persons who do not know each other's language. Is there a manual analog to that familiar sight at the United Nations—the simultaneous interpreters? Yes: persons who can hear and who know sign do interpret for deaf persons. They also "reverse interpret"; that is, they voice what deaf persons sign, when deaf persons do not speak for themselves. And there are other variations on the interpreting theme, variations that we will take up later in this chapter.

Interpreting is ancient business. Probably the earliest mention of an interpreter occurs in Exodus. Moses has been instructed to appeal to Pharaoh, but Moses is reluctant: "O Lord, I have never been a man of ready speech, never in my life, not even now that thou hast spoken to me; I am slow and hesitant to speech." God then proposes that Moses take Aaron along as his interpreter. "He will do all the speaking to the people for you, he will be the mouthpiece, and you will be the god he speaks for." So Aaron may have been the first officially appointed interpreter in recorded history. At the least, the idea of using an interpreter has biblical precedent.

THE HISTORY OF INTERPRETING IN THE UNITED STATES

The United States leads the world in the development of interpreting services for deaf persons. The reason for this leadership grows out of the Civil Rights Movement, a political trend that has been extended to handicapped people.[2] In the case of those who are deaf, it became apparent in the early sixties that if they were to fully participate in community life they would need interpreters. No other practical means of overcoming the communication barriers of deafness exist. True, many normally hearing persons are beginning to learn sign, but this development is too recent and has not spread far enough to ensure that deaf people will meet signers in the multitude of situations in which they may wish to participate. One interpreter can provide visible communication for dozens, even hundreds of deaf persons—as many as can see the interpreter—and can, of course, sign for as many speakers as address an audience, provided they speak one at a time. The interpreter, in effect, makes it possible for deaf persons to participate in any event that involves them in verbal interchanges.

Before the sixties, interpreting was usually a *favor* granted by a few knowledgeable hearing people. The Ball State Workshop on Interpreting for the Deaf, held in June 1964, signaled the change to interpreting as a *right*.[3] Instead of using any person who could hear and knew some sign, deaf people began to assert that interpreters should be trained, that they should observe a code of ethics, and that they should be paid for their services. Quite a change from what one deaf leader had seen as the minimum requirements for interpreters: "They must be able to hear; they must be able to sign; they must be willing; and they must be available."[4] The words were spoken to the delegates at the Ball State conference by the executive secretary of the National Association of the Deaf. His speech revealed the humble status of interpreting at that time.

The meeting at Ball State established the Registry of Interpreters for the Deaf (RID). That surprising move, establishing a professional organization before there was a profession, proved to be an inspired one. The RID, by its very existence, allayed questions that might have proved embarrassing and, worse, that might have impeded the growth of the interpreting movement. State officials, knowing little about deafness and less about interpreting, were easily convinced that everything was in order, simply because there was a *registry* of interpreters. They did not inquire whether the persons listed were qualified or where they had obtained their training. (Does one ask such questions of the bar association or the medical society?) Furthermore, since RID existed, there must have been a well-established demand for the service, or else why have such an organization!

The fact was that no formal training program for interpreters existed in 1964. There were only a few classes teaching sign language, almost exclusively Manual English. It was several more years before an interpreter training curriculum—first proposed at the Ball State meeting—came formally into being.

During its first year, RID had fewer than three hundred members—not very many for a *national* organization! There were barely enough to average six interpreters per state. Averages, of course, mean little: most states had only one or two RID members, and some had none. Again, the establishment of RID implied that a sufficient, or nearly sufficient, number of interpreters was available to meet the demand for their services. In a way, that proved to be the case, because in those early years there was very little demand. By holding annual meetings, RID was able to draw attention to the value of interpreters and to deaf persons' need for their services. Actually, deaf people had to be educated in the use of interpreters. Most deaf adults had no experience with them. Surely, interpreters helped a great deal, but for those who had done without them for most of their lives it took time to become used to the arrangement.

The biggest stimulus to interpreting came from the Rehabilitation Act of 1973. In that federal law was the famous Title V, "The Bill of Rights for the Handicapped." The act opened many doors to deaf people, as well as other handicapped individuals. The fourth part of Title V, the much-publicized Section 504, consists of a single sentence:

> No otherwise qualified handicapped individual in the United States . . . shall, solely by reason of handicap, be excluded from the participation in, be denied the benefit of, or be subjected to discrimination under any program or activity receiving Federal financial assistance.

The brevity of that section increases its power. Because so much activity depends on federal money, the scope of the coverage is enormous, and its example carries over to activities not specifically covered by the act. Section 504 does not define "participation," so deaf people and their advocates have taken that word to mean they have a right to communication in all federally funded meetings. In their view, the absence of interpreters in such circumstances clearly indicates discrimination against deaf people.

The probable impact of the act was immediately clear to a small group of educators and rehabilitators interested in deafness. In 1974 they formed the National Interpreter Training Consortium.[5] NITC was made up of six institutions that had already begun to prepare interpreters for the deaf. Led by New York University, NITC sought support from the Rehabilitation Services Administration. After lengthy negotiations, a five-year federal grant was awarded. It totaled $1.5 million, at a rate of about $300,000 per year—one of the best bargains ever made by the federal government.

When NITC came into existence in 1974, RID had only five hundred members. Not that there were five hundred interpreters available for duty in the United States—though even that number would have been laughably small compared to the need for them. Of the five hundred, easily half were not actually available to interpret. Some were agency executives who, while able to interpret, could hardly be expected to take time away from their administrative duties. Others were sympathetic to the RID, but could not sign well enough to provide effective service. Still others were deaf! These deaf people had joined RID as a gesture of support, not intending to be interpreters. Consider, then, the sorry state of affairs: less than 500 interpreters to serve the 450,000 deaf people in the United States who depended on sign for communication.

NITC responded to the situation by establishing three basic priorities. First, to upgrade the skills of those who were already trying to meet the demand for interpreters. (Remember, almost none had ever attended a formal program of preparation for interpreting. They had learned sign, they could hear, and they were available.) NITC set up weekend and summer programs to provide instruction on the fine points of interpreting, as well as to teach basics to those who needed them. NITC's second objective was to recruit new personnel. Toward this end, it developed a three-month training program that prepared persons with basic signing ability to become interpreters. Though none of the NITC organizers were satisfied with this brief instruction, they all realized that the situation demanded it. Third, NITC began to train trainers of interpreters, a completely new occupation. The first NITC trainers were respected interpreters who passed along their expertise to the first trainees largely on a master–apprentice basis. While that method was effective, it was too limited in the number of interpreters who could be prepared, so developing more instructors was immediately perceived as essential. In addition, NITC gave some of its funds to RID to establish a national program of interpreter certification. Teams of experts, including deaf persons representing the consumers of interpreting, began to travel around the country examining interpreters and certifying those who were deemed qualified. Certification provided an incentive to interpreters already in the field to bring their skills up to par through instruction.

NITC developed its own curriculum, one that it continued to revise and refine over the five years of its existence.[6] The entire NITC operation was of the bootstrap variety: NITC put together whatever personnel it could find, and that cadre, in turn, trained others as instructors. Equally important, NITC set out to recruit more institutions to establish interpreter training. The objective was to have at least one training program operating in every state.

How well did NITC do its work? By 1980, when its federal grant expired, RID had certified over three thousand interpreters. Many more awaited certifying examinations. The number of interpreter trainers increased from virtually none to a little over one hundred. The original six NITC members had, for company, forty-five programs throughout the United States, though not one in each state as had been hoped.

Ignoring all the other benefits of NITC—and they are substantial—the 2,500 additional interpreters cost the taxpayers an average of about $333 each. Less than the cost of many hearing aids.

The plan to develop training programs and personnel proved to be a substantial boon. In 1980, the Congress passed legislation to establish twelve training programs. The competition for the funding was open to any institution of higher education, and sixty-two applied. Though only twelve receive federal funds, fifty-three institutions now train interpreters.[7] Five years earlier only six institutions were willing to consider interpreter training. The increase in interest has been tenfold.

Sources of Interpreters

Who becomes an interpreter? At the beginning of the century, as noted, interpreters often had deaf parents. Their early exposure to Ameslan contributed to their ability to interpret. One problem with relying on the hearing children of deaf parents is that they are themselves relatively scarce. By the time they reach adulthood, they may have lost interest in being interpreters; and, naturally, many have careers that leave them little time to act as freelance interpreters. They are not likely to be available when most needed.

For the same reason, teachers of deaf students, too, are a poor source of interpreting. Being fully occupied in the classroom during the day, they are usually too tired at night to want to take on additional work. The use of teachers also presents another drawback: they have already established a role vis-à-vis the deaf person. It is an authoritarian role, suitable to the classroom but inappropriate to the passive functions of the interpreter. It is often difficult for teachers to switch from dominant to submissive relations with current and former students. A few years ago a teacher was asked to appear in court to interpret at the trial of two minors—deaf boys from his class. They had been apprehended ducking under the turnstile in a subway station and were caught by a transit patrolman. Because the transit patrolman could not communicate with them, he took them into the station house and booked them. At the juvenile court hearing, the judge listened for a few minutes to the testimony, all dutifully interpreted by the teacher, and then began to dismiss the case. At that point the interpreter stopped interpreting and said to the judge, "Your Honor, I believe you are making a mistake. These are deaf youngsters and they need to be taught a lesson." He went on in that vein, no longer interpreting, urging that they be punished. The boys could only guess that their judge was not the man sitting on the bench but the teacher who was there to interpret for them—to help them. Such behavior violates the present RID Code of Ethics.[8]

Many interpreters began as religious workers. The Episcopal Church was the first to assign a minister exclusively to a deaf congregation. He was one of Thomas Hopkins Gallaudet's sons; his other son, you will recall, founded Gallaudet College.[9] The Baptist Church has had several missions to deaf persons. In order to make these successful, the volunteers (lay missionaries) have had to learn sign. From that necessity has grown a popular book on sign, Lottie Riekehof's *Talk to the Deaf* (later revised and titled *The Joy of Signing*).[10] Other religious groups have contributed glossaries of signs, many of which are listed in Appendix A.

The religious tradition had an inhibiting effect on the growth of *professional* interpreting. First of all, those who interpreted religious services did so without monetary compensation. The work was not difficult, since church services tend to follow a fixed order, with few spontaneous utterances. Once interpreters have learned to sign "Our Father," they will sign it again and again in future services.

Even the sermons are fairly predictable; the references are generally to biblical characters and places. So religious interpreting did not put heavy demands on the interpreter; as a consequence, it did not generate any organized attempt to upgrade minimal skills and did not encourage those who knew sign to make it a career.

Outside the church, however, the interpreter was faced with entirely different circumstances. The extent of linguistic skill required was doubled and quadrupled. The vocabularies ranged widely, from odd dialects of Ameslan to precise Manual English. If called upon to interpret in a courtroom or medical setting, the interpreter encountered vocabularies for which signs were not known or little practiced. Faithfulness in interpreting was challenged when obscene and sexual terms were encountered, as they do occur in everyday conversations and in particular contexts. The interpreters' responsibility to faithfully convey both sides of a dialogue was sometimes heavily strained.

One interpreter boasted to me about her experiences as a courtroom interpreter in the 1930s and '40s. "You don't know how often I would save a deaf person by telling the judge what the deaf person *should* have said rather than what he did say!" Although a deeply religious person, she saw no reason that would bar her interference in that individual's life and felt no shame for corrupting the testimony of another person. The attitude of paternalism is one to which deaf people are very sensitive. They resent being treated like children, even when it is "for their own good." The RID Code of Ethics deals explicitly with the problem, demanding that the interpreter add and subtract nothing from the material transmitted between parties. The interpreting task requires faithful rendering of what is said to deaf people and signed by them. Nothing more and nothing less-but what a challenge that is.

Looking at the current enrollments in interpreter training programs, one can see a sharp difference between these trainees and those who formerly dominated the field. The children of deaf parents do not make up the majority of students. Teachers of deaf children seldom have the inclination—and even less, the time—to study interpreting. Religious workers are not often seen in the interpreter training programs, though they may appear frequently in sign-language classes. Applicants to the programs are now young people who seek an interesting, remunerative career. They are similar to applicants throughout the helping professions; they resemble physical therapists, counselors, teachers, and so on. Their youth and intelligence are as welcome as their lack of unshakable preconceptions about deafness and deaf persons. Their eagerness to learn and their manifest abilities promise much to the future of interpreting.

It is worth remarking that teachers and religious workers frequently attend sign classes. However, learning to sign is different from learning to interpret. Knowing sign is a prerequisite to interpreting, but knowing sign does not qualify one to interpret. Simple as that notion is, students attending sign classes need to have it repeated, because many take the classes with the idea that when they complete their studies they will be able to interpret. An interpreter not only needs consummate language proficiency but must also be conversant with the ethics, professional responsibilities, economics, and technical aspects of interpreting. Even in sign class, students should learn about cultural aspects of deafness, but the depth and range of such study are different for the language student and the interpreter.

The Nature of Interpreting

What exactly is interpreting? It may seem a simple matter: putting the words of one language into those of another. Many factors, however, make the question a complex one.

The first complicating factor is language itself. We are familiar with expressions in one language that have no direct equivalent in other languages. Take the French *faute de mieux*; an English dictionary translation hardly conveys the richness of that phrase. It means "for want of something better," and it means more than that. It carries a sense of resignation and a hint of contempt. The things one does *faute de mieux* are being downgraded. Examples of such idioms are numerous in any language.

Regardless of the language involved, linguists insist that exceptional fluency is essential in the languages one translates from and into. That may seem to go without saying, but deaf persons frequently encounter interpreters who know very little Ameslan. Even more awkward is having an interpreter whose command of both English and Ameslan is limited. That happens when the interpreter, though a native English speaker, must interpret a lecture in a technical area. Interpreters have been known to leave the scene, frustrated and embarrassed, when they cannot understand the speaker's words. The student may believe that any English-speaking person with knowledge of another language can be an interpreter. That notion will quickly evaporate when you are faced with the reality of technical vocabularies. Could you understand, let alone interpret into another language, the following passage?

A digraph is called *unipathic* if, whenever v is reachable from u, there is exactly one path from u to v. Obviously, every path in a unipathic digraph is a geodesic.

Or try signing this example from legal argument:

Plantiff realleges all of the preceding allegations as is hereinafter set forth verbatim.

Nor is vocabulary the only problem in interpreting. Context, vocal emphasis, tonal quality, pace—all of these extralinguistic features can alter the words spoken. W. R. Espy[11] recounts the story of the ancient Greek soldier who misunderstood the Delphic oracle. The prophecy, as he heard it, was "Thou shalt go, thou shalt return, never by war shalt thou perish." Unfortunately, he misinterpreted the message. He died in battle without realizing he had misplaced a comma: "Thou shalt go, thou shalt return never, by war shalt thou perish." Espy, by the way, has written a clever poem to illustrate how critical vocal emphasis is to meaning. Here is one stanza:

> *I'd be* content *could I impart*
> *The amorous* content *of my heart*
> *To you, and* intimate *we might*
> Be intimate, *some future night.*[12]

MANAGING THE SETTING

Other factors make the interpreter's task a complex one. The interpreter must exert some control over the environment, when features of the surroundings might interfere with communication. Lighting is an extremely important matter to deaf persons. The interpreter should never be placed against a bright source of light. If you do not immediately understand this point, stare at a window on a sunny day and notice how quickly your eyes fatigue. Within seconds, you will develop a negative afterimage that will interfere with your ability to see. That is what happens to deaf persons when they look at an interpreter under similar circumstances. Another visual factor is the interpreter's clothing. Gaudy shirts and dresses and glittering jewelry, which can be very distracting to the observer, should be avoided.

Interpreters must also take steps to ensure that they receive the speaker's message. But what if more than one person tries to speak at the same time? That happens often enough at conferences and meetings. And what about the speaker who mumbles or reads a list of names at a high rate of speed? Any of these circumstances can render the interpreter manually mute. As you can see, interpreters must develop a variety of tactics to handle such problems.

USING INTERPRETERS

Some common confusions in the use of interpreters are easily managed. For instance, when mediating between a deaf client and only one speaker, the interpreter always sits next to the speaker. The reason, of course, is that the deaf person needs to see the speaker *and* the interpreter at the same time, something that would be impossible if the interpreter were to sit next to the deaf person. Furthermore, the interpreter usually stands a little bit behind a public speaker, thus enabling the deaf audience to see the speaker's face and, simultaneously, the interpreter's signs. The speaker's facial expression can thus be seen by the deaf people in the audience, without the interpreter's blocking the audience's view. Seeing the speaker's face helps deaf people: the interpreter may not be able to convey, for example, the speaker's vigor, anger, or humor. Being able to see both the interpreter and the speaker, the deaf person has the opportunity to pick up these extra cues.

When using an interpreter, you should always remember to speak directly to the deaf person, not to the interpreter. That is another reason why interpreters place themselves out of the speaker's line of sight. The speaker is then less apt to say to the interpreter, "Tell the [deaf person] . . ." The speaker will annoy the deaf person by such implied condescension. How will the deaf person know the speaker is condescending? The interpreter, if acting in proper fashion, will repeat in sign the equivalent of those words: "Tell the [deaf person] . . ." The ethical interpreter does not invent dialogue or tailor an expression to suit the occasion. If the speaker is foul-mouthed, the interpreter must be prepared to curse—in sign, of course. The interpreter is not an editor, a moralist, an adviser, or a pal. The professional interpreter converts speech to sign and vice versa.

The latter—converting sign to speech—is often difficult. Some expressions in Ameslan have no immediate equivalent in English. What is more, Ameslan grammar is different from English (as we have seen in Chapter 3). Does the interpreter try to render each sign into an equivalent English term? Obviously not. To do so would result in an unintelligible pile of words, even though the deaf person is expressing a thought in grammatical Ameslan. A United Nations interpreter who rendered *faute de mieux* as "lack of better" would probably be fired on the spot. True, the separate words can be translated in that way (*faute* as "lack," *de* as "of," and *mieux* as "better"), but that is not what they mean when put together by a French speaker. For example, *faire la sourde oreille* does not mean "to do [or make] a deaf ear"! It means "to turn a deaf ear." *Faire la part des accidents* does not mean "to do the share of accidents" but rather "to make allowance for accidents." *Naviguer à la part* does not mean "steer to a place [or portion]" but rather "to divide the costs and profits of a voyage." *Aus den Fingern saugen* does not mean "to suck one's fingers" but rather "to invent." The same holds true for countless English idioms.

Interpreters who have had no training sometimes try to give advice to deaf persons or to influence their actions in other ways. Such behavior is condemned by the RID's Code of Ethics. Unfortunately, deaf people are often unaware of their rights when engaging an interpreter. They complain to each other about interpreter abuses, but seldom to the interpreters. With the advent of paid interpreters, a professional organization, and a written code of ethics, the climate is changing. Younger members of the deaf community have become accustomed to interpreting. Interpreting is no longer a favor; it is a right of citizenship. And enlightened deaf people are prepared to criticize interpreters, to discharge those who perform badly, and to seek out the well-trained, conscientious practitioners.

On the other hand, interpreters encounter deaf people who do not understand what to expect and who make unreasonable demands. Sometimes deaf college students will suggest that the interpreter take their examination for them. Or the student may ask the interpreter to fetch coffee or pick up a book for the student at the bookstore. The interpreter has little difficulty in explaining to the deaf student that *interpreting* does not include these activities. Professionals engaging interpreters also need to have the role defined. Psychologists have asked interpreters to give tests; physicians have expected the interpreter to provide the deaf patient's medical history in that patient's absence; lawyers have called on interpreters to reveal the contents of conversations in which they served only as interpreters. These situations are quickly resolved by the trained interpreter.

Somewhat more difficult is handling the deaf person's request for advice about a purchase or a medical emergency. Situations like these do occur, and interpreters may be ambivalent about keeping their professional distance. These touchy instances also illustrate why teachers, religious workers, and children of deaf parents often find a strict interpreter role difficult to maintain. The impulse to be helpful is hard to overcome, but it must be to avoid demeaning the deaf person.

INTERPRETING VARIATIONS

How does one interpret for a deaf person who cannot see? The answers are numerous: so numerous that a book has been written on the subject, *A Complete Guide to Communication with Deaf-Blind Persons.*[13] The book lists seventy-six different techniques and pieces of equipment that can be used. One of the techniques is the two-handed manual alphabet. The interpreter's right hand forms the letters on the deaf-blind person's left hand. The method can transcribe at surprisingly high speed when used by pairs familiar with it.

What about the deaf person who can see but does not know sign or finger-spelling? Some deaf persons prefer to lipread, even if they do know sign. In such cases, an *oral interpreter*, a person who is skilled at repeating what the speaker is saying, can be employed. The oral interpreter is particularly valuable when visual conditions make direct lipreading of the speaker difficult or impossible. Teachers may turn to the blackboard and continue to speak as they write on it. Sometimes deaf persons must sit too far from the speaker to permit lipreading. Some speakers have moustaches or beards that obscure their mouths. In all such circumstances, deaf persons who prefer lipreading need the services of an oral interpreter who is seated nearby and in their full view.

Up to now we have assumed that interpreting has been from English to Ameslan or vice versa. But interpreters sometimes encounter other languages. Nowadays, there is a fair demand for interpreters who know Russian or Ukrainian Sign Language. They will be kept busy in New York City interpreting for the influx of immigrants from the Soviet Union. Spanish is another popular language on both coasts, especially in California, Florida, and New York. The interpreter needs to know both Spanish Sign Language and spoken Spanish. A further confusion facing these interpreters is that Cuban and Puerto Rican versions of Spanish differ from each other, and both differ from Mexican Spanish. An interpreter's lot is not an easy one.

Interpreters' horizons have recently been broadened further by the New York City Opera. In 1981, productions of *Susannah* and *The Merry Widow* were simultaneously interpreted in sign. The 1983 season has added Janacek's *Cunning Little Vixen* and Puccini's *La Fanciulla del West* to the repertoire. At least two interpreters work the performances, one doing the female and one the male voices. They require extensive rehearsal to coordinate their signs with the music, making the transitions from sign to sign blend smoothly. The response from deaf people has been excellent, with the eighty seats reserved for them often oversubscribed. The hearing audiences have not complained, many feeling that the interpreters and the deaf members of the audience add to the excitement of the performance. And how do the interpreters feel? Very tired . . . but satisfied that they are breaking new, important ground.

INTERPRETING AS A PAYING PROFESSION

Does it pay to become an interpreter? Currently, certified sign-language interpreters charge about ten to twenty dollars per hour, while secretaries earn about six to ten dollars, and psychiatrists charge fifty to seventy-five dollars per hour. Outside the major cities, the principal difficulty facing interpreters is keeping busy. But in metropolitan areas there is a great deal of interpreting to be done and few people to do it. Traveling to the work site is a common difficulty among freelance interpreters. In sparsely populated areas, distances between assignments can mean many hours of travel time. Even in large cities, travel time eats seriously into the available working hours. Some interpreters demand portal-to-portal pay, a not unreasonable stipulation when the hours lost to traveling are considered. A few interpreters are fortunate in having positions in educational programs and industrial settings in which deaf persons come to them or where distances to the interpreting site are inconsequential.

When employed full-time, interpreters usually earn rates equivalent to those of beginning counselors or teacher aides. Vocational rehabilitation and educational programs are the principal employers of full-time interpreters. Often the interpreting position in these agencies is thought of as a lower rung on a career ladder, as an entry position. Interpreters are frequently amenable to sacrificing the higher hourly rates paid to freelance interpreters for the lower pay of a steady position. It should also be noted that there are interpreters so skillful that they can, so to speak, write their own tickets. They command guarantees of not less than $50 for half a day and $100 for a full day. Some charge $150 per day and more. But these, of course, are interpreters at the top of the field; they are exceptions.

For most, interpreting is very demanding labor. It combines considerable physical activity (often standing on one's feet and keeping one's arms in nearly constant motion for an hour or longer) and complete concentration. The combined physical and mental strain leads many interpreters to request a rest period every forty-five minutes or so. Such breaks are also welcomed by the deaf audience, since watching the interpreter carefully for long periods of time can be more fatiguing than listening is for the hearing audience. (The reason lies in the differences between eyes and ears: when eyes blink to relieve strain, vision is lost. The ears never close, so one can drift away mentally and remain fairly certain of being able to detect changes in the flow of a speech in time to refocus attention.)

Reviewing all the demands upon interpreters—the lack of experience of many deaf persons, the extreme problem of thinking in two languages simultaneously, the physical and mental demands, the employment conditions—one may conclude that their work has little glamor. Nonetheless, training programs do not lack applicants. The amount of "burnout" among those who enter the field may be high, but there are many prospective replacements. The major friction in the supply-demand equation is training: the length of training time and the limited number of training facilities. The latter deficiency should be corrected before the end of the eighties, as more and more universities and community colleges provide programs.

In the meantime, very little research is under way to find methods to improve the interpreting process and to reduce the heavy burden interpreters now carry.[14] No major breakthroughs have been made so far. Until they are, the labors of the interpreter will continue to be substantial. It is fair to state that today's interpreters certainly have their hands full.

Signing to Atypical Persons Who Can Hear

The second half of the seventies saw an interest develop in using sign language therapeutically. Researchers found that some persons who could hear but who did not develop speech could learn to sign. The discovery prompted a spate of research, by no means at an end, that has clearly established the usefulness of sign language in developing the communication abilities of several groups with whom traditional approaches have previously had little success.

Autistic children are particularly difficult to teach. They are so withdrawn that they may sit for hours staring into space, impervious to the attempts of others to attract their attention. Most critically, the children seem to have no interest in people; they appear insulated from emotional attachments to others. Penetrating the autistic wall has sometimes been regarded as beyond standard methodologies. Recently, some attempts have been made to communicate with autistic children in sign. The results have been gratifying.

Take the case of Arthur (a pseudonym). He was ten years old when he came to the Deafness Research & Training Center at New York University, in 1973. Arthur had normal hearing ability, but he had never spoken. When he wanted something, he would scream. That would activate nearby adults: Was he hungry? Hot? Cold? Did he want to go to the toilet? Remedies were proffered one after the other until Arthur stopped screaming; that would signal that his wants were, for the moment, fulfilled. The routine obviously exhausted his parents and disgusted his younger brother, who seldom received any parental attention. Arthur's parents brought him to the center because they had heard that some autistic children learned to communicate in sign. They sought the relief that such communication would bring to their family. Oddly, they also worried somewhat that Arthur's learning sign might interfere with his speech development. Pointing out the reality of his condition, however, alleviated those concerns enough to permit treatment to begin. A graduate student undertook Arthur's instruction over one summer. Within two weeks Arthur had learned five signs. By summer's end Arthur had mastered about twenty signs—all useful in indicating his daily wants. He learned the signs for *eat*, *drink*, *toilet*, and similar basic concepts. He could both make the signs and recognize them when signed to him. He seemed more responsive to visual communication than to spoken communication. Unfortunately, his parents did not continue with the sign lessons. The marked reduction in Arthur's screaming, the increase in his more tolerable means of communication, and the improvement in his general demeanor resolved their immediate problems and made home life tolerable. But the parents, both professionals, never felt comfortable signing. They disliked the idea, even though it worked.

The literature now contains a plethora of case studies much like Arthur's; the difference is that the use of sign is more widely accepted now. As a consequence, current efforts go beyond the rudimentary attempts made in Arthur's case. Sign is now used extensively to instruct some children over long periods of time. There is adequate evidence to encourage this means of establishing a relationship between autistic children and the significant adults with whom they must interact.[15]

The severely mentally retarded person is at the opposite end of the intellectual scale from many autistic children, who sometimes seem to possess average and above-average intellectual potential. The mentally retarded child who does not develop language may appear to be emotionally immature but not psychotic. The lack of speech and language development reflects a cognitive defect. Surprisingly, these children and some adults like them have been able to learn sign language, though they have not learned to speak. The signs they learned (as in the case of some autistic children) have been simple, but have proved to be very useful. The practical advantages of having some, albeit limited, communication ability include being able to live outside an institution, to enter some gainful employment, and to achieve a fair level of independence. A recent article describing the teaching of sign to groups of mentally retarded children offers great hope:

> At this point it is difficult to predict achievement levels for those students who are using Manual English. However, the Seattle program attained some remarkable results. Severely mentally retarded children learned from 1 to 65 words receptively

and expressively, including simple 2 and 3 word responses. Trainable mentally retarded children learned over 200 words and increased mean length of response and correct sequential order of words, including complicated sentence structure.[16]

Such results are far beyond what educators typically expect from children diagnosed as mentally retarded. That sign works is no longer doubted. But educators do not yet know how far they can go in developing the language abilities of these individuals previously thought to be outside the reach of instructional technology.

Aphasia is a cruel condition in which the afflicted individuals have lost the ability to express themselves orally. They may be able to think straight, but they cannot speak intelligibly. (There are other forms of aphasia, but here we will confine the discussion to expressive aphasia.) Speech therapists have found that some of these patients who cannot speak can learn to express themselves manually. Reports of sign therapy with aphasics are beginning to announce consistent success with manual communication. Attention is now being directed toward criteria for selecting patients who are more apt to benefit from sign than from the more traditional oral therapies.[17]

In addition to mental retardation, autism, and aphasia, sign's usefulness may extend to some emotional conditions like schizophrenia. The theoretical discussion of this application has begun, but not many case reports have so far made their way into the literature. The progress in communication made by the other groups, however, encourages the broadest investigation of sign's applications to the treatment of emotional disturbances.[18]

Two things impede these investigations of sign's broadened use. One is the well-documented prejudice against manual communication. As noted in the case of Arthur, parents worry about the possibility that using sign will interfere with speech development. That may seem ludicrous in the case of a ten-year-old child who has not yet spoken, but the fear is real enough, as most clinicians will attest. It may well reflect a deeper apprehension: that using manual language makes more visible the shame of having a disabled child.[19]

Interested in using sign with mentally retarded children, some British educators have developed *Makaton*. The system uses signs, many borrowed from British Sign Language, in a simplified grammatical order. The inventors have reported considerable success in developing language in children who had very little or none.

The other major impediment to the more rapid exploitation of sign for a variety of language-impaired conditions is that the number of sign-wise professionals is very small. As more learn, the use of sign in fields other than deafness will probably increase. For now, deafness claims the great majority of professionals who are skilled signers, leaving few to other conditions.

The new ideas we gain about nonverbal conditions continue to excite professionals in medicine and science. If autistic children respond to and express themselves better in sign than speech, does that mean that their disorder is related to a left-brain defect? Many authorities on infantile autism are convinced that the condition has an organic basis. Does the successful use of sign confirm the site of the organic lesion? The reasoning may be profitably extended to some severely mentally retarded individuals. Brain size does not provide a distinguishing anatomical marker for the differences in performance between intellectually normal and subnormal individuals. Perhaps the difference lies in hemisphere dominance and in the coordination between hemispheres. The fact that severely mentally retarded children, who previously learned virtually no language, can learn sign language should spur research along those lines.

The use of sign with persons who are not deaf but who have language disorders has offered employment opportunities for those who have mastered sign. Deaf persons have an unusual opportunity to enter professions that were seemingly barred to them because the work was so orally dependent. Whether working independently or in conjunction with a professional, the born-deaf person can now instruct autistic children, can do therapy with some aphasics, and can develop the language of severely mentally retarded persons. Of course, these same opportunities are open to anyone who learns to sign, but hearing people do not usually face the employment barriers that deaf people do, so the new opportunities are especially appealing to deaf people.

Altogether, then, applying sign to new situations opens exciting vistas for education, therapy, research, and employment.

Teaching Sign

Teaching others to sign has a long and distinguished history, much of which has been reviewed in Chapter 4. Today, sign's popularity has created a shortage of teachers. As might be expected (and as noted in Chapter 7), this has led to the drafting into service of individuals who either have little or no teaching preparation or who have only a passing acquaintance with sign.

The National Association of the Deaf, which pioneered sign-language instruction for the general public, has sought to remedy the situation by establishing the National Consortium of Programs Training Sign Language Instructors. The formidable set of initials NCPTSLI represents an effort to set standards for sign-language instructors and to provide a certification program through which sign teachers with appropriate training can be identified by prospective employers. NCPTSLI began operations in 1978. It has not had a strong impact upon the field, but its influence is gaining. We can expect that in the present decade NCPTSLI will achieve its principal objective: to ensure that sign-language instruction is managed by competent teachers. (See Chapter 7, Note 4.)

Sign teachers who do have the requisite knowledge and skills will find employment without difficulty. Remuneration, of course, depends on location and sponsor. It is fair to state that the present demand-supply imbalance keeps salaries in reasonably good relation to those paid to teachers of foreign languages. By and large, teaching sign offers considerable satisfactions—personal, professional, and economic—to those equipped to do it well.

Signing Before the Footlights

The notoriety given sign by the award-winning play *Children of a Lesser God* gives the impression that sign has only recently come to the stage. That is not so. Deaf persons have probably amused themselves with various forms of drama for as long as they have formed groups. Some deaf persons have also performed mime ("dumb shows") for general audiences over the centuries. Broadway plays, like *The Miracle Worker* and *Johnny Belinda*, have occasionally included characters who sign. What is new is the wide attention being given to sign in the theater and on television.

Much of the credit for the general public's acquaintance with sign language goes to the National Theatre of the Deaf. Founded in 1968, NTD has now had performances on every continent, in thirty-four countries, and in all major cities within the United States. The director of NTD, David Hays, brought the idea to the federal Office of Vocational Rehabilitation (now the Rehabilitation Services Administration), and a grant was jointly given by that office and the Bureau of Education for the Handicapped, U.S. Office of Education. The funds made it possible to hire deaf actors, provide them with instruction in the theater arts, develop plays for them, and finance the first productions. NTD's performances have run the gamut from the classics to experimental drama, and the organization has spawned a Little Theatre of the Deaf, to bring deaf actors to schoolchildren. In every respect, NTD has fulfilled its original mandates from the federal government, most important of which was to develop employment opportunities in the theater for deaf people.

Some deaf persons have left NTD to hold positions elsewhere as costumers, set designers, as well as actors. Most have aspired to become actors, and a few have succeeded.[20] Probably as small a proportion of deaf aspirants succeed as do those in the general acting profession. Among the successes the most prominent is Phyllis Frelich, a former member of the NTD troupe, who has won a Tony for her portrayal of the heroine in *Children of a Lesser God*. Phyllis, who was born deaf, graduated from Gallaudet College, the long-term home of deaf theater in the United States.

Almost from its inception in 1864, Gallaudet College has had student drama performances. These have ranged from adaptations of the classics—*The Trojan Women, Hamlet*—through productions of current favorites—*Ten Little Indians, Our Town, The Mikado*—to plays by deaf authors —*Sign Me Alice, Laurent Clerc*. Despite the popularity of drama on campus, the first drama course was not offered until 1942, and the drama department was only founded in 1969. The drama club, however, is over a hundred years old.[21] It was responsible for the student production of *Arsenic and Old Lace*, then a long-running Broadway hit, in 1942. The students' signed version was so well done that the Broadway producers, Lindsay and Crouse, invited the Gallaudet College players to replace the original cast at one New York performance. It was a stunt, but one that drew unusual critical acclaim. An example of the uniformly excellent notices is the review by the New York *Herald Tribune*'s drama critic, Helen Beebe, in which she says, in part:

> If one has never seen a performance in signs—which was your reporter's case—one thing will surprise him. Somehow the actors' hands convey differences of intonation. There are the gentle, conciliatory phrases of Miss Martha and Miss Abby. There are the staccato utterances of their brother Teddy, who imagines himself to be Teddy Roosevelt. When his fingers say, "Delighted," the word is bursting with energy. When he rushes up the stairs, one hand waving the signal, "Charge," in memory of San Juan Hill, the gesture seems to shout, though there isn't a sound. When Jonathan Brewster, the arch-villain, makes his threats, his fingers are deliberate and menacing.[22]

Her counterpart on the New York *Times*, Burns Mantle, commented:

> While the greater part of the audience was composed of deaf people trained in the difficult art of reading sign language, many were present who were not deaf. These persons of normal hearing were astounded at the lucidity of the play as presented and scarcely needed the aid of a reader who spoke the lines in a monotone while the deaf actors made their speedy signs.[23]

These laudatory comments also reveal the extent to which the critics appreciated the dramatic possibilities of sign, possibilities to which more and more people are being exposed.

Aside from the road companies of *Children of a Lesser God*, other opportunities for deaf actors have emerged on Broadway.[24] Before Phyllis Frelich made her mark on Broadway, Bruce Hlibok, a deaf teenager, developed a character in the Off-Broadway hit *Runaways*, which later moved to a legitimate theater on Broadway. Odd as it may seem, *Runaways* was a musical, but Bruce's role was entirely pantomimed. In praising his performance the reviewers were not in the least patronizing, holding his acting to the same standards as the rest of the cast. (Many persons in the audience may not even have known about his deafness, since the program made no mention of it.) No wonder he is looking forward to an acting career.

Here and there throughout the country, regional companies of deaf actors have sprung up. As yet, none have developed a sufficient following to permit the members to devote full time to acting, but they are finding increasingly greater outlets for their talents. The Fairmount Theatre of the Deaf, headquartered in Cleveland, has recently been designated as a model by the National Committee on Arts for the Handicapped, a designation that brought with it a modest grant for operations. At this writing, Rochester (New York), Washington, D.C., Los Angeles, and Seattle are some of the other cities that have groups of deaf actors performing on a regular basis. Many of the companies are connected with educational institutions in their areas.

Television is another outlet open to deaf actors. Linda Bove, a Gallaudet College graduate and former member of the National Theatre of the Deaf, has become a regular on *Sesame Street,* in which she plays, appropriately enough, the deaf person on the block. Bernard Bragg, one of the most experienced deaf actors now giving full time to acting, is readying a television program for children in which he will star as a deaf version of Superman. The program will be produced by *Beyond Sound,* an organization devoted to deaf-oriented programming on television. The company signed a contract in April 1982 with Teleprompter Cable TV to produce three and a half hours of programs per week. Earlier, Bernard Bragg had a regular program on a San Francisco educational television station. Called "The Silent Man," the program ran for two years and gained considerable popularity across the country. Bragg, like Frelich and Bove, is a Gallaudet College graduate and a National Theatre of the Deaf alumnus.

In addition to such long-term television commitments, there have been sporadic appearances by deaf actors that are worthy of note. Phyllis Frelich appeared in an episode of *Barney Miller,* first shown in 1982. In that same program, Seymour Bernstein, who is also deaf, played the part of her deaf attorney. A made-for-television movie, *My Name Is Jonah,* starred a ten-year-old deaf student, Phillip Bravin. He earned justified plaudits for his acting skills. Also, it should be noted that from time to time the National Theatre of the Deaf and some of the regional groups have appeared on television, both local and national. In 1981, Jason Robards and the NTD made for PBS "Festival of Hands," in which they discussed techniques for adapting sign to poetry. The small screen seems particularly friendly to displaying the nuances of sign.

There is not apt to be enough work to support very many deaf actors (as holds true for actors in general). However, acting is a field that should not be closed to deaf persons. A strong current of militancy has encouraged some deaf actors to picket motion pictures and television programs that have used hearing actors to portray deaf people. Amy Irving's touching performance in the motion picture *Voices* was resented by some deaf actors who recognized the excellence of her portrayal but objected to the fact that, as a hearing person, she took a role that could have been as well performed by a deaf actor. As in the case of television producers, the movie industry has taken note of this reaction and has let it be known that, in the future, deaf actors will at least be given the opportunity to audition.[25] That is, after all, the most that any actor can hope for in this highly competitive field.

The Economic Future for Sign

In our society, assigning a monetary value to an activity adds greatly to its growth potential. Now that knowledge of sign, in one way or another, can be converted into cash, its growth can be expected to soar. The impetus given sign by the discovery of its unique linguistic status will be sustained and possibly accelerated by its dollar value.

The casual use of sign by professionals and tradespeople will probably decline, because a little sign ability is not adequate to most interchanges. Signing "Hi" or "I love you" is cute, but it implies that the signer has a fuller command of sign. If that implication proves unjustified, dissatisfaction is likely to follow: the deaf person who thought that the signer knew enough to carry on a conversation is disillusioned. The signer made a promise that could not be kept. In short, a few signs can be worse than none.

The federal laws that assure handicapped persons their rightful place in society are not apt to be revoked by future administrations. Some of the laws have been supplemented by state and local statutes that expand the right of deaf people to full participation in the community's affairs. For that reason, it is safe to assert that the demand for sign-language interpreters will increase greatly over the coming decade, as will the demand for instructors. Teachers of sign will certainly benefit from the efforts to weed out those who are incompetent. The establishment of certification programs for sign teachers will upgrade instruction and encourage more persons to avail themselves of the opportunity to acquire a new language that has many applications.

The uses of sign in therapeutic and educational settings with persons who are not deaf are only beginning to be realized. As we gain a better understanding of the value of sign in treating language-impaired persons, we can anticipate a corresponding growth in the economic value of sign. The theater, television, and the movies have begun to employ deaf actors and to see the value of stories about deaf persons. This area of opportunity, too, can mean much to those who know sign.

Altogether, the economic future of sign looks bright.

9

The Deaf Community

Throughout the text, references are made to "the deaf community." The reason is, perhaps, already obvious: this book is about sign language—the lingua franca of the deaf community. In fact, we could accurately define the deaf community as a group of people bound together not by geography or family ties, but by their language. Of course, deaf people have other interests in common, but their most distinguishing feature is their mode of communication. One born-deaf lady summed it up when she said, "I look just like everybody else, until I start to sign. Then I stand out from the crowd." She meant, of course, the crowd of hearing people who do not use and seldom see sign.

Two million people in the United States cannot hear and understand speech through the ear alone.[1] In other words, they are deaf. But the deaf *community* counts only about one fourth of that number, or approximately five hundred thousand people of all ages. So being deaf does not in itself make one a member of the deaf community. To understand this, one has to remember that the distinguishing feature of membership in the deaf community is how one communicates. Those deafened at birth or in early childhood most likely use sign. Those deafened in middle age and beyond seldom learn to sign. The earlier one loses hearing, the more likely one communicates by sign and thus speaks the language of the deaf community.

Another important consideration in determining the effects of hearing impairment is the amount of hearing that is lost. Deafness is not an all-or-none condition; most deaf people can hear some sounds, especially if they are loud enough. What deaf people cannot hear well enough to understand is what people say to them. Because deafness entails neither legal penalties nor benefits, it is not defined in our laws.[2] Nor do all professions use the term in the same way; some apply it to any degree of hearing impairment; others apply it only to those whose losses occurred early in childhood; and there are even further variations.[3] Professionals agree that deafness is relatively rare. But whether it affects almost one of every hundred Americans or only about two per thousand depends upon how it is defined. The definition of deafness most accepted now is the one given above: *inability to hear and understand speech, with all possible correction.* It was used in the National Census of the Deaf Population, from which most of the statistics in this chapter are drawn. That ascertainment of the deaf population was completed in 1972, and it provides the most up-to-date detailed information about this disability.[4] It estimates that almost 1 percent of the population is deaf, but that only 0.2 percent (about half a million people) lost their hearing before nineteen years of age. The latter persons make up the bulk of the deaf community—a small minority group within our society and the group that signs.

Where is the deaf community located? Many sociologists consider people to have formed a community when they live in geographical proximity to each other. That is not the case with the deaf community.[5] We use the term to mean people with common interests who may or may not live near each other. In the United States, deaf people reside in every state. Yet, despite their dispersion, early-deafened people in this country constitute a relatively cohesive interest group. They subscribe to publications distributed nationally; they join organizations whose scope transcends state and local boundaries; they attend functions at great distances from their homes to be with other deaf people. In short, the deaf community's boundaries are conceptual, not spatial.

Family Life

Most deaf adults have parents who could hear. The actual statistics show that nine out of ten persons born deaf or deafened in childhood have no other deafness in their families. What that means is that most deaf children grow up like strangers in their own households. They do not readily participate in family discussions; they are usually unaware of plans for family events, and they may not even know the names of other people in their home. One deaf man characterized his early years as "living in a glass box." He could see others, and they could see him, but they did not communicate.

In a study of conversations between normally hearing mothers and their deaf children, researchers found that almost all discussions concerned things that were immediately visible. These mothers did not sign, so they limited their remarks to the things at hand. Restricting conversation in that way means that abstract issues must be eliminated along with announcements of things to come ("To-morrow we are going to visit granny"). This limitation may not be much of a handicap with a very young child, but it plainly hampers later child rearing. It is nearly impossible, without language, to discuss the consequences of future actions or to justify discipline after a misdemeanor has occurred.[6]

Added to the difficulties in communicating are the parents' emotional reactions to having a deaf child. The diagnosis often comes after long delays in which harried pediatricians dismiss the parents' concerns as being without foundation, inducing parents to worry that their child is mentally retarded ("slow"). Despite the advances in pediatric audiology, an early, correct diagnosis of deafness is still not common.[7] When telling parents that their child has a severe hearing impairment, the professional often delivers the information in a manner suggesting that the child is *dead* rather than deaf. The news of a disability in a young child is never welcome, but professionals who are responsible for giving parents such bad news need more training in counseling. The parents go through predictable phases of shock, denial, guilt, anger, and grief—until, if they are fortunate, they can accept their child's condition and begin to cope with it constructively. Most importantly, where deafness is concerned, the emotional climate generated by the disability adds further disruption to communication.

Well-intentioned advisers may urge parents to treat deaf children *normally*—that is, to ignore their inability to hear and to continue speaking to them. This approach is supposed to lead to children's developing speech and lipreading, although experts who recommend this method concede that much highly skilled professional involvement is also necessary to achieve such a result. Until recently, these experts told parents that they must not sign or gesture to the deaf child. Now more emphasis is being placed on making communication effective, rather than on how to communicate.[8] Where parents elect to learn sign, they face difficulties in acquiring the skill; and by doing so they are admitting that their child is deaf—something perhaps even more difficult. What they gain is not only the early establishment of communication with their deaf child, but also the clear demonstration to the child of their affection. Demanding that deaf children make all the accommodations is likely to arouse their resentment when they realize that other communication options were available to their parents. The relationship that emerges between signing parent and deaf child can be particularly helpful in the turbulent teen years.

What about the 10 percent of deaf children who have deaf parents? The research shows that these children achieve better in school and appear to be emotionally better adjusted.[9] Why? Early and effective communication is part of the answer. Most deaf parents of deaf children sign to them in the same way that hearing parents talk to their infants. The result is generally a rapid development of language, as noted earlier. The scientists who have reviewed these studies point out that another factor comes into play: most deaf parents readily accept their children's deafness. At the time when the children are struggling to establish an identity, their parents are not rejecting them. The combination of early communication and full emotional acceptance probably accounts for the superior academic performance of deaf children of deaf parents over those who have hearing parents. This, however, does not mean that hearing parents cannot successfully raise a deaf child and that deaf parents always can. Neither is true. Hearing parents can manage deaf children very well, and some deaf parents, like some hearing parents, do not. Still, the general finding is important, for it points out ways to smooth the psychoeducational development of the majority of deaf children. That the solution of deaf children's developmental problems does not rest entirely upon signing to them should be no surprise. After all, parents who speak to their hearing children still have problems raising them. But without the ability to maintain a fluent interchange with one's child, parenting is a nearly impossible task.[10]

When deaf children grow up, what kinds of families do they create? Most early-deafened people marry other deaf people. Only about one of every ten deaf persons marries a person who can hear. Among the reasons given for choosing a deaf spouse, one that is generally included is the desire to have a mate with whom communication will be convenient. By and large, marriages are as successful among deaf people as among the general population. What about the children who emerge from these pairings? Most of the children born of such marriages can hear. There are genetically deaf persons who transmit their deafness to their children, but most early-deafened persons do not have a dominant genetic deafness that would directly affect their offspring's hearing. Genetics aside, what is interesting about this finding is that the deaf couple typically come from families in which no one is deaf, and then have children, all of whom can hear. As a result, these deaf couples are surrounded by a communication gulf in their immediate families.

Most deaf parents use sign at home, and their children usually acquire it effortlessly, as children raised in a bilingual home acquire both the language of the country and their parents' language. The situation is not without its difficulties. Children are sensitive to what they perceive as weaknesses in their parents; hearing children of deaf parents sometimes are ashamed of their parents' lack of hearing. Not all are, however. A few years ago a deaf father told me how his young son handled the taunting of a neighborhood bully. When the bully sneered, "Your father can't even talk," the deaf man's son promptly retorted, "Yeah, well your old man can't sign!"

The research so far done on the hearing children of deaf parents agrees that the children do as well as others in their socioeconomic class. A great concern of some turns out not to be warranted: despite the fact that their parents may not speak at all (though most deaf parents make some attempt to do so when it seems appropriate to them), the hearing children usually develop good speech. One study even found their articulation to be above average. Their vocabulary may sometimes be below average when they enter school, but most hearing children of deaf parents quickly make up such deficiencies.[11]

Roots of the Deaf Community

Surrounded as they are by people who hear, deaf people nonetheless find each other. For most, the first contact with other deaf persons comes in school, since the majority of deaf children attend special schools and classes with other deaf children. It is the special school, then, that provides the deaf community's seedbed. There, most deaf students learn Ameslan—from the other students. They do not learn it from any formal courses, because schools for deaf children do not teach them to sign. The schools that use sign do that and nothing more: they *use* sign, but they do not *teach* it in a formal course. At least, none have done so up to now. The schools that do teach sign teach it to adults—mostly hearing adults—because the schools see their responsibility to be that of passing on the dominant culture and its language. They have been content to ignore deaf culture up to now, and it does not seem to occur to educational administrators that there is any good reason to teach their deaf students to sign correctly. Imagine what would happen to English if our schools did not devote a significant portion of the curriculum to it. No matter that we have spoken English all of our lives, we still must take a course in English every year in elementary and secondary school. Ameslan is not given that much attention by any public or private school in the United States. Students learn from each other, and Ameslan, in most instances, is passed along from child to child, rather than from adult to child. The situation is unusual among modern languages.

In the development of the deaf community, the school is important as the place where sign is learned, not taught. The special schools also provide for deaf children the first environment adapted to them instead of requiring that they adapt to the majority. It is illuminating to correlate the emergence of organizations of deaf people with the establishment of their schools. Before 1817, there is no record of any organization of deaf adults. The New England Association of the Deaf was founded in 1837, twenty years after the first permanent school for deaf students opened in Hartford, Connecticut. The Congress chartered the National Deaf Mute College (later renamed Gallaudet College) in 1864, and sixteen years later the National Association of the Deaf came into being. These are but two of many instances of the relationship between the schools and the organizations of deaf persons.

The current trend toward "mainstreaming" (putting disabled children into regular classes) will alter and perhaps delay the meetings of deaf children with each other. These delays, though likely to have an effect on the individual children, will probably not affect the deaf community in any substantial way. Most deaf people react favorably to meeting others like themselves. One deaf adolescent who had never before met another deaf person remembers his feelings when he entered a class of deaf children for the first time: "I wanted to reach out and hug them all." Writing about the experience years later, he went on to say that "at long last I began to come home. It was literally a love experience. For the first time, I felt less like a stranger in a strange land and more like a member of a community."[12]

While the national trend is away from special schools for disabled grade-school children, there are more opportunities than ever for deaf students to meet each other in college. Recent federal laws bar discrimination in the higher education of disabled people. Deaf students formerly could find few programs adapted to them; indeed, some colleges refused them admittance altogether. The situation has changed dramatically for the better, with dozens of colleges and universities now inviting deaf students to attend.[13] The broadened opportunities for deaf people to meet each other will, more than likely, strengthen the deaf community and invigorate its leadership.

How did the United States attain leadership in the higher education of deaf students? Edward Miner Gallaudet dreamed, almost from the time he came to Washington, D.C., of a college for deaf students. He chose a most unlikely time to pursue his dream. In 1863, while the country was struggling for its existence, Gallaudet proposed to the Congress that it give his school the authority to award college degrees. He lobbied well, and in the winter of 1863, with civil war raging, Congress passed the legislation establishing the National Deaf Mute College (renamed Gallaudet College in 1880). The first diplomas issued in 1864 were signed by the college's original patron, Abraham Lincoln. Thereafter, the college's diplomas have been signed by the President of the United States. Over a hundred years later, the United States remains the only country to have a liberal arts college exclusively for the education of deaf students.[14]

The federal government, which finances a major portion of Gallaudet College's activities, also underwrites the cost of the National Technical Institute for the Deaf, at the Rochester Institute of Technology. Only recently established (1968), NTID has already demonstrated the value of education for deaf students and, not incidentally, the effectiveness of sign language for instructional purposes. On the West Coast, another program for deaf students has had only sporadic federal support but has enjoyed the consistent backing of the state. California State University at Northridge—known affectionately as CSUN—accepts about a hundred deaf undergraduates annually. Interpreters are present in all their classes to facilitate the transfer of knowledge. CSUN has also had a Leadership Training Program for the Deaf since 1964. Joining NTID and Gallaudet College, the program has become one of the principal sources of leaders for the deaf community's organizations and the administration of special schools. Like the general community, the deaf community seeks out its officers and administrators from the ranks of the college-educated, and the colleges that the majority of deaf leaders attend contribute to their sign skills along with their education in other areas. For deaf people, a "Gallaudet College accent" is identifiable in a graduate's signing. Like the distinctive speech of a graduate from, say, an Ivy League college, the sign of deaf college students sets them apart, though not usually in a pejorative sense. The style of signing particularly suits public presentations, a leader's frequent task.

The Organized Side of Deafness

Deaf people seem to welcome any occasion to mingle with each other. Announce a sporting event—a bowling tournament, for example—and they will flock to it from neighboring towns, even though they may have no interest in the particular activity. What they seek are opportunities to relax and exchange news with their friends. With the mails slow and the telephone difficult (or impossible) for them to use, deaf people must meet in person to share information that hearing persons can easily transmit by telephone. The desire for companionship shared by all humans leads deaf people to join their clubs and other organizations in which they conduct their business by sign.

Visit almost any metropolitan area in the United States and you will find a deaf club. It may not be extravagantly decorated; indeed, it probably will not be, for most deaf people do not do as well financially as their hearing age peers. The typical club occupies rented rooms in an unfashionable part of the city, though it is usually easily reached. Enter it and you will note that the quarters are sparsely furnished, but well maintained. The interior design suggests the premises' main function: to facilitate personal interactions. The walls are not covered with pictures; the television set, if there is one, does not dominate the room; the furnishings can be shifted readily to form conversation groups. The quarters will almost certainly house a bar and a raised platform. The former needs no explanation; the latter is for speakers, skits, or whatever activities are intended to be viewed by the group as a whole. The club is clearly a place for seeing people.

Originally, these organizations were strictly social centers. But the example of other minority groups in the fifties and sixties led deaf people to become more active in obtaining their civil rights, so the clubs have become rallying points for political activism. As a group, deaf people are not as militant as some other minorities, but they have become much more openly aware of their social disadvantages and of what they need to do to overcome them. The clubs form a steady base from which the members can launch themselves into the local political arena.

The state associations are very much like the local clubs. They, too, were essentially created for social purposes. Many state associations functioned solely to prepare for the next state convention. Now, however, most state associations have become more active in working for the general welfare of their members. They are gaining the attention of their states' legislatures, and in several instances have succeeded in getting them to establish commissions on deafness—such as the commissions that blind people have had for most of this century but deaf people have only had in a few states since 1970.[15]

Most of the state associations have joined the National Association of the Deaf, the organization that has represented the interests of deaf people since 1880. NAD came into being as a reaction to the Milan Conference's attack on sign language (see Chapter 4). That critical point can be easily overlooked today, especially when one visits the modern office building the NAD owns in the Washington, D.C., suburb of Silver Spring, Maryland. Enter the headquarters, however, and there is no question that it is the National Association *of* the Deaf. Every administrative position—including that of executive secretary, of president, of member of the board—is filled by a deaf person. Everyone who works for NAD signs. Clearly, sign is the organization's official language.

NAD was the first national organization of disabled people in the United States. A companion organization is the National Fraternal Society of the Deaf. It was founded in 1901, again as a reaction against discrimination. At the time, deaf people found themselves being overcharged by life insurance companies (something that is no longer true for most of the companies). A few deaf leaders pooled their resources and set up a cooperative life-insurance plan. Today, NFSD fills the deaf community's need for fairly priced life insurance, and does so with a success that is the envy of the trade. NFSD has 120 chapters in the United States and Canada that serve both business and social functions. It offers scholarships to deaf students and does other good work. As in the case of NAD, the affairs of NFSD are conducted in sign.

There are other, younger organizations in the deaf community that manifest its independence. When barred from activities or benefits by organizations of the general community, deaf people have tended to establish their own separate organizations that cater to themselves and, most important, are managed by themselves. The fact that all their administrators sign symbolizes that apartness. Of course, signing is essential to rapid, accurate communication in these organizations, but signing also reinforces the self-reliance of the deaf community. They use their language to forward their affairs.

Do all born-deaf people know sign? No. There are deaf people who are raised in an oral tradition and rely on speechreading and speech for communication. Modern hearing aids assist many of them to make optimal use of whatever hearing they may have. The hearing aids do not restore their ability to understand what is said, but do improve lipreading and keep them in auditory contact with the environment. (Of course, hearing aids and signing are not incompatible; many deaf people both wear hearing aids and sign.) Since access to the deaf community is limited for those who do not sign, oral deaf people tend to associate with each other. The Oral Deaf Adults Section of the Alexander Graham Bell Association for the Deaf is the principal organization representing them. Persons deafened in adulthood have tended to remain unorganized and largely unrepresented. In 1978, a national organization was founded by a former hearing-impaired FBI agent, Rocky Stone. He established Self Help for Hard of Hearing People, Inc., which identifies itself by the acronym SHHH. As an advocacy group, SHHH neither opposes nor supports the use of sign language. Naturally, since most of its members do not know sign, it emphasizes communication techniques that depend on amplification and lipreading.

Advocacy

In the United States, deaf people have been their own best advocates. Through the NAD, they have had a prominent voice before Congress in the last two decades. At the state level, the state associations of deaf people have had varying success. Many state legislators and administrators look to their educational institutions for assistance with technical matters; for example, in Minnesota, the St. Paul Technical-Vocational Institute has been highly effective in improving interpreter services. Increasingly, however, at all levels of government, deaf people are demanding that their voices be heard.

The United States has no comparable organization to Great Britain's Royal National Institute for the Deaf (RNID). Originally called simply the National Institute for the Deaf, RNID became "royal" in 1958, when His Royal Highness Prince Philip, Duke of Edinburgh, became its patron. In a letter, dated 23 October 1983, from the Prince's secretary to RNID Director Roger Sydenham, the appropriateness of the Duke's support becomes clear:

> Thank you for your letter of 19th October. The Duke of Edinburgh has no objection to references being made to Princess Andrew and his own subsequent interest in the R.N.I.D.
>
> His Royal Highness points out that Princess Andrew did not become deaf but was born deaf and of course that his Patronage of the R.N.I.D. was influenced by the realisation of the value of the work it undertakes.

(For readers unfamiliar with the Royal Family, Princess Andrew of Greece is Prince Philip's mother.) His sensitivity to the distinction between early- and late-deafened people, as indicated in the letter, speaks highly for his understanding of deafness.

Occupations and Income

Deaf people have been employed in virtually every occupation in our country, except for those specifically requiring hearing. Deaf people own their own businesses and manage the businesses of others. They are accountants, architects, barbers, butchers, cosmeticians, dentists, and lawyers. They have often faced discrimination, not only at occupational entry points but also in gaining promotions. They have compiled excellent records and have still met opposition to further advancement. As a group, deaf workers have not found remuneration consistent with their efforts. They tend, on the average, to earn less than the general population does in the same or similar occupations.

How are these discrepancies explained? When considering the matter at all, management usually justifies poor treatment of deaf workers on the basis of communication difficulties. They are left in entry-level jobs, because it is too difficult to train them for better positions in the company. They cannot take executive roles, because these require the use of the telephone. Or they cannot be placed in work that requires rapid communication. The excuses are many and varied, and so are deaf workers' responses. The experiences of deaf executives and professionals belie the supposed insurmountability of communication barriers. One study of high-achieving deaf men demonstrates how well they have met and conquered the obstacles they have encountered in their work.[16] But prejudices do not quickly disappear. While they remain, they press hard on the deaf pocketbook. Perhaps, as sign becomes more widespread, the early-deafened person will find greater acceptance as a worker.

Athletics

Sports figure prominently in the deaf community. The major national organization serving its athletic interests is the American Athletic Association of the Deaf. AAAD organizes and encourages competitions between local clubs. It sponsors a national basketball tournament annually that draws deaf spectators by the thousands—although, as noted above, many who attend come for the socializing rather than the competition. In fact, one of AAAD's stated purposes is to "provide social outlets for the members and their friends." Another, more specialized group is the National Deaf Bowling Association, which holds regional and national competitions. Most state residential schools participate in their states' football and basketball tournaments. At the international level, the Comité International des Sports Silencieux, headquartered in Paris, France, sponsors the World Games for the Deaf every four years. Patterned after the Olympic Games, the deaf games attract athletes from as many as thirty different nations. CISS also arranges Winter Games for the Deaf—an event which, like its Olympic counterpart, is growing in popularity.

The emphasis on the social aspects of athletics should not obscure the fact that a number of deaf athletes have done well in competition with normally hearing peers. At least fourteen major league baseball players have been deaf. At one time, in 1900, the New York Giants had three deaf pitchers on the team, one of whom, Luther "Dummy" Taylor, led them to two pennants (1904 and 1905) and a World Series (1905). William E. Hoy played for Cincinnati, New York, and Chicago, in the major leagues. Hoy is credited with initiating the practice of umpires' signaling balls with the left hand and strikes with the right hand, so he could follow the count when at bat. His distinguished career spanned eighteen years in organized baseball and earned him a place in baseball's Hall of Fame.

Eugene "Silent" Hairston is one of several deaf boxers to have become professionals. Hairston won the 1946 National AAU and Golden Gloves championships and then turned professional, ranking second in the middleweight division to Sugar Ray Robinson, one of the great champions of this century. Hairston was unhampered by his inability to hear the roar of the crowd.

Deaf football players have left an indelible mark on the game. Most historians attribute the invention of the huddle to deaf teams' need to hide their discussions before each play, especially when playing another deaf team that could read their signs. Gallaudet College is generally believed to be the first college team to use the huddle in a regulation game. Defending the deaf priority, historian Jack Gannon writes: "Logic for the invention of the huddle is on the side of deaf players, unfortunately there is no printed documentation."[17]

The Arts

The deaf community generates substantial cultural activity, mirroring the general community in vigor but having its unique aspects. Deaf people have ample outlets for their creative energies, and they seem to make good use of them. To picture members of the deaf community as lonely, isolated figures deprived of contact with their fellows bears no relation to the facts. The deaf isolate is more likely the late-deafened individual who has not adjusted to hearing loss and its social consequences. The early-deafened person typically joins the deaf community and its active social life.

Deaf authors and artists have made significant contributions to society. Melville Ballard, for example, never developed usable speech, but he wrote fluently in English. He also developed amazing proficiency in Latin and French. Among his accomplishments was a French political pamphlet that he translated for General James Garfield, later President of the United States. The General was so impressed by Ballard's work that he rewarded him with a handsomely bound set of Caesar's Commentaries, in French.[18]

One of the foremost drypoint etchers in the world, Cadwallader Washburn, became a war correspondent despite his deafness. During the Mexican revolution he succeeded in interviewing, with pad and pencil, President Madero. Earlier, Washburn had covered the Russo-Japanese conflict. He made his major mark on paper, but with drawings rather than words.

Another renowned deaf artist was the sculptor Douglas Tilden. His works are prominently displayed throughout his home state of California; for example, his massive sculpture "The Mechanics" dominates the intersection of Market and Battery Streets in San Francisco. Though he gained international acclaim by winning a prize at an exhibition in Paris, he had little commercial success during his lifetime, depending on his salary as a teacher at the California School for the Deaf.

Not all deaf writers and artists are in the past. To name a few who are living, Rex Lowman (*Bitterweed*), Kathleen Schreiber (*Dear Beth*), and Linwood Smith (*Silence, Love and Kids I Know*) are all published poets and all still productive. Two of the many successful deaf painters are William Sparks and Kelly H. Stevens. There are many, many more; some have achieved commercial recognition, and others must await the judgment of history as to their longtime artistic worth. What this tiny sample makes clear, however, is that artistic talent can flourish in silence.

Most moviegoers never realized that some of the performers on the "silent screen" were truly silent. Before sound was added to film, a number of actors were deaf. Among them were Granville Redmond, Emerson Romero, Louis Weinberg, Carmen de Arcos, and Albert Ballin. Some actors, like Charlie Chaplin, signed well, and some actors and directors learned to fingerspell. When the movies became "talkies," the deaf actors lost their positions, and deaf audiences lost the captions that made the movies so entertaining for them.

Religion

No religion can prevent deafness. Whatever the faith, it has deaf persons among its members. Deaf congregants do not receive the same treatment from individual religious groups; some groups make extensive provisions for those who cannot hear, while others tend to ignore their deaf coreligionists. None, however, is openly hostile toward deaf people.

Historically, the Catholic Church ranks at the top among religions that have given particular attention to deafness. As noted in Chapter 4, Catholic churchmen led the early attempts to educate deaf children, freeing them from the constraints of ancient dogma. Pablo Bonet, Pedro de Ponce, the Abbé de l'Epée, and Sicard pioneered in the use of manual communication. Today, in the United States, the Catholic Church has nine parochial schools for deaf students: St. Mary (Buffalo), Holy Trinity (Chicago), St. Rita (Cincinnati), St. John (Milwaukee), St. Francis de Sales (New York City), St. Joseph (New York City), Archbishop Ryan (Philadelphia), DePaul Institute (Pittsburgh), and St. Joseph (St. Louis). The Lutheran Church sponsors schools for deaf children in Detroit and on Long Island. In New York City, the Hebrew Academy for the Deaf includes material on Jewish life in its educational program. The fact that more Protestant denominations do not sponsor schools for deaf children reflects their dedication to public education more than their rejection of the children. Many Protestant groups provide Sunday school classes and other special programs for deaf children, ranging from summer camps to drug treatment centers. Most religious groups also have programs for deaf adults, such as counseling, social get-togethers, and housing for the elderly.

Within the churches, great variations occur in the preparation of deaf persons as ministers. The Episcopal Church leads all other denominations in the United States with forty-five priests—all of whom were deaf before ordination. At the other extreme, there is only one deaf Catholic priest, Reverend Thomas Coughlin, who was ordained in 1977. There are no deaf rabbis, though one young deaf man, Alton Silver, was studying for the rabbinate in 1963 when he died during surgery. The number of deaf ministers in other religious groups varies between these extremes, with most denominations having one or two.

The early church influences on sign language emerged through its use by clergymen in teaching deaf children, but religious use has extended well beyond the classroom. In the United States, sign has become a commonplace in the conduct of church services wherever deaf people gather in sufficient numbers. When the minister does not sign, interpreters make the service visible to the deaf congregants. Until very recently, the churches were the principal employers of interpreters (most of whom, however, volunteered their services). These interpreters contributed to the shaping of signs, particularly those used in religious services.

Almost every religious concept has one or more signs. The particular choice of signs depends on the religious order and, of course, the signer. For example, *baptism* is signed as shown in Figure 91. The sign is supposed to convey the idea of immersion, the movement reminiscent of ducking someone under water. In churches that do not subscribe to that form of baptism, the sign in Figure 92 might be used, since it suggests the act of sprinkling water.

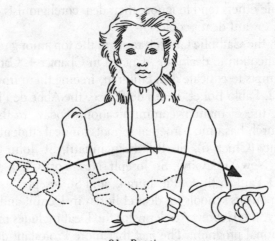

91. *Baptism*

92. *Baptism*

Another sign variation is in the designation of *bible*. A long-standing version combines the two signs shown in Figures 93 and 94, which separately mean *Jesus* and *book*. The signs in Figures 95 and 94 stand separately for *God* and *book*, and together for *bible*. The latter combination is preferred by some to signify the Old Testament. Other versions combine *holy* or *Moses* with *book* to achieve the same meaning of *bible*. These latter variants are relatively new.

93. *Jesus*

94. *Book*

95. *God*

Names for religious denominations can be amusing or, for some, prejudicial. The sign for *Methodist* (Figure 96) also means *eager* and *enthusiastic*. Methodists do not seem to object to the implied reference to their founder's evangelical spirit. Jews, on the other hand, dislike one form of the sign sometimes used to designate them: it is like the acceptable sign that appears in Figure 97, except that as the fingers leave the chin they curl into a tight fist. In the version shown, the sign is the same as that used for *beard*. In the former, it means "stingy" and "Shylock." Obviously, neither definition is pleasing to Jewish people. It is fascinating to note, however, that the dictionary of Israeli signs[19] uses the sign depicted in Figure 97 and also glosses it as "the beards." The American Congress of the Jewish Deaf has undertaken the preparation of signs for use in religious rituals. Some Judaic religious concepts (like blowing the *shofar*) have no present sign in Ameslan, though the Israelis do have most such signs. Other religious groups have depended upon the enterprise of interested members, like the Baptists' Dr. Lottie Riekehof, to compile signs relevant to their services.

96. *Methodist*

97. *Jewish*

That sign has a spiritual aspect should not surprise anyone, especially if one considers its use by silent religious orders and by priests in the education of deaf children. What must be seen to be fully appreciated, however, is its singular appropriateness for religious worship. The depth of expression that can be achieved by signing defies accurate description. The Academy Award won by Jane Wyman in 1948 for her portrayal of a deaf girl in *Johnny Belinda* undoubtedly owed much to her beautiful (and accurate) rendering of the Lord's Prayer in Ameslan.

It is perhaps in the church service that the beauty of sign becomes most evident. Some churches have sign choirs. Watching the robed members sign in unison can be an awe-inspiring experience. The movements impart vigor to the service and add a spirituality that words alone do not often engender. Two Gallaudet College chaplains, Rudolph Gawlik, a Catholic priest, and Daniel Pokorny, a Lutheran minister, formed a group to present gospel songs in sign, to the accompaniment of a rock band. The results brought them nine years of performances at deaf functions, during which they never failed to arouse their audiences to high levels of participation in the "sign-sing," as well as appreciation of sign's power to make the gospel message come alive.

To illustrate a problem of being deaf and a member of a religious minority, one deaf young man tells of his religious confusion as a child. Though Jewish, he was sent to a Catholic residential school that specialized in educating deaf children. The first night home on Christmas vacation, the boy followed the bedtime ritual he learned in school: he knelt by his bedside, folded his hands and bowed his head, and began to recite the Lord's Prayer. Without warning, his mother grabbed his hair and pulling him upright said in slow words he could lipread, "Jews don't kneel!" As he later reported, "That is how I discovered I was a Jew." Lack of information about their religion is all too common among deaf youngsters . . . and not a few deaf adults.

Humor Among the Deaf

Perhaps it is already apparent—but cannot hurt to say—that the deaf community is not a somber place: silent, yes, but not morose. What is its humor like, then? In many ways, what makes deaf people laugh is as obvious and inexplicable as what makes any other group of people laugh. Certainly, a major theme derives from the frustrations of being deaf in a world designed for people who can hear. Deaf people enjoy telling stories about the foolish things that happen to them because they cannot hear. One cartoon depicts a deaf man at a bus stop being approached by a stranger obviously asking some questions. The deaf man signals that he cannot hear. After a moment's pause, the stranger circles around to the deaf man's other ear and continues to shout his questions. Funny? Yes: to deaf people who have repeatedly experienced that sort of situation, the display of how ridiculous it can be becomes emotionally cathartic.

Deaf people also like jokes showing that their lack of hearing is not so bad after all. One college skit that has been performed countless times, and is probably still performed, depicts a deaf man again waiting at a street corner. He is approached by a blind man, tapping along with his cane. The deaf man is horrified by the blind man's attempts to speak with him. How can he show a blind person that he does not hear or speak? The situation is played out in accordance with the performer's skills, but the denouement is swift and always draws appreciative guffaws from the deaf audience. The deaf man gives the well-dressed blind man a coin and walks quickly away.

These stories say, "Deafness is not the worst thing that could happen to one," and they are perennial favorites. They may mean little to persons outside the deaf community (just as is true of much ethnic humor), but they serve the purposes of humor, relieving stress and making life a bit easier to bear.

Sign play is another aspect of humor in the deaf community that parallels word play in spoken languages. Puns are possible in sign, as are other aspects of linguistic humor: minimalization, exaggeration, and so on. Once, a number of years ago, I was interpreting for a very intelligent deaf lady at a very dull meeting. With barely discernible signs she signaled me to stop conveying the speaker's remarks. In response to my questioning look, she signed by placing her index finger against her nose as she curled her little finger in the manner of one daintily holding a teacup. When I said I had never seen that sign and asked what it meant, she replied by spelling b-o-r-i-n-g. I protested that her execution of the sign threw me off (see Figure 8 for the usual handshape). Her quick reply was that she was simply being ladylike!

In their delightful essay on iconicity in sign, Edward Klima and Ursula Bellugi recall how one elderly deaf storyteller made sure that his viewers got the idea that a long time had elapsed. The sign is usually made by drawing the index finger along the inner surface of the arm from the wrist to the elbow. In his account, the storyteller made the sign by touching his left shoe with his index finger and bringing it through the air to a point over his right shoulder. Very long, indeed.[20]

The Dynamics of Sign

No one studying sign can fail to be impressed by its dynamic character. Today's Ameslan has moved as far from Ameslan at the turn of the century as today's English has from that of Shakespeare. The reason that sign has changed more swiftly is twofold: sign is not yet being written, and it is seldom taught to those who use it most. The changes that have occurred and are occurring in sign proclaim its vigor. The world is changing, so language changes also. Sign can keep pace with new events as readily as any language, though it has less of one advantage that spoken languages have: they can borrow words and expressions from each other. Open an English dictionary and count the words that have been recently taken from another tongue: atoll, blitzkrieg, cosmonaut, zaftig . . . And English returns the favor. Ameslan has few sources from which to take signs, so signs have been invented. These inventions are particularly prevalent in the teaching of college courses. The new signs that come out of university classrooms are not always warmly greeted by deaf people, who resent what they see as tampering with their language by insensitive outsiders.

Deaf people have recently come to appreciate their linguistic heritage. Where once they hesitated to be seen signing in public, they now have a sense of pride in their language. They have shifted from a defensive posture to a confident stance. Sign is their language, and they love it. One of the foremost leaders of deaf people in the twentieth century, the late Frederick C. Schreiber, reflected the changes in an editorial he wrote about the new attitudes toward sign:

> Of course, we are glad that finally, after all these years of frustration and dogged determination to keep what was ours, we have achieved recognition. We have overcome to the extent that education finally has come to grips with the problem and agreed that we, the deaf people, were right after all.

He then reveals the depth of feeling that language can arouse when he comments on what he sees as outsiders tampering with Ameslan:

> If that were the end of the matter, it would be great. And as in fairy tales, we could all "live happily ever after." But that isn't all. With the acceptance of signs, everybody got on the bandwagon. So many people got on this bandwagon that there suddenly were too many and some had to be pushed off and guess who they were? The deaf, of course. Now everybody is in the business of improving sign language, everybody knows more about it than the people who have been using it for a hundred years and more. It was bad enough when we found that every Tom, Dick, and Harry was inventing signs for words without regard for the deaf community and for that matter without regard for each other, but it became the height of the ridiculous when they began to "improve" on signs that were already in existence. It seems high time that the deaf community ought to get up in arms and suggest politely or not so politely, if you wish, that this is our language.[21]

Dr. Schreiber's cry of "our language" may lack the panache of a Charles de Gaulle singing the "Marseillaise," but it is similarly motivated and no less sincere. As executive secretary of NAD, Schreiber expected his readers to recall that the organization had been founded in reaction to the attack upon sign by the delegates to the Milan conference in 1880 (see Chapter 4). For one hundred years, NAD held as one of its principal aims the preservation of Ameslan. Small wonder that after years of bitter struggle deaf leaders resented the Johnny-come-latelies who embraced sign. But for most deaf people the bitterness has quickly receded. What remains is pride in their language.

Sign has survived neglect and active onslaught. It has proved to be remarkably robust, growing without the nourishment of formal instruction and without the support of a written form. It flourishes in the eager hands of little deaf children; it goes cleverly to school with them; it leaps vigorously to meet the requirements of the workplace; it adapts to the shifting demands of time; and it rests comfortably in the tender care of elderly deaf people, telling and retelling their stories of yesterday.

Can you sing in sign? Can you tell jokes? Recite poetry? Court, argue, curse, and bless? Yes, to all of these. "Sign-sings" are popular with deaf people. The lyrics are translated into signs that must be adjusted to fit the music's rhythm (the deaf performers get the beat from vibrations, which is why heavily accented music, like rock or country, is greatly enjoyed). The adept sign-singer creates a smooth flow of signs that follows the melodic line, imparting a special quality to the song. Observing a signed version of the national anthem, for example, may be far more emotion-provoking than hearing it sung.

Whatever can be said or sung can be signed. No wonder so many deaf people are passionate in their regard for their language. Ameslan gives them back what deafness takes away: the ability to communicate with their fellow human beings.

Scientists may find sign fascinating and rewarding to study. Many hearing persons regard it as an object of curiosity. But for those who are deaf from childhood, sign is simply essential.

The history of sign predicts a secure future for it. The science of sign is developing rapidly, adding not merely to our knowledge of manual language but to our understanding of all languages. The high art of sign, which has always had its enthusiasts in the deaf community, is also finding appreciation outside of it. Now, increasingly, the general community has the opportunity to observe and to learn a linguistic art form, one that cannot be called new (we have seen that) but whose wider appreciation in the general community is a fresh and burgeoning phenomenon.

Those who have kept sign alive deserve the gratitude of all humankind. To all those farsighted, evenhanded individuals, we can offer a sign from Ameslan. It is the concluding illustration—easily learned and, at this juncture, most appropriately signed: Thank you!

98. *Thank you*

NOTES

CHAPTER 1

N.B.: Citations in these notes are by author and year of publication. The complete citations will be found in References, beginning on page 165.

1. For more about the numbers and characteristics of deaf people in the United States, see Chapter 9.

2. A review of sign dictionaries appears in Appendix A.

3. This discussion is based on the article by Cutting and Kavanagh (1975).

4. Another term for a new language that emerges from persistent contact between two groups speaking different languages is *creole*. Further discussion of pidgins and creoles will be found in Chapter 5.

5. Wescott 1974, p. iv. Jerome Bruner and Carol Feldman (1982, p. 34) take a different view of that professional censorship: "If language seems like a miraculous, proliferating tree, most guesses about its roots have been notoriously unproductive and singularly dull . . . Small wonder the Société de Linguistique of Paris banned the topic of origins from its meetings in the late nineteenth century."

6. In May 1980, the New York Academy of Sciences published the proceedings of a conference on animal communication. The editors commented: "Deep scholarship was leavened with strong affect . . ." (Sebeok and Rosenthal 1981, p. vii). The proceedings cannot convey fully the emotions to which the editors refer, but the papers are well worth reading for their intellectual content. Several will be cited in later chapters.

7. Brennan and Hayhurst 1980, p. 234.

8. Lewis 1982, p. A33.

9. Bickerton 1981 puts strongly his views on our earlier conceptions of the role of language in culture: "According to 19th-century racists, languages and people alike were ranged along a scale of being from the primitive Bushman with his clicks, grunts, and shortage of artifacts, to the modern Western European with his high pale brow and plethora of gadgets. That was when everyone, racist or anti-racist, did believe that Western Man was superior; the only argument was about how nasty this superiority permitted him to be toward 'lesser' breeds. Now that we are rapidly disabusing ourselves of this kind of mental garbage, it becomes possible to uncouple language from 'level of cultural attainment' and look at it developmentally without any pejorative implications" (p. 299).

CHAPTER 2

1. The first use I could find of the acronym *Ameslan* is in Fant 1972. Others prefer *ASL*. It is a matter of taste. But Fant deserves credit, I believe, for coining the term.

2. Stokoe, Casterline, and Croneberg 1965.

3. Klima and Bellugi 1979.

4. Stokoe, Casterline, and Croneberg 1965, p. xxxi.

5. Hewes 1974, p. 13.

6. Frishberg 1976.

7. Woodward 1979.

8. Woodward 1979, pp. 1–2.

9. Woodward 1980. This collection of drug-related signs ranges from AA (Alcoholics Anonymous) to *wack* (angel dust or PCP).

10. For example, Kannapell, Hamilton, and Bornstein 1969. A further listing will be found in Appendix A.

11. Woodward 1980.

12. Sternberg 1980. The dictionary contains 5,200 English words, for which there are 7,200 illustrations, according to the publisher.

13. *Variety*'s critic wrote, "There is much dramatic impact and force in the performances which are spoken with the fingers, hands, and arms. . . . The performers play the play. Their faces speak even if their lips do not, and there were no excessive dramatics or overdone acting. It was in fact, a remarkable professional job by college students" (cited by Tadie 1978, p. 308).

14. Meadow 1977.

15. Hoemann 1975; Klima and Bellugi 1979; Wilbur 1979.

16. Signs for particular concepts differ substantially from language to language. For instance, Klima and Bellugi 1979 demonstrated as many differences between signs in Ameslan versus Chinslan as between words in English and

Chinese. Battison and Jordan 1976 and Jordan and Battison 1976 determined the ability of native signers from various countries to comprehend signs from other countries. Lifelong users of Ameslan, Danislan, Franslan, Chinslan (Hong Kong version), Italislan, and Portuslan viewed videotapes in their own and the other five languages. The researchers modestly conclude that "deaf signers can understand their own sign language better than they can understand sign languages foreign to them" (Jordan and Battison 1976, p. 78). For a discussion about International Sign Language, see Chapter 5.

17. Battison 1978, pp. 177–78. Further discussion of the origins of signs will be found later in this chapter.

18. Frishberg 1975.
19. Klima and Bellugi 1979.
20. Hoemann 1978.
21. Riekehof 1978.
22. Riekehof 1978, p. 73.
23. Crystal 1980, p. 81.
24. Crystal 1980, p. 100.

CHAPTER 3

1. Mallery 1881, p. 332.
2. Stokoe 1972 has a fine methodological review. He is particularly well-worth reading, since he is the premier sign researcher. Some additional perspectives into the methods used by students of sign will be found in Hoemann 1978, Klima and Bellugi 1979, Lane and Grosjean 1980, and Wilbur 1979. Even if you do no more than leaf through these volumes, you will surely be impressed by the diversity of approaches in the various disciplines that have begun to study sign.
3. Sources of videotapes and films illustrating signs are listed in Appendix C.
4. Tervoort 1975.
5. Goldin-Meadow and Feldman 1977.
6. Hoemann and Lucafo 1980.
7. Prinz and Prinz 1979.
8. Holmes and Holmes 1980.
9. Maestas y Moores 1980.
10. Battison 1978.
11. Baker 1976.
12. Stokoe, Casterline, and Croneberg 1965 anticipated this point in their pioneering work. Recent studies, such as those reported in Wilbur 1979, support their premonition about the grammatical role of facial expression in Ameslan.
13. The creators of the titles, in corresponding order, are Frishberg 1978,

Frishberg and Gough 1973, Friedman 1977, Supalla and Newport 1978, Battison, Markowicz, and Woodward 1975, Baker 1976, and Woodward and Markowicz 1975. All of the authors, by the way, were under forty years of age when they chose these intriguing headings, boding well for the future of sign scholarship.

14. Mallery 1881.

15. Woll, Kyle, and Deuchar 1981.

16. Valerie J. Sutton has invented a notational system for sign. She has founded the Center for Sutton Movement Writing, which publishes a newspaper that uses her symbols and English in parallel columns. The center's address is The Movement Shorthand Society, Inc., P.O. Box 7344, Newport Beach, Cal. 92660-0344. Cohen, Namir, and Schlesinger 1977 have used the Eshkol-Wachmann Movement Notation System, created to record dance routines, to display Israeli Sign Language. Their book, translated into English, serves as a guide to the sign used by deaf Israelis as well as to the transcription system. George Sperling 1978 has proposed that ideographs, like those used to write Japanese and Chinese, be composed for Ameslan. He has illustrated what such a system would look like, but has not developed this intriguing idea beyond the demonstration sample.

17. In her discussion of pronominalization, Wilbur 1979 cites ten recent studies that have examined various aspects of this single grammatical construction. Stokoe's 1972 analysis of the pronoun in Ameslan, though written much earlier than Wilbur's, should not be overlooked by any serious student of this subject. Stokoe recognized the critical fact that "sign language, unlike English, often contains the subject or object reference, or more rarely both, implicitly in verb signs" (p. 71). He also succinctly described the signer's use of space to signify various persons and objects, a point that additional research has confirmed.

18. Dyer 1976.

19. Baker and Cokely 1980.

20. Crystal and Craig 1978.

21. Padden 1981.

22. The sign in Figure 29, for example, is familiar to anyone who has watched a baseball umpire signal "You're out!" Was the sign borrowed from Ameslan? As you will see in Chapter 9, early deaf baseball players, like Luther "Dummy" Taylor, caused umpires to adopt the convention of signaling balls with the left hand and strikes with the right. The same may be true of the hand signals used to indicate "safe" and "out." Another sign gaining rapidly in popularity—it was used by Jimmy Carter during his presidential campaign, in 1976—is the one-handed sign meaning "I love you" (Figure 77).

23. Baker and Cokely 1980.

24. For example, see Hansen 1980 and Deuchar 1981.

CHAPTER 4

1. The book edited by Wescott (1974) and the article by Hewes (1977) provide thorough coverage of present thinking about the beginnings of language. Obviously, when experts reconstruct unrecorded historical events, they can be expected to disagree. These two references fairly present most extant thought on the topic, while advancing the authors' own viewpoints.

2. Hewes (1974b, p. 14) reasons that "the onset of serious manual gesture communication would have had to wait until our ancestors were mostly bipedal." That point explains why animal communication researchers prefer chimpanzees to gorillas, since the latter tend to keep their hands in contact with the ground to balance themselves when in motion. For a more detailed treatment of early hominid anatomy in relation to language, see Hill 1974.

3. Additional references may be found in the bibliography appended to Wescott 1974.

4. Fouts and Mellgren 1976, p. 342. Van Cantfort and Rimpau (1982) came to the same general conclusion from their positions as comparative psychologists; they urged greater rigor in the design and analysis of animal communication studies.

5. Terrace 1980.

6. Gaustad 1981.

7. Terrace 1982, pp. 179–80.

8. Gaustad 1982, p. 181.

9. F. M. Muller, *Lectures on the Science of Language* (London, 1861). Cited in Bonvillian 1982.

10. Bonvillian 1982, p. 13.

11. Hill 1977, p. 48.

12. Gould 1975, p. 692.

13. Sarles 1976, p. 167. Commenting on another controversial experiment in animal communication, a linguist writes: "A further telling, if oblique, bit of evidence comes from Gill and Rumbaugh (1974), who report that it took Lana 1,600 trials to learn the names for *banana* and *M&M*, but that the next five items were acquired in less than five trials each—two of them in two only. This stunning and instantaneous increment is inexplicable in terms of Lana's having 'learned how to learn' in the course of those 1,600 trials; learning curves just don't jump like that. It is much more plausible to suppose that for a long time Lana simply couldn't figure out what her trainers were trying to do, and then suddenly it clicked: 'My God, they're feeding me concept names—why couldn't they have *told* me, the dummies?' The concepts had been there all the while, and only the link between them and these mysterious new things that people were doing to her needed to be forged" (Bickerton 1981, p. 236).

14. Refer to the discussion of children's acquisition of sign language in Chapter 3. Schlesinger and Meadow 1972 report extensive data on young deaf children's

communication behavior. These children are being followed as they grow, with the anticipation of some exciting findings about language development and deafness as further reports are made.

15. Brown 1973, p. 97.

16. Kushel 1973.

17. Hewes 1974a, p. 28.

18. A sampling of cross-cultural studies of sign turns up investigations of sign used in China (Klima and Bellugi 1979; Youguang 1980), France (Sallagoity 1975; Woodward and DeSantis 1977), Grand Cayman, British West Indies (Washabaugh 1981), Providence Island, Colombia (Washabaugh 1980a, 1980b; Woodward 1979b), Scotland (Brennan and Colville 1979), and Yuendumu, Northern Territory, Australia (Kendon 1980). Woodward 1978 compared the kinship terms used in twenty different sign languages, ranging from Adamorobe to Taiwanese, and observed some regularities—for example: "All sign languages have a term for offspring"; and, "If a sign language has a basic term for father, it will also have one for mother, but not conversely." This kind of research can yield a better understanding of the characteristics of manual languages as distinguished from spoken languages, and these distinctions in turn can lead to a firmer grasp of linguistic principles that are independent of the code used.

19. So far, studies of the acquisition of sign language by young deaf children agree that their acquisition patterns parallel those of hearing children, though sign tends to develop earlier than speech. See the discussion in Chapter 3.

20. Hewes 1977, p. 97.

21. Bender 1981 translates Aristotle's comment: "Those who become deaf from birth also become altogether speechless. Voice is certainly not lacking, but there is no speech" (p. 20). She notes that later translations, glossing the Greek *eneos* (speechless) as "dumb or stupid," altered the remark to read, "Those who are born deaf all become senseless and incapable of reason" (p. 21). Thus the overwhelming authority of Aristotle may have been perverted by his translators, with disastrous consequences for generations of born-deaf persons.

22. Romeo 1978, p. 356.

23. Flint 1979, p. 22, and Silverman 1978, p. 423.

24. Barakat 1975.

25. For the quotation and much of this history, I am indebted to the excellent article by Chaves and Soler (1975).

26. Some historians now offer Manuel Ramírez de Carrión, not Bonet, as the successor to Pedro de Ponce. Chaves and Soler 1975 characterize Carrión as "the first one to make a living in this profession." He hid his methods of instructing deaf children so assiduously that little is directly known of what he did; but apparently he did have great success. "His method was incorporated definitely in the history of western culture only when Juan Pablo Bonet, observing the progress of Don Luis [a born-deaf child of the nobility], and snatching information where

he could [,] put the method down in writing and published it in 1620" (Chaves and Soler 1975, p. 244).

27. Pertinent references to the Abbé will be found in Bender 1981, Flint 1979, Lane 1976 and 1977, and Silverman 1978.

28. Cited by Lane 1976, p. 79.

29. Lane 1977, p. 4.

30. Lane 1977, p. 4. For a slightly different version, see Bender 1981, p. 78.

31. Groce 1980, p. 12. See the earlier discussion in this chapter of sign languages that have emerged among isolated groups of people.

32. Like the size of the deaf population, the number of deaf schoolchildren depends upon the definition used. This estimate is actually the count of deaf and hard-of-hearing students issued by the Bureau of Education for the Handicapped, U.S. Department of Education, for 1982-83.

33. Lane (1980) has compiled a detailed, step-by-step account of attempts to suppress sign in France and in the United States. It is a dismal record, occasionally lightened by brave attempts to promote the use of sign in contradiction to prevailing sentiments. Lane expresses some bitterness of his own in a sardonic "Acknowledgments" that he has appended to that account: "I want to thank the individuals and federal agencies, notably the National Library of Medicine and the National Endowment for the Humanities, who, by maintaining that the deaf have neither a community nor a language but only a handicap and gestures, have redoubled my efforts to trace the social history of the American Sign Language of the Deaf" (p. 159).

34. The quotation and much of the factual material about Gallaudet College appear in its official history, prepared by then Chairman of the Board Albert W. Atwood on the occasion of the college's hundredth anniversary (Atwood 1964).

35. Christopher Garnett (1968) has brought together and translated the correspondence between Heinecke and Epée. The letters provide a fascinating account of two brilliant, opposing intellects.

36. The National Association of the Deaf and other organizations founded by deaf people are discussed in Chapter 9.

37. Conrad 1981, p. 13. See also the related discussions in Chapter 5.

38. The quotation is from Kannapell 1975. Her personal reminiscences may be found in Kannapell 1980. A sample: "Indirectly they [the hearing educators] communicated to me that if I wanted to succeed in a hearing world, I must talk well or at least write English well. I know that I was an 'oral failure' in the eyes of those people. I did not feel good about my speech and my English skills, but I tried hard to communicate with hearing people on their terms. I limited my facial expressions and body movements, was worried about using correct English, tried to use my voice, and was anxious to end conversations with them. Hearing people in general were always interested in how well I talked or heard or wrote

English. They didn't seem to be interested in making friends with me. The teachers always corrected the errors I made in writing or talking . . . They never sat down for a moment to chat with me or other students as friends" (pp. 106–7).

39. Stokoe 1980, pp. 266–67.

40. Eastman 1980, p. 32.

CHAPTER 5

1. Terminology related to sign language has not been standardized, a condition that reflects sign's recent attraction to scholars. In addition to *Manual English*, a term that was probably first used at the Washington State School for the Deaf (1972), you will see such names as *Manually Encoded English*, *Signed English*, *Siglish*, as well as the other names for artificial systems discussed in this chapter. Whatever the name, however, all of these terms indicate the same attempt to render English by signs, as opposed to *Ameslan*, which is a separate manual language. See Note 7 for more details on nomenclature.

2. Paget 1951 is not available in the United States and probably is out of print in England. The interested reader can obtain the current version of the system (Paget and Gorman 1968) from the Royal National Institute for the Deaf, 105 Gower Street, London WC1E 6AH.

3. David Anthony's original manuscript, completed while he was a student at the University of Michigan, has not been published. The updated version (Anthony 1971) was printed by the Anaheim (California) schools while he was a teacher there.

4. The statement that Ameslan lacks signs for certain function words is not completely accurate, as noted in Chapter 3. However, indicators such as gaze (used to designate the person being discussed) are not presently considered signs— that is, conventional manual expressions. Manual English systems provide specific hand signals for most such missing elements.

5. Gustason, Pfetzing, and Zawolkow 1972.

6. Wampler 1971.

7. *Siglish* is the creation of Lou Fant (1972b), who also coined *Ameslan*. *Signed English* is a term introduced at Gallaudet College (Bornstein et al. 1973). David Watson (1964) thought up the acronym *Ameslish*.

8. Statewide Project for the Deaf 1978.

9. Harry Bornstein and Karen Saulnier (1981) found that deaf children who were taught SEE did not use the complex markers regularly. They urge a more exploratory approach to the application of such systems to learning English. Another review criticizes Manual English for being much slower than Ameslan without a corresponding increase in information communicated (Caccamise et al. 1978). Gerilee Gustason, one of the creators of SEE II, reviews the research and her own data on that coding system; she concedes the evidence is mixed and

"raises far more questions than it answers," but feels it is too early to judge the potential efficacy of her system (Gustason 1980).

10. Barbara Kannapell (1975, 1980) has been a particularly strong proponent of *diglossia* (bilingualism). In a recent review of the research so far published on diglossia, Dorothy Lee finds the issues not yet resolved from a linguistic standpoint (Lee 1982). Stokoe 1976 explains why a resolution is not rapidly forthcoming: "The constant use of two languages . . . may be looked at from either end of a sociolinguistic telescope. In the broad view, it is a complicated social and political problem with a linguistic center and a very explosive potential, if peoples of two language stocks must live under one government. It is also, if looked at closely, a valuable skill of an individual person" (p. 22). Educationally, however, the decision to teach deaf children both English and Ameslan may well prove to be the best option for them and for society.

11. Much of the research has been summarized in Schlesinger and Meadow 1972 and Moores 1978. Of course, on an issue so critical to the welfare of children and so generally formulated, more evidence can be expected and, indeed, should be forthcoming. Thomas Kluwin has wisely cautioned against too early an appraisal of the concept underlying the use of Manual English: "The answer is not to say that because these systems do not work no system for representing English can work, but rather to say that since these systems have failed in the ways described above, a better system should be developed" (Kluwin 1981, p. 185). Deaf children differ widely among themselves, educational settings and their objectives are greatly disparate from place to place and time to time, and, as I hope this text has demonstrated, manual communication is not a unitary method but rather a number of different approaches that have all been subsumed under that one title. Thus, a single study or even a small group of studies cannot be expected to indicate decisively the best method to be used in educating a particular child in a particular subject at a particular time. Ignoring children's individual differences is the antithesis of Special Education.

12. Mead 1976.

13. Unification of Signs Commission 1975. The commission members were Josif Guejlman, U.S.S.R.; Allan B. Hayhurst, Great Britain; Willard J. Madsen, U.S.A.; Francesco Rubino, Italy; and, until his death, Ole M. Plum, Denmark. Perhaps because the committee's work was divided between five persons only, it accomplished the astonishing task of overcoming national linguistic prejudices and agreeing on a basic set of 1,470 signs in less than two years. The *lack* of funds, from government or other sources, and the great distances that separated committee members may also have contributed to the speed with which they worked.

14. Madsen 1976.

15. Unification of Signs Commission 1975 (Foreword).

16. Ibid.

CHAPTER 6

1. Guillory 1966.

2. Harry Hoemann 1978 and Charlotte Baker and Dennis Cokely 1980 comment on the role of fingerspelling in the curriculum for persons learning sign as a second language or new code. Both books recommend that its use be withheld until instruction in sign is well under way.

3. Caccamise and Blasdell 1978. An interesting comparison is with speechreading. For persons with normal vision, lipreading scores remain fairly constant up to a distance of about twenty to twenty-four feet (Berger 1972). Thus, when distance is the governing parameter, reading fingers is about three times more legible than reading lips.

4. Abernathy 1959.

5. Battison 1978.

6. How did Battison know the "correct" origin of the sign, especially if some native signers had a different explanation? His procedures are somewhat complex, but essentially they depend on asking informants for their independent judgments. These are then carefully analyzed until the consensus becomes clear. Battison also makes use of historical accounts to buttress his interpretations. When a large group of signs is analyzed in this way, the results are impressive in the regularity with which patterns emerge. It is the systematic nature of the data that justifies their claim to validity—a claim that a single example could not make.

7. Scouten 1967.

8. Cited in Scouten 1967, pp. 52–53.

9. McIntyre 1977.

10. The late Boris V. Morkovin (1968) brought back firsthand reports of Russian teaching methods. He emphasized the necessity of visitors' knowing Russian if they want to obtain an accurate perception of the activities shown them. As a White Russian officer who escaped after the Russian Revolution began, Morkovin had full command of the language; as a professional who had devoted most of his life to educating deaf children, he was also eminently able to understand from a heuristic vantage what he was observing. Regrettably he died before he had the opportunity to disclose fully his views of an extensive tour he made of Russian educational facilities for deaf students.

11. For an extensive treatment of all aspects of speechreading (or lipreading, as it is also called), see Berger 1972.

12. Cornett 1967.

13. Moores 1978 and Nash 1973 are two sources of Cued Speech criticism. Cornett has occasionally replied to denigrators of his approach (1973), but his principal response to opponents has been to persist in his efforts to disseminate and research it. A newsletter, *Cued Speech News*, keeps those interested up to date about the technique. It can be ordered from Cued Speech Programs, Gallaudet College, Washington, D.C. 20002.

14. Ling 1976.

15. One was Friar Bernard of Saint Gabriel, the other a Monsieur Fourcade (Wilbur 1979).

16. Wilbur 1979.

17. Romeo 1978.

18. Kendon 1975.

19. In fairness, I must confess that the curator of the Daniel Chester French home-studio, in Stockbridge, Massachusetts, disagrees with the "Lincoln's hands story." He regards it as an attractive myth, and referred me to Packard 1965. Packard concluded that the A hand results from the model's holding a broomstick. About the L hand, Packard has no convincing explanation. That French was aware of Amanubet is not disputed. There the argument must rest, since the only indisputable authority on the story's truth, French, is dead.

20. Romeo 1978.

21. A thorough presentation of methods and devices used to communicate with persons whose vision *and* hearing are severely diminished or absent will be found in Kates and Schein 1980.

CHAPTER 7

1. This statement about the difficulties of sign vs. speech learning is somewhat ambiguous, because it covers three problems: learning sign as a first language, learning sign as a second language, and comparing the perceptuo-motor abilities required by each. As the chapter proceeds, the issue should become clearer.

2. Madsen 1976b. For a brief account of the first classes funded by the federal government to teach sign to the general public, see Schein 1981.

3. Brennan and Hayhurst 1980.

4. Karl Diller sagely notes that "a warm, nonthreatening, supportive environment is more important than method in language learning" and that "the teacher's focus should be more on morale than on linguistic content" (1981, p. 79).

5. For a current listing of qualified teachers in your area, write to Communicative Skills Program, National Association of the Deaf, 814 Thayer Avenue, Silver Spring, Md. 20910. The director of that program has also published advice on selecting a sign class (Carter 1981).

6. Bernice Feldman 1978 has described the New York University experience with intensive sign-language instruction. Various linguistic researchers have acknowledged the potency of intensive or "immersion" approaches to other foreign-language learning (Diller 1981; Lambert 1981).

7. A survey of 7,181 classes for deaf students in the United States found that 4,774 (about two thirds) were using manual communication. Of these, nearly two thirds had changed to some form of manual communication in the period

1968–75, offering substantial evidence of the trend toward its use in the classroom (Jordan, Gustason, and Rosen 1976).

   8. Winitz 1981.

   9. Lambert 1981.

   10. McLaughlin 1981. Another reviewer cites a study suggesting that "college students may be five times faster than nine-year-olds in learning foreign languages" (Diller 1981, p. 76).

   11. Diller 1981, p. 84.

   12. Studies have found that individuals who score high on empathy scales score higher than others on the ability to speak a second language (Taylor et al. 1971). The data from that research coincide with H. Douglas Brown's position that affective variables—empathy being among the most influential of these—play a sizable role in determining achievement in second-language acquisition (Brown 1973). Motivation, too, is an emotion. With rare exceptions (and these exceptions are considered pathological), children display a strong desire to acquire their native language. That tendency probably plays a large part in their obvious ability to learn other languages (Diller 1981). Babies born in one culture and moved at infancy to another will learn the language of the second culture. Children raised in bilingual homes, provided the two languages are both socially acceptable, will learn both. What appears to be genetic in humans is the motivation to communicate and, hence, to acquire languages.

   13. Kinsbourne 1981.

   14. Lambert 1981, p. 19.

CHAPTER 8

   1. For more information about rehabilitation practices in the United States, see Schein 1980.

   2. This thesis was advanced in two books by the same author, Frank Bowe (1978, 1980). Dr. Bowe, himself deaf, was the first director of the American Coalition of Citizens with Disabilities. The ACCD has tried to bring together all disabled people in their struggle for civil rights.

   3. Smith 1964.

   4. Frederick C. Schreiber in Schein 1981, p. 50.

   5. Lauritsen 1976 and Romano 1975. Because the National Technical Institute for the Deaf (at Rochester Institute of Technology) only trained interpreters for service in its own classrooms, it declined to join the consortium. NTID's contributions to research on interpreting and to preparation of interpreters, however, should not be overlooked.

   6. Possibly the first published curriculum for interpreter training was Sternberg, Tipton, and Schein 1973. That it appeared only so recently is a measure of the public's and the professionals' neglect of interpreting.

7. Registry of Interpreters for the Deaf 1980.

8. A provocative article by Carol Tipton (1974) influenced the revision of RID's Code of Ethics. Copies of the current standards can be obtained from RID, 814 Thayer Avenue, Silver Spring, Md. 20910.

9. By 1912, in the United States, the Episcopal Church had ordained eighteen deaf ministers; the Lutheran Church, six; the Methodist Church, four; and the Baptist Church, one. The Catholic Church, despite its seminal educational programs for deaf children, did not ordain a deaf priest until 1977.

10. *Talk to the Deaf* (Riekehof 1963) was preceded by J. W. Michaels' *A Handbook of the Sign Language of the Deaf* (1923), also sponsored by a Baptist organization.

11. Espy 1972, p. 203.

12. Espy 1972, p. 272.

13. Kates and Schein 1980.

14. The January 1974 issue (Vol. 7, No. 3) of the *Journal of Rehabilitation of the Deaf* contains twelve articles on interpreting, only two of which are on research. Since that issue, it has printed only one other study of interpreting. In the last five years, *American Annals of the Deaf* did not publish a single research article on interpreting. Also interesting by their absence are studies on the attitudes of deaf persons toward the interpreting process and interpreters.

15. Most of the literature contains reports of single cases of autistic children who have been aided by signed communication (for example, Casey 1978; Cohen 1981; Webster et al. 1973; Wolf 1979). An unusual study is the report of sign used with nineteen mute autistic children (Miller and Miller 1973). All learned to sign and respond to signs; some later developed usable speech. Nonetheless, the researchers felt compelled to conclude their recitation of the excellent outcome with a defense of sign: "We suggest that the inability of a mute autistic child to attain meaningful speech via signs does not invalidate their use. The signs offer such children the means of understanding both signs *and* spoken language as well as the possibility of communicating with other people. Without such human contact, most mute autistic children tend to lapse into states in which they pass their days rocking back and forth and twiddling objects" (p. 84). A review of data on over one hundred mute autistic children confirms their ability to acquire expressive and receptive sign, an astonishing affirmation of the value of this approach to one of psychiatry's most difficult syndromes (Bonvillian, Nelson, and Rhyne 1981).

16. Grinnell, Detamore, and Lippke 1976, p. 124. Contrasting mentally retarded with autistic children proves confusing when an estimated three fourths of autistic children also receive diagnoses of mental retardation. The important point: both autistic and mentally retarded children who do not speak learn sign.

17. Caplan 1977, Hanson 1976, Markowicz 1973, Wepman 1976, and Winitz 1976. These scientists advance evidence of the effectiveness of nonvocal ap-

proaches, generally sign, with aphasic patients, and they offer several theoretical rationales to explain why vocal therapies may fail where nonvocal therapies succeed, even with patients who had previously mastered speech.

18. Fristoe and Lloyd (1978) and Goodman, Wilson, and Bornstein (1978) conducted surveys that reveal the widespread use of sign with a variety of severe communication problems. Benson Schaeffer (1978 and 1980) has added curricular emphasis to the literature, with empirical and theoretical support for the use of sign with all nonvocal persons.

19. The depth of revulsion from sign is revealed in the statement of one speech clinician who writes in a respected professional journal: "It is, of course, difficult for family members to comprehend that a handicapped person may lack skills which a lower animal possesses" (Stengelvik 1976, p. 471). An article in the same journal is entitled "If a chimp can learn sign language, surely my nonverbal client can too" (Mayberry 1976). In spite of its title, however, the article soberly considers the possibilities for using sign in clinical practice and, while cautioning it is not a panacea, does acknowledge the evidence of its efficacy.

20. The National Theatre of the Deaf publishes biographies of deaf actors and makes them available for casting purposes.

21. Tadie 1978.

22. Cited in Tadie 1978, p. 204.

23. Cited in Tadie 1978, p. 205.

24. How well deaf actors respond to the opportunities given them is shown by Elizabeth Quinn, who replaced Phyllis Frelich in the London production of *Children of a Lesser God*. Quinn won the Society of West End Theatre Critics' Actress of the Year Award (the British equivalent of the Tony), an amazing achievement in view of the high quality of the competition and the fact that she was an alien.

25. See "Home Office Notes" in *The Deaf American*, September 1979.

CHAPTER 9

1. These and subsequent data in this chapter are taken from Schein and Delk 1974, unless otherwise noted. The estimates used are rounded off. Readers wishing more precise figures should consult the sources cited.

2. This statement is no longer strictly true. Some state laws have been passed recently to lower telephone rates for users of telephones adapted for the deaf consumer, and there may be other, somewhat obscure laws, such as the one in New York State that gives some privileges to deaf persons in recreation programs. Most such laws do not define deafness; they only name it. The same holds true for federal laws that mention deaf persons but do not specify the criteria for judging who is deaf.

3. For a lengthy exposition of the definitional problem, see Schein 1968 or Schein and Delk 1974.

4. In addition to Schein and Delk 1974, the National Center for Health Statistics occasionally publishes information about deafness from its National Health Survey. (The government publications, however, contain little or no social or psychological data.) Also, Gallaudet College gathers statistics on hearing-impaired children in schools through its voluntary Annual Survey of Hearing Impaired Children and Youth. See Appendix C for its address.

5. Paul Higgins (1980), a sociologist, sets three criteria for membership in the deaf community: identification (acknowledging one's deafness), shared experiences (particularly during the formative years), and participation in the community's affairs.

6. Kathryn Meadow (1980) reviews the development of the deaf child, citing these and other studies, to highlight the hearing parent–deaf child communication problems.

7. Several studies have noted this, and the medical profession is taking steps to remedy the situation. Eugene Mindel and McCay Vernon (1971) and Hilde Schlesinger and Kathryn Meadow (1972) are excellent beginning points for further study of this and related points. The misdiagnosis of deaf infants and young children remains a serious concern. In January 1982, the New York State Court of Claims awarded $2.5 million to Donald Snow, a seventeen-year-old deaf boy who had been diagnosed an "imbecile" at two years of age and put into an institution for the mentally retarded until he was almost eleven years old. At that age he was transferred to another institution, where a routine psychological examination revealed he was "at least of normal intelligence." The monetary restitution by the state can hardly compensate him for the nine years he lost during his developing years.

8. Three Canadian doctors have recently published a text strongly urging the use of sign with deaf children (Freeman, Carbin, and Boese 1981). Another view suggests that parents' decision on how to communicate with their child should not be based on general recommendations, but on consideration of their particular child (Naiman and Schein 1978). The issues are complex and stimulate a great deal of emotion. Indisputably, parent-child communication, however achieved, is vital.

9. One of the earliest investigations of deaf children of deaf parents was done by Kathryn Meadow; her book (cited in Note 6) is a good source of related material.

10. History has shown how unwise it can be to apply general solutions to an individual's problems. How to manage a deaf child should be determined only with regard to that child. Deafness does not homogenize people.

11. McCay Vernon (1974) summarizes the evidence, and Louis Fant and John Schuchman (1974) add personal recollections of their experiences as hearing children of deaf parents.

12. The quotation is from a speech to parents of deaf children made by Frank

Bowe (1973), who never saw another deaf child until he was a college student;
he was educated, as educational jargon now puts it, "in the mainstream."

13. A directory of these programs can be obtained from Gallaudet College
(Rawlings, Trybus, and Biser 1981). An article portraying the situation from 1900
to 1960 revealed that proportionally more deaf students went on to college earlier
in the century than later (Schein and Bushnaq 1962). That is no longer the case.

14. The official account of the college's first hundred years was written on
the occasion of its centennial by its then chairman of the board, Albert Atwood
(1964). Another, briefer account will be found in the book by Jack Gannon (1981).

15. The following states now have special agencies devoted to deafness (with
the year of their founding shown in parentheses): Arizona (1977), Connecticut
(1975), Iowa (1972), Kansas (1982), Kentucky (1982), Louisiana (1981), Massachusetts (1971), Michigan (1979), Nebraska (1979), New Jersey (1977), North
Carolina (1976), Oklahoma (1976), Tennessee (1978), Texas (1971), Virginia
(1972), and Wisconsin (1980). These agencies are legal entities set up by the
states' legislatures. They should not be confused with state associations of deaf
people, which are voluntary groups.

16. Substantial amounts of information were gathered in interviews with
eighty-seven early-deafened executives. Their responses confirmed the prejudices
they faced and divulged their techniques for overcoming the barriers placed in
the way of their advancement (Crammatte 1968).

17. Gannon 1981. This excellent history of deafness in the United States
provided much of the information on deaf sports figures cited here; it also contains
a wealth of data on the social and cultural lives of deaf people.

18. Over a ten-year period, Reverend Guilbert C. Braddock wrote one
hundred biographies of eminent deaf men, Ballard among them. The Gallaudet
College Alumni Association gathered them together and published them with
funds subscribed to celebrate the centennial of their alma mater, in 1964 (Braddock
1975).

19. Cohen, Namir, and Schlesinger 1977.

20. In addition to humor, poetry can be signed in a way that gives its expression
another dimension of meaning (Klima and Bellugi 1979).

21. The quotation is from Dr. Schreiber's collected papers, which were published in conjunction with his biography (Schein 1981).

REFERENCES

Abernathy, E. A. "An historical sketch of the manual alphabets," *American Annals of the Deaf*, 1959, *104*, 232–40.

Anthony, David. *Seeing Essential English*. Vols. I and II. Anaheim, Cal.: Anaheim Union School District, 1971.

Atwood, Albert W. *Gallaudet College: Its First One Hundred Years*. Washington, D.C.: Gallaudet College, 1964.

Babbini, Barbara E. *An Introductory Course in Manual Communication*. Northridge, Cal.: San Fernando Valley State College, 1965.

Baker, Charlotte. "What's not on the other hand in American Sign Language." In S. Mufwene, C. Walker, and S. Steever (eds.), *Papers from the Twelfth Regional Meeting of the Chicago Linguistic Society*. Chicago: University of Chicago Press, 1976.

Baker, C., and R. Battison. *Sign Language and the Deaf Community*. Silver Spring, Md.: National Association of the Deaf, 1980.

Baker, Charlotte, and Dennis Cokely. *American Sign Language: A Teacher's Resource Text on Grammar and Culture*. Silver Spring, Md.: TJ Publishers, 1980.

Barakat, Robert A. "On ambiguity in the Cistercian sign language," *Sign Language Studies*, 1975, *8*, 275–89.

Battison, Robin. *Lexical Borrowing in American Sign Language*. Silver Spring, Md.: Linstok Press, 1978.

Battison, Robin, and I. K. Jordan. "Cross-cultural communication with foreign signers: Fact and fancy," *Sign Language Studies*, 1976, *10*, 53–68.

Battison, Robin, Harry Markowicz, and James Woodward. "A good rule of thumb." In R. Shuy and R. Fasold (eds.), *New Ways of Analyzing Variation in English II*. Washington, D.C.: Georgetown University Press, 1975.

Bender, Ruth E. *The Conquest of Deafness* (3rd ed.). Danville, Ill.: Interstate Printers & Publishers, 1981.

Berger, K. W. *Speechreading Principles and Methods*. Baltimore: National Educational Press, 1972.

Bickerton, Derek. *Roots of Language*. Ann Arbor, Mich.: Karoma Publishers, 1981.

Bonvillian, John D. "Review of *The Education of Koko*," *Sign Language Studies*, 1982, 34, 7–14.

Bonvillian, John D., Keith E. Nelson, and Jane M. Rhyne. "Sign language and autism," *Journal of Autism and Developmental Disorders*, 1981, 11, 125–37.

Bornstein, H., and L. Hamilton. "Some recent national dictionaries of sign language," *Sign Language Studies*, 1972, 1, 42–63.

Bornstein, H., L. Hamilton, B. Kannapell, H. Roy, and K. Saulnier. *Basic Pre-School Signed English Dictionary*. Washington, D.C.: Gallaudet College, 1973.

Bornstein, Harry, and Karen L. Saulnier. "Signed English: A brief follow-up to the first evaluation," *American Annals of the Deaf*, 1981, 126, 69–72.

Bowe, Frank G. "Crisis of the deaf child and his family." In *The Deaf Child and His Family*. Washington, D.C.: Rehabilitation Services Administration, 1973.

Bowe, Frank G. *Handicapping America*. New York: Harper & Row, 1978.

Bowe, Frank G. *Rehabilitating America*. New York: Harper & Row, 1980.

Braddock, Guilbert C. *Notable Deaf Persons*. Washington, D.C.: Gallaudet College Alumni Association, 1975.

Brennan, Mary, and Martin Colville. "A British Sign Language research project," *Sign Language Studies*, 1979, 24, 253–72.

Brennan, Mary, and Alvin B. Hayhurst. "The renaissance of British Sign Language." In Charlotte Baker and Robin Battison (eds.), *Sign Language and the Deaf Community*. Silver Spring, Md.: National Association of the Deaf, 1980.

Brown, H. Douglas. "Affective variables in second language acquisition," *Language Learning*, 1973, 2, 231–34.

Brown, James S. *A Vocabulary of Mute Signs*. Baton Rouge, La.: Morning Comet, 1856.

Brown, Roger. "Development of the first language in the human species," *American Psychologist*, 1973, 28, 97–106.

Bruner, Jerome, and Carol F. Feldman. "Where does language come from?" *The New York Review of Books*, June 24, 1982, 34–36.

Bulwer, John B. *Chirologia or the Natural Language of the Hand*. London: Tho. Harper, 1644.

Bulwer, John B. *Philocophus, or the Deafe and Dumbe Man's Friend*. London: Humphrey Moseley, 1648.

Caccamise, F., and R. Blasdell. "Distance and reception of fingerspelling," *American Annals of the Deaf*, 1978, *123*, 873–76.

Caccamise, Frank, Robert Ayers, Karen Finch, and Marilyn Mitchell. "Signs and manual communication systems: Selection, standardization, and development," *American Annals of the Deaf*, 1978, *123*, 877–99.

Caplan, Bruce. "Cerebral localization, cognitive strategy and reading ability." Doctoral dissertation. New York University School of Education, Health, Nursing and Arts Professions, 1977.

Carter, S. Melvin. "On selecting a sign language class—Part II," *The Deaf American*, 1981, *34*(2), 23–25.

Casey, LaDeane O. "Development of communicative behavior in autistic children: A parent program using manual signs," *Journal of Autism and Childhood Schizophrenia*, 1978, *8*, 45–60.

Chaves, Teresa L., and Jorge L. Soler. "Manuel Ramirez de Carrión (1579–1652?) and his secret method of teaching the deaf," *Sign Language Studies*, 1975, *8*, 235–48.

Clark, W. P. *The Indian Sign Language*. Philadelphia: L. R. Harmsley, 1884.

Cohen, Einya, Lila, Namir, and I. M. Schlesinger. *A New Dictionary of Sign Language*. The Hague, Netherlands: Mouton, 1977.

Cohen, Morris. "Development of language behavior in an autistic child using Total Communication," *Exceptional Children*, 1981, *47*, 379–81.

Conrad, R. "Sign language in education: Some consequent problems." In B. Woll, J. Kyle, and M. Deuchar (eds.), *Perspectives on British Sign Language and Deafness*. London: Croom Helm, 1981.

Cornett, R. O. "Cued Speech," *American Annals of the Deaf*, 1967, *112*, 3–13.

Cornett, R. O. "Comments on the Nash case study," *Sign Language Studies*, 1973, *3*, 93–98.

Crammatte, A. B. *Deaf Persons in Professional Employment*. Springfield, Ill.: Charles C Thomas, 1968.

Crystal, D., and E. Craig. "Contrived sign language." In I. M. Schlesinger and L. Namir (eds.), *Sign Language of the Deaf*. New York: Academic Press, 1978.

Crystal, David (ed.). *Eric Partridge in His Own Words*. New York: Macmillan, 1980.

Cutting, J. E., and J. F. Kavanagh. "On the relationship of speech to language," *Asha*, 1975, *17*, 500–6.

Dee, A., I. Rapin, and R. J. Ruben. "Speech and language development in a parent-infant Total Communication program," *Annals of Otology, Rhinology & Laryngology*, 1982, *91* (5, Supplement 97), 62–72.

Deuchar, Margaret. "Variation in British Sign Language." In B. Woll, J.

Kyle, and M. Deuchar (eds.), *Perspectives on British Sign Language and Deafness*. London: Croom Helm, 1981.

Diller, Karl. " 'Natural methods' of foreign-language teaching: Can they exist? What criteria must they meet?" *Annals of the New York Academy of Sciences*, 1981, 379, 75–86.

Dyer, Eugene R. "Sign Language agglutination: A brief look at ASL and Turkish," *Sign Language Studies*, 1976, *11*, 133–48.

Eastman, Gilbert C. "From student to professional: A personal chronicle of sign language." In C. Baker and R. Battison (eds.), *Sign Language and the Deaf Community*. Silver Spring, Md.: National Association of the Deaf, 1980.

Fant, Louie J. *Ameslan*. Silver Spring, Md.: National Association of the Deaf, 1972a.

Fant, Louie J. "The American Sign Language," *California News*, 1972b, 83(5), 18–21.

Fant, Louie J., and John S. Schuchman. "Experiences of two hearing children of deaf parents." In Peter J. Fine (ed.), *Deafness in Infancy and Early Childhood*. New York: MEDCOM Press, 1974.

Feldman, Bernice K. "An investigation of the relationship among some demographic and psychological factors and the acquisition of sign language by physically normal adults enrolled in manual communication training programs." Doctoral dissertation. New York University, 1978.

Fine, Peter J. (ed.) *Deafness in Infancy and Early Childhood*. New York: MEDCOM Press, 1974.

Flint, Richard W. "History of education for the hearing impaired." In L. J. Bradford and W. G. Hardy (eds.), *Hearing and Hearing Impairment*. New York: Grune & Stratton, 1979.

Fouts, Roger S., and Roger L. Mellgren. "Language, signs, and cognition in the chimpanzee," *Sign Language Studies*, 1976, *13*, 319–46.

Freeman, Roger D., Clifton F. Carbin, and Robert J. Boese. *Can't Your Child Hear?* Baltimore: University Park Press, 1981.

Friedman, Lynn A. *On the Other Hand*. New York: Academic Press, 1977.

Frishberg, Nancy. "Arbitrariness and iconicity: Historical change in American Sign Language," *Language*, 1975, *51*, 676–710.

Frishberg, Nancy. "Some aspects of the historical development of signs in American Sign Language." Doctoral dissertation. University of California at San Diego, 1976.

Frishberg, Nancy. "The case of the missing length." In R. Wilbur (ed.), *Sign Language Research*. Special issue of *Communication and Cognition*, 1978.

Frishberg, Nancy, and Betty Gough. "Time on our hands." Paper delivered at the Third Annual California Linguistics Conference. Stanford, Cal., 1973.

Fristoe, Macalyne, and Lyle L. Lloyd. "A survey of the use of non-speech systems with the severely communication impaired," *Mental Retardation*, 1978, *16*, 99–103.

Gannon, Jack R. *Deaf Heritage*. Silver Spring, Md.: National Association of the Deaf, 1981.

Garnett, Christopher B. *The Exchange of Letters Between Samuel Heinecke and Abbé Charles Michel de l'Epée*. New York: Vantage Press, 1968.

Gaustad, Gregory R. "Review of *Nim*," *Sign Language Studies*, 1981, 30, 89–94.

Gaustad, Gregory R. "Reply to Herbert S. Terrace," *Sign Language Studies*, 1982, 35, 180–82.

Gill, T., and D. Rumbaugh. "Mastery of naming skills in a chimpanzee," *Journal of Human Evolution*, 1974, 3, 482–92.

Goldin-Meadow, Susan, and Heidi Feldman. "The development of language-like communication without a language model," *Science*, 1977, 197, 401–3.

Goodman, Linda, Paula S. Wilson, and Harry Bornstein. "Results of a national survey of sign language programs in special education," *Mental Retardation*, 1978, 16, 104–6.

Gould, James L. "Honey bee recruitment: The dance-language controversy," *Science*, 1975, 189, 685–92.

Grinnell, Mary F., K. L. Detamore, and B. A. Lippke. "Sign it successful— Manual English encourages expressive communication," *Teaching Exceptional Children*, 1976, 8, 123–24.

Groce, Nora. "Everyone here spoke sign language," *Natural History*, 1980, 89(6), 10–16.

Guillory, LaVera M. *Expressive and Receptive Fingerspelling for Hearing Adults*. Baton Rouge, La.: Claitor's Bookstore, 1966.

Gustason, Gerilee. "Does Signing Exact English work?" *Teaching English to the Deaf*, 1980, 7(1), 16–20.

Gustason, Gerilee, D. Pfetzing, and E. Zawolkow. *Signing Exact English*. Rossmoor, Cal.: Modern Signs Press, 1972.

Hansen, Britta. "Research on Danish Sign Language and its impact on the deaf community in Denmark." In C. Baker and R. Battison (eds.), *Sign Language and the Deaf Community*. Silver Spring, Md.: National Association of the Deaf, 1980.

Hanson, Wayne R. "Measuring gestural communication in a brain-injured adult." Videotape demonstration. American Speech and Hearing Association Convention, November 22, 1976.

Hewes, Gordon W. "Gesture language in culture contact," *Sign Language Studies*, 1974a, 4, 1–34.

Hewes, Gordon W. "Language in early hominids." In Roger W. Wescott (ed.), *Language Origins*. Silver Spring, Md.: Linstok Press, 1974b.

Hewes, Gordon W. "A model for language evolution," *Sign Language Studies*, 1977, 15, 97–168.

Higgins, Daniel D. *How to Talk to the Deaf*. St. Louis: Private publication, 1923.

Higgins, Paul C. *Outsiders in a Hearing World*. Beverly Hills, Cal.: Sage, 1980.

Hill, Jane H. "Hominid protolinguistic capacities." In Roger W. Wescott (ed.), *Language Origins*, Silver Spring, Md.: Linstok Press, 1974.

Hill, Jane H. "Apes, wolves, birds, and humans: Toward a comparative foundation for a functional theory of language evolution," *Sign Language Studies*, 1977, *14*, 21–58.

Hoemann, Harry W. "The transparency of meaning of sign language gestures," *Sign Language Studies*, 1975, 7, 151–61.

Hoemann, Harry W. *Communicating with Deaf People*. Baltimore: University Park Press, 1978.

Hoemann, Harry, and Rosemarie Lucafo. *I Want to Talk*. Silver Spring, Md.: National Association of the Deaf, 1980.

Holmes, Kathleen M., and David W. Holmes. "Signed and spoken language development in a hearing child of hearing parents," *Sign Language Studies*, 1980, 28, 239–54.

Jordan, I. King, and Robin Battison. "A referential communication experiment with foreign sign languages," *Sign Language Studies*, 1976, *10*, 69–80.

Jordan, I. King, Gerilee Gustason, and Roslyn Rosen. "Current communication trends at programs for the deaf," *American Annals of the Deaf*, 1976, *121*, 527–32.

Kannapell, Barbara M. "The effects of using stigmatized language." In *Deafpride Papers: Perspectives and Options*. Washington, D.C.: Deafpride, Inc., 1975.

Kannapell, Barbara M. "Personal awareness and advocacy in the deaf community." In C. Baker and R. Battison (eds.), *Sign Language and the Deaf Community*. Silver Spring, Md.: National Association of the Deaf, 1980.

Kannapell, Barbara M., Lillian B. Hamilton, and Harry Bornstein. *Signs for Instructional Purposes*. Washington, D.C.: Gallaudet College Press, 1979.

Kates, L., and J. D. Schein. *A Complete Guide to Communication with Deaf-Blind Persons*. Silver Spring, Md.: National Association of the Deaf, 1980.

Kendon, Adam. "Gesticulation, speech, and the gesture theory of language origins," *Sign Language Studies*, 1975, 9, 349–73.

Kendon, Adam. "The sign language of the women of Yuendumu: A preliminary report on the structure of Warlpiri Sign Language," *Sign Language Studies*, 1980, 27, 101–12.

Kinsbourne, Marcel. "Neuropsychological aspects of bilingualism," *Annals of the New York Academy of Sciences*, 1981, 379, 50–58.

Klima, E., and U. Bellugi. *The Signs of Language*. Cambridge, Mass.: Harvard University Press, 1979.

Kluwin, Thomas N. "A rationale for modifying classroom signing systems," *Sign Language Studies*, 1981, 31, 179–87.

Kushel, Rolf. "The silent inventor: The creation of a sign language by the only deaf-mute on a Polynesian island," *Sign Language Studies*, 1973, 3, 1–28.

Laird, Charlton. "Language and the dictionary." In David B. Guralnik (ed.), *Webster's New World Dictionary* (2nd ed.). New York: The World, 1970.

Lambert, Wallace E. "Bilingualism and language acquisition," *Annals of the New York Academy of Sciences*, 1981, 379, 9–22.

Lane, Harlan. *The Wild Boy of Aveyron*. Cambridge, Mass.: Harvard University Press, 1976.

Lane, Harlan. "Notes for a psycho-history of American Sign Language," *The Deaf American*, 1977, 29(1), 3–7.

Lane, Harlan. "A chronology of the oppression of sign language in France and the United States." In H. Lane and F. Grosjean (eds.), *Recent Perspectives on American Sign Language*. Hillsdale, N.J.: Lawrence Erlbaum Associates, 1980.

Lane, Harlan, and Francois Grosjean (eds.). *Recent Perspectives on American Sign Language*. Hillsdale, N.J.: Lawrence Erlbaum Associates, 1980.

Lauritsen, Robert R. "The National Interpreter Training Consortium." In F. B. and A. B. Crammatte (eds.), *Seventh World Congress of the World Federation of the Deaf*. Silver Spring, Md.: National Association of the Deaf, 1976.

Lee, Dorothy. "Are there signs of diglossia? Re-examining the situation," *Sign Language Studies*, 1982, 35, 127–52.

Lewis, Flora. "Speaking in tongues," New York *Times*, February 4, 1982, A33.

Ling, D. *Speech and the Hearing-Impaired Child: Theory and Practice*. Washington, D.C.: A. G. Bell Association for the Deaf, 1976.

Long, J. Schuyler. *The Sign Language: A Manual of Signs*. Council Bluffs, Iowa: Private publication, 1909.

Madsen, Willard J. "Report on the International Dictionary of Sign Language." In F. B. and A. B. Crammatte (eds.), *Seventh World Congress of the World Federation of the Deaf*. Silver Spring, Md.: National Association of the Deaf, 1976a.

Madsen, Willard J. "The teaching of sign language to hearing adults." In F. B. and A. B. Crammatte (eds.), *Seventh World Congress of the World Federation of the Deaf*. Silver Spring, Md.: National Association of the Deaf, 1976b.

Maestas y Moores, Julia. "Early linguistic environments: Interactions of deaf parents with their infants," *Sign Language Studies*, 1980, 26, 1–13.

Mallery, Garrick. "Sign language among North American Indians." In J. W. Powell (ed.), *First Annual Report of the Bureau of Ethnology to the Secretary of the Smithsonian Institution, 1879–80*. Washington, D.C.: Government Printing Office, 1881.

Markowicz, Harry. "Aphasia and deafness," *Sign Language Studies*, 1973, 3, 61–71.

Mayberry, Rachel. "If a chimp can learn sign language, surely my nonverbal client can too," *Asha*, 1976, *18*, 223–28.

McIntyre, Marina L. "The acquisition of American Sign Language hand configurations," *Sign Language Studies*, 1977, *16*, 247–66.

McLaughlin, Barry. "Differences and similarities between first- and second-language learning," *Annals of the New York Academy of Sciences*, 1981, *379*, 23–32.

Mead, Margaret. "Unispeak: The need for a universal second language," *Mainliner*, 1976 (July), 17–18.

Meadow, Kathryn P. "Name signs as identity symbols in the deaf community," *Sign Language Studies*, 1977, *16*, 237–46.

Meadow, Kathryn P. *Deafness and Child Development*. Berkeley, Cal.: University of California Press, 1980.

Meissner, Martin, and Stuart B. Philpott. "A dictionary of sawmill workers' signs," *Sign Language Studies*, 1975, *9*, 309–47.

Michaels, J. W. A *Handbook of the Sign Language of the Deaf*. Atlanta: Southern Baptist Convention, 1923.

Miller, A., and Eileen E. Miller. "Cognitive-developmental training with elevated boards and sign language," *Journal of Autism and Childhood Schizophrenia*, 1973, *3*, 65–85.

Mindel, E. D., and M. Vernon. *They Grow in Silence*. Silver Spring, Md.: National Association of the Deaf, 1971.

Moores, Donald F. *Educating the Deaf*. Boston: Houghton Mifflin, 1978.

Morkovin, Boris V. "Language in the general development of the preschool deaf child: A review of research in the Soviet Union," *Asha*, 1968, *10*, 195–99.

Naiman, D., and J. D. Schein. *For Parents of Deaf Children*. Silver Spring, Md.: National Association of the Deaf, 1978.

Nash, Jeffrey E. "Cues or sign: A case study in language acquisition," *Sign Language Studies*, 1973, *3*, 79–92.

Packard, Harry. "The incident of the broom handle," *Yankee Magazine*, 1965, *10*, 17–19.

Padden, Carol. "Some arguments for syntactic patterning in American Sign Language," *Sign Language Studies*, 1981, *32*, 239–59.

Paget, Richard. *The New Sign Language*. London, England: The Welcome Foundation, 1951.

Paget, Richard, and Pierre Gorman. A *Systematic Sign Language*. London, England: Royal National Institute for the Deaf, 1968.

Prinz, Philip M., and Elizabeth Prinz. "Simultaneous acquisition of ASL and spoken English (in a hearing child of a deaf mother and hearing father)," *Sign Language Studies*, 1979, *25*, 283–96.

Rawlings, Brenda W., Raymond J. Trybus, and James Biser. A *Guide to College/Career Programs for Deaf Students*. Washington, D.C.: Gallaudet College, 1981.

Registry of Interpreters for the Deaf, Inc. *A Resource Guide for Interpreter Training for the Deaf Programs*. Silver Spring, Md.: Private publication, 1980.

Riekehof, Lottie L. *Talk to the Deaf*. Springfield, Mo.: Gospel Publishing House, 1963.

Riekehof, Lottie L. *The Joy of Signing*. Springfield, Mo.: Gospel Publishing House, 1978.

Romano, F. "Interpreter consortium; A sign for the future," *Social and Rehabilitation Record*, 1975, 2(1), 10.

Romeo, Luigi. "For a medieval history of gesture communication," *Sign Language Studies*, 1978, 21, 353–80.

Rosen, Lillian. *Just Like Everybody Else*. New York: Harcourt Brace Jovanovich, 1981.

Sallagoity, Pierre. "The sign language of Southern France," *Sign Language Studies*, 1975, 7, 181–202.

Sarles, Harvey B. "On the problem: The origin of language," *Sign Language Studies*, 1976, 11, 149–81.

Schaeffer, Benson. "Teaching spontaneous sign language to nonverbal children: Theory and method," *Sign Language Studies*, 1978, 21, 317–52.

Schaeffer, Benson. "Teaching signed speech to nonverbal children: Theory and method," *Sign Language Studies*, 1980, 26, 29–63.

Schein, J. D. *The Deaf Community*. Washington, D.C.: Gallaudet College Press, 1968.

Schein, J. D. "The deaf community." In H. Davis and S. R. Silverman (eds.), *Hearing and Deafness*. New York: Holt, Rinehart & Winston, 1978.

Schein, J. D. *Model State Plan for Rehabilitation of Deaf Clients* (2nd revision). Silver Spring, Md.: National Association of the Deaf, 1980.

Schein, J. D. "Society and culture of hearing-impaired people." In L. J. Bradford and W. G. Hardy (eds.), *Hearing and Hearing Impairment*. New York: Grune & Stratton, 1979.

Schein, J. D. *A Rose for Tomorrow: Biography of Frederick C. Schreiber*. Silver Spring, Md.: National Association of the Deaf, 1981.

Schein, J. D., and S. M. Bushnaq. "Higher education of the deaf in the United States: A retrospective investigation," *American Annals of the Deaf*, 1962, 107, 416–20.

Schein, J. D., and M. T. Delk. *The Deaf Population of the United States*. Silver Spring, Md.: National Association of the Deaf, 1974.

Schein, J. D., and M. M. Miller. "Rehabilitation and management of auditory disorders." In Frederic J. Kottke (ed.), *Krusen's Handbook of Physical Medicine and Rehabilitation* (3rd ed.). Philadelphia: W. B. Saunders, 1982.

Schlesinger, H., and K. P. Meadow. *Sound and Sign*. Berkeley, Cal.: University of California Press, 1972.

Scouten, E. L. "The Rochester Method, an oral multisensory approach for instructing prelingual deaf children," *American Annals of the Deaf*, 1967, 112, 50–55.

Sebeok, T. A., and R. Rosenthal (eds.). "The Clever Hans phenomenon," *Annals of the New York Academy of Sciences*, 1981, 364.

Silverman, S. Richard. "From Aristotle to Bell—and beyond." In H. Davis and S. R. Silverman (eds.), *Hearing and Deafness*. New York: Holt, Rinehart & Winston, 1978.

Smith, Jess M. *Workshop on Interpreting for the Deaf*. Muncie, Ind.: Ball State Teachers College, 1964.

Sperling, George. "Future prospects in language and communication for the congenitally deaf." In L. Liben (ed.), *Deaf Children: Developmental Perspectives*. New York: Academic Press, 1978.

Spradley, Thomas S., and James P. Spradley. *Deaf Like Me*. New York: Random House, 1978.

Statewide Project for the Deaf. *Preferred Signs for Instructional Purposes*. Austin, Tex.: Texas Education Agency, 1978.

Stengelvik, Maren L. "Old sign language," *Asha*, 1976, 18, 471.

Sternberg, M. L. A., C. C. Tipton, and J. D. Schein. *Curriculum Guide for Interpreter Training*. Silver Spring, Md.: National Association of the Deaf, 1973.

Stokoe, William C. *Semiotics and Human Sign Languages*. The Hague, Netherlands: Mouton, 1972.

Stokoe, William C. "The study and use of sign language," *Sign Language Studies*, 1976, 10, 1–36.

Stokoe, William C. "Afterword." In C. Baker and R. Battison (eds.), *Sign Language and the Deaf Community*. Silver Spring, Md.: National Association of the Deaf, 1980.

Stokoe, William C., D. C. Casterline, and C. G. Croneberg. *A Dictionary of American Sign Language on Linguistic Principles*. Washington, D.C.: Gallaudet College Press, 1965.

Supalla, Ted, and Elissa Newport. "How many seats in a chair?" In P. Siple (ed.), *Understanding Language Through Sign Language Research*. New York: Academic Press, 1978.

Tadie, Nancy B. "A history of drama at Gallaudet College: 1864 to 1969." Doctoral dissertation. New York University School of Education, Health, Nursing and Arts Professions, 1978.

Taylor, Linda L., John C. Catford, Alexander Z. Guiora, and Harlan T. Lane. "Psychological variables and the ability to pronounce a foreign language," *Language and Speech*, 1971, 14, 146–57.

Terrace, Herbert S. *Nim*. New York: Knopf, 1979.

Terrace, Herbert S. "Comment on Gaustad's review of *Nim*," *Sign Language Studies*, 1982, 35, 178–80.

Tervoort, Bernard T. *Developmental Features of Visual Communication*. New York: American Elsevier, 1975.

Tipton, Carol. "Interpreting ethics," *Journal of Rehabilitation of the Deaf*, 1974, 7(3), 10–16.

Tomkins, William. *Universal Indian Sign Language of the Plains Indians of North America*. San Diego, Cal.: Private publication, 1937.

Umiker-Sebeok, D. J., and T. A. Sebeok. *Aboriginal Sign Languages of the Americas and Australia*. Vol. I. New York: Plenum Press, 1978.

Unification of Signs Commission, World Federation of the Deaf. *Gestuno: International Sign Language of the Deaf*. Carlisle, England: British Deaf Association, 1975.

Van Cantfort, Thomas E., and James B. Rimpau. "Sign language studies with chimpanzees and children," *Sign Language Studies*, 1982, 34, 15–72.

Vernon, McCay. "Effects of parents' deafness on hearing children." In Peter J. Fine (ed.), *Deafness in Infancy and Early Childhood*. New York: MEDCOM Press, 1974.

Wampler, Dennis. *Linguistics of Visual English*. Santa Rosa, Cal.: Early Childhood Education Department, Santa Rosa City Schools, 1971.

Washabaugh, William. "The organization and use of Providence Island Sign Language," *Sign Language Studies*, 1980a, 26, 65–92.

Washabaugh, William. "The manu-facturing of a language," *Sign Language Studies*, 1980b, 29, 291–330.

Washabaugh, William. "The deaf of Grand Cayman, British West Indies," *Sign Language Studies*, 1981, 31, 117–34.

Washington State School for the Deaf. *An Introduction to Manual English*. Vancouver, Wash.: Private publication, 1972.

Watson, David O. *Talk with Your Hands*. Menasha, Wis.: George Banta, 1964.

Webster, C. D., H. McPherson, L. Sloman, M. A. Evans, and E. Kuchar. "Communicating with an autistic boy by gestures," *Journal of Autism and Childhood Schizophrenia*, 1973, 3, 337–49.

Wepman, Joseph M. "Aphasia: Language without thought or thought without language?" *Asha*, 1976, 18, 131–36.

Wescott, R. W. (ed.). *Language Origins*. Silver Spring, Md.: Linstok Press, 1974.

Wilbur, R. B. *American Sign Language and Sign Systems*. Baltimore: University Park Press, 1979.

Winitz, Harris. "Full-time experience," *Asha*, 1976, 18, 404.

Winitz, Harris (ed.). "Native language and foreign language acquisition," *Annals of the New York Academy of Sciences*, 1981, 379.

Wolf, Enid G. "Development of improved communication skills in autistic children through use of sign language," *Tijdschrift voor Zwakzinnigheid, Autisme en andere Ontwikkelingsstoornissen*, 1979, 16, 50–54.

Woll, B., J. Kyle, and M. Deuchar (eds.). *Perspectives on British Sign Language and Deafness*. London: Croom Helm, 1981.

Woodward, James. *Signs of Sexual Behavior*. Silver Spring, Md.: TJ Publishers, 1979a.

Woodward, James. "The selflessness of Providence Island Sign Language: Personal pronoun morphology," *Sign Language Studies*, 1979b, 23, 167–74.

Woodward, James. *Signs of Drug Use*. Silver Spring, Md.: TJ Publishers, 1980.

Woodward, James. "All in the family: Kinship lexicalization across sign languages," *Sign Language Studies*, 1978, 19, 121–38.

Woodward, James, and Susan DeSantis. "Two-to-one it happens: Dynamic phonology in two sign languages," *Sign Language Studies*, 1977, 17, 329–46.

Woodward, James, and Harry Markowicz. "Some handy new ideas on pidgins and creoles." Paper delivered at International Conference on Pidgin and Creole Languages. Honolulu, 1975.

Yarnall, Gary D. "Preferred methods of communication of four deaf-blind adults: A field report of four selected case studies," *Journal of Rehabilitation of the Deaf*, 1980, 13(3), 1–8.

Youguang, Zhou. "The Chinese finger alphabet and the Chinese finger syllabary," *Sign Language Studies*, 1980, 28, 209–16.

APPENDIX A

Annotated List of Sign Dictionaries

This listing is arranged alphabetically by author to indicate that the entries are not competing with each other. They serve different purposes. Some are general presentations of Ameslan; some describe special sign systems; others concentrate on particular sign collections. The entries are briefly annotated and include estimates of the size of the vocabulary. As pointed out in the text, counting signs can be misleading, because a particular sign may stand for several words in English; for example, the sign in Figure 1 can be glossed as "work," "working," "worked," "labor," "laboring," "labored," and so on. It could, therefore, be counted as one sign, or six, or more. On the other hand, one word may be represented by two or more signs; for example, "husband" in Figure 14 is made up of the signs for "man" and "marry." The estimated number of signs, then, is only intended to give some idea of the extent of the coverage.

Probably the first published dictionary of signs in the United States was James S. Brown's *A Vocabulary of Mute Signs*, printed in 1856 by a Louisiana newspaper, the *Morning Comet* of Baton Rouge. In 1884, L. R. Harmsley & Co. (Philadelphia) published W. P. Clark's *The Indian Sign Language*, which contained about one thousand entries verbally described and relating each to the equivalent Ameslan sign, thus making it a dictionary of both Indian and American sign. No other significant work appeared until 1909, the year *The Sign Language: A Manual of Signs* was published by J. Schuyler Long, then a principal at the Iowa School for the Deaf. Daniel D. Higgins followed, in 1923, with *How to Talk to the Deaf*, which he published himself. These four dictionaries are now largely of historical interest, since many of the signs depicted have been altered so much that they are as archaic to the modern signer as Chaucerian speech is to modern English speakers. Since 1960, there has been an explosion of sign dictionaries, with more than thirty collections published. Not every currently available compilation appears below, the idea of this listing being to introduce the range of possible sources, not to delimit them. For some other examples, see the review prepared by Bornstein and Hamilton (1972).

In reviewing these sign dictionaries one should be tolerant, as they strive to counter the long neglect of semiology. It might be well to keep in mind the wise words of the scholar Charlton Laird when referring to dictionaries generally he says:

> A dictionary, at its best, is a mine of incomplete answers, but in a world where profound answers are vague and most answers are partly wrong, a collection of well-founded answers about man's most useful tool, language, can be a boon. *

*Laird 1970, p. xxx.

Anthony, D. *Seeing Essential English*. Vol. I and II. Anaheim, Cal.: Educational Services Division, Anaheim Union School District, 1971. One of the earliest versions of Manual English in this country, illustrated by line drawings of 1,000 signs.

Babbini, Barbara E. *An Introductory Course in Manual Communication*. Northridge, Cal.: San Fernando State College, 1965. The student version of this work, though not precisely a dictionary, can be useful for self-study; teachers will have no difficulty seeing its relevance to them. Arranged in twenty-two lessons are 600 signs, which are carefully described but not illustrated.

Becker, V. A. "Sign language," *Silent Worker*, 1956, 8(7), 4–7. Describes forty signs for use under water by skindivers. The U.S. Navy has trained underwater demolition teams to sign.

Charlip, Remy, Mary Beth Miller, and George Ancona. *Handtalk: An ABC of Finger Spelling & Sign Language*. New York: Parents Magazine Press, 1974. A picture book to introduce children to manual communication. Each letter of the alphabet is illustrated by color photographs of its fingerspelled equivalent and of a sign with the same initial letter for the English translation. Pictorial sequences also illustrate occasional signed sentences.

Cohen, E., L. Namir, and L. Schlesinger. *A New Dictionary of Sign Language*. The Hague: Mouton, 1977. The 1,400 Israeli signs are arranged by handshape and body part. In place of illustrations, English words and the Eshkol-Wachmann Movement Notation are used to describe the signs. The book demonstrates fully the notational system for those with an interest in representing signs in print.

Fant, L. J. *Ameslan: An Introduction to American Sign Language*. Northridge, Cal.: Joyce Motion Picture Co., 1977. Lou Fant is an accomplished actor familiar to TV viewers; his photographs not only depict the 400 signs but also clearly illustrate the role of facial expression in signing. Like Babbini (above), Fant has arranged the book in the form of lesson plans; he emphasizes putting the signs together meaningfully, rather than presenting them in isolation.

Gestuno: International Sign Language of the Deaf. Carlisle, England: British Deaf Association, 1975. An official publication of the World Federation of the Deaf, the book contains 1,470 signs depicted in photographs, each of which is defined by one French and one English word, and indexed in French, English, and Italian. A brief text describes the work of the WFD's Unification of Signs Commission and gives some clues to use of the signs in multilingual settings.

Gustason, G., D. Pfetzing, and E. Zawolkow. *Signing Exact English*. Rossmoor, Cal.: Modern Signs Press, 1972. This is the official guide to SEE II. It contains line drawings of 3,000 signs, including suffixes and prefixes.

Hackett, B. *Emergency Words for the Deaf and Hearing*. One of many collections of survival or emergency signs, this collection differs from most others in putting the signs into sentences such as "Don't move, you are hurt; breathe slowly." Because the author is a fireman, the signs tend to be those useful at a fire, but apply to medical emergencies as well. (Contact the sources in Appendix C for other lists or check with your local police, fire, or health department for emergency signs that may be in use in your locale.)

Jamison, S. L. *Signs for Computing Terminology*. Silver Spring, Md.: National Association of the Deaf, 1983. About 800 signs contributed by a panel of experts on computers and sign.

Kannapell, B., L. Hamilton, and H. Bornstein. *Signs for Instructional Purposes*. Washington, D.C.: Gallaudet College Press, 1969. Grouped under headings corresponding to college subjects, the 500 signs are those that have been invented at Gallaudet College for instruction of its students. Brief verbal descriptions accompany the line drawings. Indexed in English and French.

Kates, L., and J. D. Schein. *A Complete Guide to Communication with Deaf-Blind Persons*. Silver Spring, Md.: National Association of the Deaf, 1980. While not a dictionary, this book does introduce the seventy-five different ways now used to communicate with those who are both deaf and blind. In addition to describing each of the devices and methods, the book discusses some techniques for easing communication with and selecting a method suited to a particular deaf-blind person.

Meissner, M., and S. B. Philpott. "A Dictionary of Sawmill Workers' Signs," *Sign Language Studies*, 1975, 9, 309–47. The 150 signs are illustrated and described, with indications of their context. The signs are used not by deaf people but by Canadian sawmill workers, who need a visual system to communicate while the mill is operating. The signs are not limited to the transmission of technical, work-related information; they are also used for social conversation. The authors gathered the signs on the spot. They guess that other noisy workplaces (like steel rolling mills) also have spontaneously generated sets of signs. The study is relevant for those considering the genesis of signs.

O'Rourke, T. J. *A Basic Course in Manual Communication*. Silver Spring, Md.: National Association of the Deaf, 1979. One of the two most popular sign dictionaries (Riekehof's being the other). The 750 entries are arranged by lessons and illustrated by line drawings, supplemented by verbal instructions for their reproduction by students.

Oléron, P. *Language Gestuel des Sourds-Muets*. Paris, France: Editions du Centre National de la Recherche Scientifique, 1974. The 1,000 signs are first described verbally and then illustrated by photographs. Since the dictionary is entirely in French, it will probably appeal to those interested in cross-cultural sign studies or planning a visit to France.

Riekehof, L. *The Joy of Signing*. Springfield, Mo.: Gospel Publishing House, 1978. See O'Rourke (above) for the other bestselling dictionary of sign. This version is Riekehof's third. Each of the 1,500 signs is illustrated by a line drawing, described in words, and usually given a mnemonic (or etymological) clue.

Skelly, M., L. Schinsky, R. Donaldson, and R. W. Smith. *Handbook of Amerind Sign*. St. Louis: Veterans Administration Workshop, 1973. These one-handed signs were selected for use with aphasic veterans. The authors regard these signs as more suited to speech therapy than Ameslan or Manual English.

Springer, C. J. *Talking with the Deaf*. Baton Rouge, La.: Redemptorist Fathers, 1961. As a Catholic priest, Springer naturally includes signs for all concepts of importance in that religion. The 1,000 signs are shown in photographs accompanied by verbal descriptions. This work updates the popular text by Higgins (1942).

Statewide Project for the Deaf. *Preferred Signs for Instructional Purposes*. Austin, Tex.: Texas Education Agency, 1976. The 2,000 drawings are glossed in Spanish and English. The entries include affixes used in Manual English. The system is an attempt to standardize the use of signs in Texas classes for deaf students.

Stokoe, W., D. Casterline, and C. Croneberg. *A Dictionary of American Sign Language on Linguistic Principles*. Washington, D.C.: Gallaudet College Press, 1965 (copyright has now passed to Linstok Press, 9306 Mintwood Street, Silver Spring, Md. 20901). This book sets the standard against which to judge all other dictionaries in this field. The illustrations only explain the notational system invented by the authors (see Appendix B). It, rather than drawings, is used to describe the 2,000 entries. They are ordered by the elements of the system: tab, dez, sig. Those desiring to master this method of writing sign must begin with this book. A delightful bonus are its essays on Ameslan; they read as well today as they did at the beginning of the sign revolution.

Watson, D. *Talk with Your Hands*. Vols. I and II. Menasha, Wis.: George Banta, 1973. David Watson is a professional cartoonist who has combined his artistic skill with his interest in sign. He has chosen a cartoon format, with entire stories told in Ameslan. To tell these stories he uses about 3,000 signs. The book can be read without reference to the English captions, making it helpful in learning to read sign.

Woodward, J. *Signs of Sexual Behavior*. Silver Spring, Md.: TJ Publishers, 1979. The 150 signs displayed are carefully drawn. The verbal material focuses on when to use the signs rather than on how to make them. The collection is especially important to interpreters who work in medical-psychological settings.

Woodward, J. *Signs of Drug Use*. Silver Spring, Md.: TJ Publishers, 1980. As in the preceding book, the 150 signs are drawn, not described. This collection of signs will be of greatest value to those who work with teenagers and young adults.

APPENDIX B

Table of Symbols Used
for Writing the Signs
of American Sign Language

Tab Symbols

1. ∅   zero, the neutral place where the hands move, in contrast with all places below
2. ◯   face or whole head
3. ⌒   forehead or brow, upper face
4. ⊔   mid-face, the eye and nose region
5. ∪   chin, lower face
6. ʒ   cheek, temple, ear, side-face
7. π   neck
8. []   trunk, body from shoulders to hips
9. ⌄   upper arm
10. ✓   elbow, forearm
11. ɑ   wrist, arm in supinated position (on its back)
12. ɒ   wrist, arm in pronated position (face down)

Dez symbols, some also used as tab

13. A   compact hand, fist; may be like 'a', 's', or 't' of manual alphabet
14. B   flat hand
15. 5   spread hand; fingers and thumb spread like '5' of manual numeration
16. C   curved hand; may be like 'c' or more open
17. E   contracted hand; like 'e' or more clawlike
18. F   "three-ring" hand; from spread hand, thumb and index finger touch or cross
19. G   index hand; like 'g' or sometimes like 'd'; index finger points from fist
20. H   index and second finger, side by side, extended
21. I   "pinkie" hand; little finger extended from compact hand

22.	K	like G except that thumb touches middle phalanx of second finger; like 'k' and 'p' of manual alphabet
23.	L	angle hand; thumb, index finger in right angle, other fingers usually bent into palm
24.	3	"cock" hand; thumb and first two fingers spread, like '3' of manual numeration
25.	O	tapered hand; fingers curved and squeezed together over thumb; may be like 'o' of manual alphabet
26.	R	"warding off" hand; second finger crossed over index finger, like 'r' of manual alphabet
27.	V	"victory" hand; index and second fingers extended and spread apart
28.	W	three-finger hand; thumb and little finger touch, others extended spread
29.	X	hook hand; index finger bent in hook from fist, thumb tip may touch fingertip
30.	Y	"horns" hand; thumb and little finger spread out extended from fist; or index finger and little finger extended, parallel
31.	8	(allocheric variant of Y); second finger bent in from spread hand, thumb may touch fingertip

Sig symbols

32.	∧	upward movement	⎫
33.	∨	downward movement	⎬ vertical action
34.	N	up-and-down movement	⎭
35.	>	rightward movement	⎫
36.	<	leftward movement	⎬ sideways action
37.	z	side to side movement	⎭
38.	T	movement toward signer	⎫
39.	⊥	movement away from signer	⎬ horizontal action
40.	I	to-and-fro movement	⎭
41.	α	supinating rotation (palm up)	⎫
42.	ʊ	pronating rotation (palm down)	⎬ rotary action
43.	ω	twisting movement	⎭
44.	ŋ	nodding or bending action	
45.	□	opening action (final dez configuration shown in brackets)	
46.	#	closing action (final dez configuration shown in brackets)	
47.	ℓ	wiggling action of fingers	
48.	∅	circular action	
49.	)(	convergent action, approach	⎫
50.	×	contactual action, touch	⎪
51.	⊓	linking action, grasp	⎬ interaction
52.	∓	crossing action	⎪
53.	⊙	entering action	⎪
54.	÷	divergent action, separate	⎭
55.	''	interchanging action	

APPENDIX C

Sources of Information
and Material About Sign

The particular items that become available change from day to day; some go out of print or leave the supply trail, while others enter it. For a list of lasting value, then, preference goes to naming sources from which a substantial amount of sign-related material can be expected over time. These sources have a basic interest in deafness and manual communication; hence they tend to keep material in circulation longer than more general suppliers, and they usually respond to requests knowledgeably and enthusiastically.

National Association of the Deaf, 814 Thayer Avenue, Silver Spring, Md. 20910. In addition to its Communication Skills Program, NAD has a mail-order service that supplies books, pamphlets, games, videotapes, and other specialized materials. A free catalogue can be obtained by requesting it. Note, also, that NAD publishes books on deafness, sign language, and related matters of interest to its members. One unusual but helpful item is a hand-cranked viewer that can be loaded with film clips of signs. The device requires no electricity, only the existing light and an agile wrist. NAD can also be called upon to ship items published by others, something it usually will do.

Gallaudet College, 7th & Florida Avenue, N.E., Washington, D.C. 20002. The college bookstore maintains a large stock of sign books and related materials. Like NAD, it will typically sell materials that it must obtain from other sources. The bookstore should be particularly helpful in providing materials published by Gallaudet College Press, another segment of the college's activities. Also, the college maintains a National Information Center on Deafness that welcomes any legitimate, relevant request for information. In addition, the college houses the Linguistics Research Laboratory, headed by William Stokoe, and the Office of Demographic Studies, which conducts the Annual Survey of Hearing Impaired Children and Youth. To keep abreast of developments in sign research, which is actively being pursued in at least twelve different countries, the reader is urged to subscribe to *Signs for Our Times*, which is distributed at nominal cost by the Linguistic Research Laboratory, Gallaudet College, Washington, D.C. 20002. The laboratory provides an international way station for those interested in sign.

Linstok Press, 9306 Mintwood Street, Silver Spring, Md. 20901. If this company did nothing more than publish *Sign Language Studies*, it would still be invaluable to students of Ameslan. But it does do more: it publishes books on sign. Regarding the quality of its publications, it is only necessary to note that its owner is William Stokoe.

National Technical Institute for the Deaf, One Lomb Memorial Drive, Rochester, N.Y. 14623. NTID is a federally funded school within the Rochester Institute of Technology. Like Gallaudet College and NAD, NTID publishes its own books, videotapes, and materials used by deaf students; however, NTID does not seem to be a general source for materials prepared by others. A free resource catalogue is available for the asking.

Other

Cassette videotapes offer an excellent opportunity to see signs in action. An intriguing item is "Signs Not Found in Books," which was compiled by Bonnie Grossbauer, Michigan School for the Deaf, in Flint. Contact the school for information about how to obtain the videotape. "Shabbat in Sign Language" shows deaf students at a sabbath dinner and service. Produced by the Hillel Outreach Program, California State University at Northridge (CSUN), the videotape can be purchased from Four Seasons Media, 5456 Cahuenga Boulevard, North Hollywood, Cal. 91601.

INDEX

Music, 145, 147–48
My Name is Jonah, 128

NAD. *See* National Association of the Deaf
Name, 43
Names
    fingerspelling, 27, 86, 87
    signs, 27
National Association of the Deaf (NAD)
    and American Sign Language, 147
    certification for sign instructors, 103, 125
    function of, 136, 138
    office of, 137
    origin of, 61, 134
National Committee on Arts for the Handicapped, 127–28
National Consortium of Programs Training Sign
        Language Instructors (NCPTSLI), 125
National Deaf Bowling Association, 139
National Deaf Mute College, 60, 134, 135
National Fraternal Society of the Deaf (NFSD), 137
National Institute for Deaf-Mutes, 56
National Interpreter Training Consortium (NITC), 113–14
National Technical Institute for the Deaf (NTID), 135
National Theatre of the Deaf (NTD), 126, 128
NCPTSLI. *See* National Consortium of Programs
        Training Sign Language Instructors
Necking, 11
Negating statements, 42
Neo-oralism, 95
New England Association of the Deaf, 134
New York City Opera, 121
NFSD. *See* National Fraternal Society of the Deaf
NITC. *See* National Interpreter Training Consortium
Nose, use of in sign, 18–19
Not yet, 34–35
Now, 40, 41, 75
NTD. *See* National Theatre of the Deaf
NTID. *See* National Technical Insitute for the Deaf
Numbers, 53–85

Occupations, 138–39, 141
"Oral approach," 60
Oral Deaf Adults Section of Alexander Graham Bell
        Association for the Deaf, 137
Oral interpreter, 120
Ordinal position, 85
Organizations, in the deaf community, 136–37
Orientation, and sign, 37
Our Town, 126

Padden, Carol, 43
Paget, Sir Richard, 66
Paget-Gorman Sign System (PGSS), 66, 72
Painters, 140
Parochial schools, 141
Parrots, 4
Partridge, Eric, 30
Past, 39
PBS, 128
PGSS. *See* Paget-Gorman Sign System
Philip, Prince, 138
Pidgin, 5–6, 65–66
Pidgin English, 74
Pluralizing words, 20, 37, 41–42
Poets, 140
Pokorny, Daniel, 145
Portuguese Manual Alphabet letter A, 94
Posture, use of in sign, 22
Prefixes, in Manual English, 68
Prehistoric communication, 47, 51

Prejudice, 138, 139
Proactive inhibition, 105
Professions, 138–39, 141
Pronouns, 39, 69–70
Puccini, *La Fanciulla del West*, 121
Puns, 25–26

Questions, asking in sign, 24, 43–44

Rain, 45
Ramapithecine, 47
Reading sign vs. signing, 108
Redmond, Granville, 141
Registry of Interpreters for the Deaf (RID), 112, 113, 114
    Code of Ethics, 115, 116, 119
Rehabilitation Act Amendments of 1978, 111
Rehabilitation Act of 1973, 113
Rejection, 42
Religion, 141–145
    and ministers, 141
    parochial schools, 141
    and sign choirs, 145
    sign language in services, 142
    signs for religious terms, 142–44
Religious leaders, 141
Religious orders
    education of the deaf in, 53–54
    silent, and manual communication, 52–53
Rennell (island), 49–50
Repetition of signs, 20, 37
Research, linguistic, 32–35
RID. *See* Registry of Interpreters for the Deaf
Riekehof, Dr. Lottie, 144
    Talk to the Deaf (rev. ed., *The Joy of Signing*), 115
Right, 73
River, 70–71
RNID. *See* Royal National Institute for the Deaf
Road, 71
Robards, Jason, 128
Rochester Method of fingerspelling, 86
Romeo, Luigi, 52
Romero, Emerson, 141
Royal National Insitute for the Deaf (RNID), 102, 138
Runaways, 127
Russian Manual Alphabet, 91–93
Russian method of fingerspelling and speech, 95

Sarles, Harvey, 49
Schizophrenics, teaching sign to, 124
Schools
    and colleges, 59–60, 135
    first for the deaf, 53
    first in the U.S., 58
    importance of for contact with others, 134
    "mainstreaming" in, 134
    parochial, 141
    special, 58–59, 134–35
    See also Education
Schreiber, Frederick C., 147
Schreiber, Kathleen, *Dear Beth*, 140
Second-language learning, 105–8
SEE. *See* Seeing Essential English
Seeing Essential English (SEE I), 66
Seeing vs. hearing, 5
Self Help for Hard of Hearing People, Inc. (SHHH), 137
Semiology, 6–7
Sentences, creating, 42–43
Sesame Street, 128
Sexual signs, 25